Routledge Revivals

Developing Competent Teachers

First published in 1996, *Developing Competent Teachers* aims to explore the implications of different ways of thinking about the professional competences of teachers. It does so through case studies of competence frameworks used in a number of teacher education contexts – and, for comparative insights, in social work, nursing and police training. The intended readership is all involved in teacher education: in particular, Higher Education tutors; mentors and senior staff in schools.

Developing Competent Teachers

Approaches to Professional Competence in Teacher Education

Edited by David Hustler and Donald McIntyre

First published in 1996
By David Fulton Publishers Ltd.

This edition first published in 2024 by Routledge
4 Park Square, Milton Park, Abingdon, Oxon, OX14 4RN
and by Routledge
605 Third Avenue, New York, NY 10017

Routledge is an imprint of the Taylor & Francis Group, an informa business

© David Fulton Publishers 1996

All rights reserved. No part of this book may be reprinted or reproduced or utilised in any form or by any electronic, mechanical, or other means, now known or hereafter invented, including photocopying and recording, or in any information storage or retrieval system, without permission in writing from the publishers.

Publisher's Note
The publisher has gone to great lengths to ensure the quality of this reprint but points out that some imperfections in the original copies may be apparent.

Disclaimer
The publisher has made every effort to trace copyright holders and welcomes correspondence from those they have been unable to contact.

A Library of Congress record exists under ISBN: 1853463833

ISBN: 978-1-032-74456-8 (hbk)
ISBN: 978-1-003-46930-8 (ebk)
ISBN: 978-1-032-74462-9 (pbk)

Book DOI 10.4324/9781003469308

DEVELOPING COMPETENT TEACHERS

Approaches to Professional Competence in Teacher Education

edited by
David Hustler and Donald McIntyre

David Fulton Publishers
London

David Fulton Publishers Ltd
2 Barbon Close, London WC1N 3JX

First published in Great Britain by David Fulton Publishers 1996

Note: The right of David Hustler and Donald McIntyre to be identified as the editors of this work has been asserted by them in accordance with the Copyright, Designs and Patents Act 1988.

Copyright © David Fulton Publishers

British Library Cataloguing in Publication Data

A catalogue record for this book is available from the British Library

ISBN 1-85346-383-3

All rights reserved. No part of this publication may be reproduced, stored in a retrieval system or transmitted, in any form, or by any means, electronic, mechanical, photocopying, recording or otherwise, without the prior permission of the publishers.

Typeset by The Harrington Consultancy Ltd
Printed in Great Britain by the Cromwell Press Ltd, Melksham

Contents

Contributors v
Acknowledgements viii
1   Introduction
    David Hustler and Donald McIntyre 1

PART ONE: CASE STUDIES OF INITIAL TEACHER EDUCATION COURSES

2   Designing a Competency Based Framework for Assessing Student Teachers: The UEA Approach
    Roy Barton and John Elliott 9
3   Profiling in Practice: The Goldsmiths' Experience
    Pat Mahony and Vee Harris 28
4   Diversity, Change and Continuity: Developing Institutional Policy at The Manchester Metropolitan University
    Jack Hogbin, Pat Cockett and David Hustler 41
5   Trying to Make Profiling Useful for Teacher Education: The Oxford Experience
    Anna Pendry and Donald McIntyre 56

PART TWO: CASE STUDIES OF NATIONAL INITIATIVES

6   'Competence' Guidelines in Scotland for Initial Teacher Training: 'Supercontrol' or 'Superperformance'?
    Ian Stronach, Peter Cope, Bill Inglis and Jim McNally 72
7   Professional Competences and Professional Characteristics: The Northern Ireland Approach to the Reform of Teacher Education
    Geoff Whitty 86
8   Professional Standards for Teachers in Australia
    James Walker 98

PART THREE: GOING BEYOND INITIAL TEACHER EDUCATION

9   Competence Frameworks and Profiles for Newly-Qualified Teachers
    Peter Earley 114
10 Competency in the Mathematics Classroom – The Example of Equal Opportunities
    Leone Burton and Hilary Povey 128

11 Competences and the First Year of Teaching
    Pat Mahony 141

PART FOUR: OTHER PROFESSIONS APPROACH COMPETENCES

12 The 'ASSET' Programme: The Development of a Competence-Based Honours Degree in Social Work
    Richard Winter and Maire Maisch 153
13 Exploring Competence in Nursing and Midwifery
    John Schostak 168
14 The Role of a Small-Scale Research Project in Developing a Competency Based Police Training Curriculum
    John Elliott 183
15 Concluding Comments
    Donald McIntyre and David Hustler 199

Index 213

Contributors

Roy Barton is a Lecturer in Education at the University of East Anglia and has a special interest in initial teacher training. He was closely involved in setting up the new partnership arrangements for initial training with local schools, particularly in the development of the assessment arrangements. His research interests relate mainly to the application of information technology to the teaching of science. He has been involved in curriculum development and has published a number of articles in this area.

Leone Burton is Professor of Education (Mathematics and Science) at the University of Birmingham, UK. Her teaching, research and publications offer a challenge to make mathematics education at every level accessible, critical and stimulating to all learners.

Pat Cockett is Head of Primary Education at the Didsbury School of Education, The Manchester Metropolitan University. Her work in ITE and CPD has involved piloting models of partnership with schools, developing profiles for NQTs, exploring the recognition and accreditation of school-based professional development, publishing professional development materials for use in schools in connection with Inspection and the SEN Code of Practice and publishing classroom materials for teaching Primary Mathematics.

Peter Cope is a Senior Lecturer in Education and Director of Initial Teacher Education at the University of Stirling. He has research interests in Information Technology and Education as well as teacher development.

Peter Earley worked for many years at the National Foundation for Educational Research undertaking a number of projects in the areas of school management and professional development. After a spell at the Institute of Education University of London, he is now based at the Oxford Centre for Education Management, Oxford Brookes University.

Professor John Elliott is the Director of the Centre for Applied Research in Education (CARE), at the University of East Anglia. He was a founding member of CARE and has directed a number of action research projects involving local teachers and schools. He has designed in-service courses for teachers which support reflective practices in schools and directed research projects on teachers' jobs and lives, pupil autonomy in learning with micros, the assessment of experiential learning, competency based professional education, and teachers as researchers in the context of award bearing higher education. He is a consultant for the OECD, helping to support international curriculum development in environmental education. In 1984 John Elliott was a member of a Home Office commissioned review of Police recruit training and has continued to undertake research and consultancy work in the field of Police Education.

Vee Harris is the Modern Languages tutor on the Postgraduate (Secondary) programme at Goldsmiths College. She was involved in the first pilot of the profile of teacher competences and has published in the field of Partnership In Initial Teacher Education. She has also published in the areas of pupil autonomy and learner strategies in modern language learning. She is a member of the National Teacher Education Working Group at the Centre for Information on Language Teaching and Research.

Jack Hogbin is the BEd (Hons) Course Leader at the Didsbury School of Education, The Manchester Metropolitan University. He has undertaken and supervised research into the School's survey of newly qualified teachers and has been part of a team investigating school experience supervision. He has responsibility throughout the School for Quality Assurance and Primary course development. He is Chair of NaPTEC (National Primary Teacher Education Conference).

David Hustler is Professor of Education at the Didsbury School of Education, The Manchester Metropolitan University. He convened the ESRC Research Seminar Group on Competences and Teacher Education which informed this book. He has commitments to professionally-focused research and formative styles of evaluation, with particular interest in teaching and learning styles and 14+ education.

Bill Inglis is a Senior Lecturer in Education at the University of Stirling. His research interests include Initial Teacher Education, the continuing development of teachers and the history of education.

Pat Mahony worked for many years in Initial Teacher Education before becoming Head of the Department of Educational Studies at Goldsmiths College. She has recently moved to a senior research post at Roehampton Institute London where she is enjoying the luxury of researching government policy rather than trying to manage the effects of it. She has published in the areas of equal opportunities and teacher competence and is currently researching the ways in which new public management is affecting the work of headteachers and those involved in teacher education.

Maire Maisch is Principal Lecturer in Social Work at Anglia Polytechnic University. She worked with Richard Winter on the development of the ASSET project and then as Director of the Asset Programme, the honours degree course for qualified social workers established by the project. Previously, she worked in several Social Services Departments and voluntary agencies as a social work practitioner, Team Leader and Child Protection Training Officer.

Donald McIntyre is Professor of Education at the University of Cambridge. As Reader in Education at Stirling University from 1977 to 1985 and Reader in Educational Studies at the University of Oxford from 1986 to 1995, his priority concerns have been with research and development in teacher education, and with research on curriculum teaching.

Jim McNally is a Lecturer in Education at the University of Stirling. His research interests relate to teacher education, and in particular, mentoring activities.

Anna Pendry is Lecturer in Education at the University of Oxford. As co-ordinator of the Development Group which planned the Oxford Internship Scheme and later as co-ordinator for several years of the PGCE course itself, she has been at the centre of thinking and developing practice of the Oxford scheme. Her D.Phil. degree and her major subsequent research have been concerned with the development of beginning teachers' pedagogical thinking.

Hilary Povey is a Senior Lecturer in Mathematics Education at Sheffield Hallam University, UK where she works in initial teacher education. In her teaching, writing and research she is committed to social justice and its implementation in the mathematics classroom.

John Schostak as a professor in the School of Education and Professional Development at the University of East Anglia has been involved in educational research in nursing, midwifery, policing and schooling and maintains interests in youth cultures and the media.

Ian Stronach is Research Professor in Education at The Manchester Metropolitan University. He was formerly Professor of Education at the University of Stirling. He is interested in policy critique and programme education.

James Walker is Professor of Curriculum and Teaching, and Dean of the Faculty of Education at the University of Western Sydney. With a background in both educational philosophy and ethnographic educational research, he has played a leading role in the development of Australian thinking, policy and practice relating to the description of competency and professional standards for teaching.

Geoff Whitty is the Karl Mannheim Professor of Sociology of Education and Chair of the Department of Policy Studies at the Institute of Education, University of London. He was formerly Professor and Dean of Education at Bristol Polytechnic and the Goldsmiths' Professor of Policy and Management in Education at Goldsmiths' College, University of London. He chaired a Working Party on Competence-based Teacher Education for the Council for National Academic Awards and a Working Group on Competences in Teacher Education for the Department of Education in Northern Ireland. He is currently co-director of the ESRC-funded Modes of Teacher Education (MOTE) research project.

Richard Winter is Professor of Education at Anglia Polytechnic University. He worked for many years in teacher education before working with Maire Maisch as co-ordinator of the ASSET project. He is the author of *Learning From Experience*, a book concerned with professional development through practitioner action research and joint editor of the journal *Educational Action Research*.

Acknowledgements

We wish to express our thanks to the ESRC for supporting the work of the Competences and Teacher Education Seminar Group. We also thank those core members of the group who have not contributed chapters to this book, but whose work and ideas were certainly important in the thinking of the group – i.e. Andrew Pollard, Jean Rudduck, Rob Moore and in particular Michael Eraut – who brought to the group his very extensive experience of work in this field. Several people made contributions to ESRC seminars and we express our appreciation to all of these and especially to Sally Brown.

1

Introduction

David Hustler and Donald McIntyre

Developing competent teachers seems to be a good title for a book and a pretty good ambition generally. Many readers, however, will feel that such terminology already raises some serious questions regarding the nature of teaching as a profession and the applicability of the notion of competence to both initial teacher education and continuing professional development.

This book has its roots in a variety of questions in this area which were being posed by some members of the British Educational Research Association (BERA) during 1990 and 1991. In particular, BERA had established a series of educational policy research groups of which one was concerned with teacher education. This group became increasingly involved in discussions concerned with the growing policy initiatives pointing to both the demand that initial teacher education should be more school-based and that it should focus on the competences required of beginning teachers (DES, 1989). At this time a series of articles and reports addressing competences and teacher education were also beginning to appear (CNAA, 1991; Eraut, 1989; Whitty and Willmott 1991). Whitty and Willmott amongst others made it clear that competence-based and performance-based approaches to teacher education were not new, but pointed to the large range of issues 'that will have to be addressed if progress is to be made in this field'. Like that paper, the CNAA report was typical of a number of publications at this time in usefully overviewing 'viewpoints and issues'.

The BERA Teacher Education Policy Research group felt that there was an urgent need to establish a network which might enhance research development, advance theoretical understanding and potentially play some part in informing policy in this field. Consequently a successful bid was made to the Economic and Social Research Council for funding under their Research Seminar programme. The bid was a collaborative proposal from members of BERA associated with Oxford University, Sheffield University, The University of East Anglia, the University of Stirling, Bristol Polytechnic (now University of the West of England) and Manchester Polytechnic (The Manchester Metropolitan University) and each of these institutions hosted a seminar. One of the central aims for the planned series of seminars was to: 'enhance research development regarding competence-based teacher education generally, and in particular to promote publication activity in this field by both academic researchers and practitioner researchers'. This book is in large part one product of the working of those seminars, but before moving to the structure and general rationale for this book it may be useful to sketch in some of the additional background to the functioning of these seminars, since this has informed that rationale.

The seminar series ran from the beginning of 1993 to the end of 1994 and included a 'core group' of regular participants who represented a range of interests and positions regarding competency-based approaches. The mix of participants and the time-scale for the seminars are both worth briefly commenting on. The core group consisted of: Professor Leone Burton, Mr Peter Earley, Professor John Elliott, Professor Michael Eraut, Ms Pat Mahony, Mr Donald McIntyre, Professor Andrew Pollard, Professor Jean Rudduck, Professor Ian Stronach, Professor Geoff Whitty, Professor Richard Winter, Mr Rob Moore (who joined the group later) and Mr David Hustler who was the convenor for the seminar group series.

Some readers will recognise that this group contains a number of people with a strong commitment to professionally focused research generally. Such members brought with them a concern that the group should attempt to gain access to some of the most current attempts to address and utilise a competence-based approach within teacher education. As policy initiatives gathered pace it seemed crucial to capture and debate examples of developing course and institutional practice together with the arguments informing such approaches. In addition, many members of the group were themselves involved in their own institutions, in initial teacher education and continuing teacher education course developments. As noted earlier, several publications had addressed the issues and viewpoints relating to competences and teacher education: as a research group, with a concern to enhance and inform developing practice, the ESRC group members wished to keep abreast of that practice, relate to it and contribute to it. As will be seen, this concern is a central aspect of the informing rationale for this book. Within the group were members who have taken somewhat more critical and negative positions regarding the relevance of competences to teacher education, as well as those who have adopted a more positive and embracing approach to competency-based teacher education. The group also contains members who have written extensively about competences and/or considered the applicability of competency-based approaches in professional areas outside of teacher education. Interestingly the group contained some members who had considered competency approaches in relation to Employment Department initiatives, rather than the DfE. This added important dimensions to the group's thinking, since it is generally recognised that the major policy and practice initiatives associated with competences during the 1980s were in the areas of employment and training primarily associated with the Employment Department and bodies such as the CBI Task Force on Training (Burke, 1989; Jessup, 1991).

The time-scale during which the seminars took place is important to take account of, because (as foreseen) the Department for Education did instigate a variety of dramatic changes to the system for teacher education during this period. There emerged, just prior to the first meeting of the group, one of the more important documents in this area: Circular 9/92, which introduced new criteria and procedures for the accreditation of courses of initial training in England and Wales for secondary school teachers. This circular contained a set of competency statements which 'specify the issues on which the case for approval will be considered' (regarding institutions providing initial teacher training) whilst asking individual institutions to develop 'their own competence-based approaches to the assessment of students'. The circular also required that schools should become full partners with higher education institutions in Initial Teacher Training. Many of the studies in this book are intimately concerned with this particular policy context and many of them have drawn on the ESRC seminar group discussions which took place during this period of turbulent change in teacher education. As such, these studies often represent thinking and practice as it is moving through a process of change and development, rather than finished refined products. Whilst some readers might regret this flavour to the studies, the rationale behind their publication here is that it is precisely because they raise questions grounded in developing practice that they are relevant and will continue to be relevant to teacher education. The questions they raise, at their most fundamental level, are to do with what we might understand by the profession of teaching and how best to serve the development of that profession. We return to this later.

As will be apparent from the above, this book presents a series of case studies rather than papers addressing only the conceptual issues and matters of principle associated with competence-based teacher education. These latter issues are, however, not neglected and the reader will find these considered in the context of why and how a particular development emerged. We will return to some of the major recurring issues in our concluding chapter, rather than preview them here. It is our strong view that the great strength of the studies is that in the reading of them we find how matters of deep conviction, matters of conceptual complexity and matters of practical possibility to do with teacher education and the teaching profession are being worked through in a variety of settings. In short, it is not appropriate to abstract them from those contexts through some overarching overview in this introduction.

The book is divided into four groupings of case studies. The first section focuses on studies from initial teacher education associated with four institutions of higher education and their partners in schools. All four studies relate to the policy context established via Circular 9/92, but the studies vary in their particular focus, institutional context and the arguments they marshall in relation to their developing practice. Barton and Elliott's study (Chapter 2) spells out and critiques the approach towards competences associated with that Circular and then moves into how colleagues associated with the University of East Anglia have developed their particular competence-based assessment framework in partnership with schools. Mahony and Harris (Chapter 3) focus on how the commitments at Goldsmith's College to a development profiling process have interrelated with competency-based teacher education. Hogbin, Cockett and Hustler (Chapter 4) pursue issues to do with policy construction and staff development in a very large initial teacher education partnership context. Pendry and McIntyre (Chapter 5) first describe the rationale for a particular general approach to the articulation of competences and other qualities in the context of the Oxford PGCE programme; but then go on to explore some of the problems and practicalities which led to new theoretical concerns in trying to implement the scheme.

The ESRC group contained within it members who were reasonably well informed regarding some of the subtle and not so subtle differences of approach to competences and teacher education which were beginning to emerge at a policy level across the UK contexts of: England and the DfE; Scotland with the Scottish Office Education Department; and Northern Ireland with the Department of Education in Northern Ireland. These differences of approach became the substance of several seminar discussions and need to be taken account of, because they point to somewhat different positions and interpretations concerning competency-based approaches and the development of the teaching profession. The study from Stronach *et al.*, (Chapter 6) and Whitty's study (Chapter 7) consider, respectively, the Scottish and Northern Ireland contexts. It has been suggested that thinking about teacher education and competences in these two settings has been more open to discussion with other parties, including teacher educationists, than the DfE position as expressed in Circular 9/92. Not only did it seem important to include studies of differing national initiatives for the comparative insights they might bring, it is also clear that several partnership approaches to competences in England have found the Scottish and Northern Ireland debates of relevance to their own thinking and development. Another helpful comparative perspective is offered by Walker's account (Chapter 8) of developments regarding professional standards for teachers in Australia. In this account we find an interesting discussion of how teachers and teacher educationists have contributed significantly to debates concerning the relevance of holistic models to a competency framework.

One point made a number of times in the studies from the first two sections concerns the dangers of viewing initial teacher education and continuing professional development as separate worlds. The ESRC seminar core group contained within it members who also argued this position as well as some who had a particular concern for teacher education after initial training. The next section to the book 'Going Beyond Initial Teacher Education' addresses these concerns with three studies. The first, by Earley (Chapter 9), draws on NFER research into how LEAs were moving towards competence-based profiles for newly qualified teachers. Burton and Povey (Chapter 10) focus on two newly qualified teachers of mathematics in relation to equal opportunity issues. Mahony's chapter (11) looks in considerable detail at one particular scheme concerned with what a profile of competence might or should mean to the various parties involved in school-based induction in the first year of teaching and the mentoring process.

The final section of case studies considers some examples of how other professions are addressing competences. It is of interest to note that the very first ESRC Group seminar involved contributors working with competences in the nursing profession and with the police. Two of the case studies, from Schostak and Elliott (Chapters 13 and 14, respectively), look at developments in these professions. In addition, within the group there was considerable experience of competency-based approaches across a range of occupational areas including competency-based approaches in social work training. Winter's work which has been received with considerable interest by teacher educators, is represented here by the case study from Winter and Maisch (Chapter 12) in this final section. Particularly interesting, from the point of view of the ESRC Group's concerns, was that some of the competency-based developments in other professional areas seemed to be moving away from what some would see as the atomistic, check-list, fragmented, narrowly skills-based and potentially de-professionalising approaches which some viewed Circular 9/92, and the DfE more generally, as encouraging and which some viewed as weaknesses in the American experience during the 1970s.

These last comments, concerning the supposed dangers of atomistic, fragmented etc. approaches, are on the edge of moving into issues which will be pursued in the concluding chapter (15). They also, however, relate quite closely to some discussions which took place at the third meeting of the ESRC Seminar Group and in particular to a contributing paper from Professor Sally Brown. This paper and the ensuing discussion helped to reshape the dynamic of the ESRC Group and in doing so also helped indirectly to inform aspects behind the rationale and structuring of this book. Sally Brown, having not been to earlier ESRC seminars but commenting on the seminar papers produced up to that time, sensed anxiety and unease in those papers. She characterised the earlier discussions in relation to competences as seeming to be not so much a developing debate but 'more in the realm of exchanges between defence lawyers and law enforcers', with a tendency to the reactive rather than the proactive. Sally Brown suggested that this anxiety or unease was expressed in at least four ways and we reproduce here most of this section of her paper:

(1) Will we be engulfed by, taken in by, identified with: simple-minded 'official' constructs of competence; crude behaviourist concepts or mechanistic prescriptions for occupations; armchair polemicist views; Total Quality Management approaches; competence models from other (e.g. economic, management) contexts; atomistic models of competence; decontextualised statements about competence?

(2) Will we be able to: maintain/reconstruct our concepts of teacher professionalism; avoid straightforward prescriptions for 'best practice' and continue to include the broader views – critical, evaluative, reflective, analytical, personal qualities, attitudes, understandings, commitments, values and is it appropriate to include these within the construct of competence; go beyond performance as inferred by the other qualities; describe differences in quality rather than be trapped in minimum competence?

(3) Will the competences: focus only on outcomes and be directly translated into assessment systems; commandeer virtually all the ITE (and INSET?) curriculum rather than be treated as just the minimum requirement; turn out to be a way of edging out the moral practice, cognitive and interpersonal aspects of teaching i.e. drown ideas about the complexity of teachers' work and the multifaceted nature of learning to teach; ignore the processes of children's and student teachers' learning; be seen as very attractive, especially in their simplest forms, to everyone outside the teacher education in-group?

(4) Where do ideas about competences to be identified come from: beliefs (government, ultra-Right) about competent practitioners; collecting views about competent practitioners; job descriptions, statements of aims; functional analysis – specific/generic lists of competences; analysis of professional processes or roles; HMI/civil servant armchair exercises; political assertions?

Sally Brown concluded her paper by asking 'Is there a place for addressing fundamental questions of what it means to be a competent teacher and what it means to learn to teach?' and arguing that in terms of being proactive and creative there were:

> three strands in the discourse that turn up frequently as indicators of how progress in this area might be made:
> - the concern that ITE has to be seen as part of a continuum from student to beginning teacher to experienced professional, and that any competence model has to reflect the centrality of movement from dependence to independence to routinization;
> - The recognition that ideas about competences have themselves to be dynamic – entrenched lists of competences constructed in ways that inhibit 'moving on' are dangerous;
> - any constructs of competence have to support continuing learning and offer something to teacher development.

In the case studies which follow we would argue that we do find the questions posed in Sally Brown's (1)–(4) list being pursued. We would also argue that, perhaps in more proactive mode, we also find those last three strands being addressed in a variety of ways. Even for those most opposed to competency-based approaches to teacher education, it might be reasonably argued that the competency movement has invited all those with a concern for teacher education to revisit, clarify and perhaps reformulate, fundamental principles to do with what we understand by the profession of teaching and how that profession can be enhanced. It is worth speculating, for example, as to whether UCET, the Universities' Council for Teacher Education, would have felt the need to produce a pamphlet, *Our Teachers*, in the absence of the government's policy directives in this area. Interestingly enough that pamphlet does not use the word competence once, though we are not presenting this as a critique! Not all those teacher educators invited have taken up the challenge (although most courses have embraced competences in some form). Our somewhat biased view, as editors, is that the contributors to this volume of case studies have been proactive and constructive in their approaches to competences, albeit in various ways. In part, therefore, our position regarding what follows in this book, is that these studies represent contextualised examples of teacher educators 'addressing fundamental questions of what it means to be a competent teacher and what it means to learn to teach'.

References

Burke, J. W. (ed.) (1989) *Competency-Based Education and Training*. Lewes: Falmer.
CNAA (1991) *Competence-Based Approaches to Teacher Education: Viewpoints and Issues*. London: CNAA.
DES (1989) *Criteria for the Approval of Courses of Initial Teacher Training* (Circular 24/89). London: HMSO.

DfE (1992) *Initial Teacher Training (Secondary Phase)* (Circular 9/92). London: HMSO
Eraut, M. (1989) 'Initial teacher training and the NVQ model', in Burke, J. W. (ed.) *Competency-Based Education and Training*. Lewes: Falmer.
Jessup, G. (1991) *Outcomes: NVQs and the Emerging Model of Education and Training*. Lewes: Falmer
UCET (1995) *Our Teachers*. London: UCET
Whitty, G. and Willmott, E. (1991) 'Competence-based teacher education: approaches and issues', *Cambridge Journal of Education*, **21** (3), 309–18.

Part One
Case Studies of Initial Teacher Education Courses

2

Designing a Competency Based Framework for Assessing Student Teachers: The UEA Approach

Roy Barton and John Elliott

The DfE Framework of Competences (Circular 9/92): A Critique

Although DfE Circular 9/92 goes out of its way to point out the distinction between specifying criteria for accrediting competency based courses and criteria for planning and assessing students' learning experiences, it fails to explore the accreditation issues posed for teacher education institutions in developing their own approaches to competency based training. There is no discussion of the assumptions which underpin the accreditation framework and the extent to which they are consistent with some models of teacher professional development rather than others. In the absence of such discussion and guidance it is not surprising to discover that many institutions are using the accreditation framework to plan their secondary teacher training, and fine-tuning it to accommodate additional elements.

Circular 9/92 organises the criteria in the following categories: subject knowledge, subject application, class management, assessment and recording of pupils' progress, further professional development.

The competency statements are listed and numbered under each category. The accreditation framework is unsatisfactory as a framework for curriculum planning and student assessment for the following reasons:

- The main categories of competence are not internally coherent and consistent.

- It would imply a dubious account of the relationship between the acquisition of relevant knowledge and the development of practical abilities.
- The list of competences appears to have been compiled without much thought being given to how they can be validly and reliably assessed.

Coherence and consistency

Two of the categories (Management and Assessment) refer to functions inherent in the teaching role. Other functions are either ignored or referred to in, and confused with, particular statements of competence. If the framework was used as a basis for curriculum planning and student assessment it would neglect a range of competences which are necessary conditions of being able to perform some essential pedagogical functions well. In other words a curriculum or assessment system planned on the basis of the framework would distort the development of teaching competence. The category of Further Professional Development appears to contain a rag-bag of competences. Compare the following items:

1. 'an understanding of the school as an institution and its place within the community';
2. 'an ability to develop effective working relationships with professional colleagues and parents, and to develop their communication skills';
3. 'an awareness of individual differences, including social, psychological, developmental and cultural dimensions';
4. 'a self-critical approach to diagnosing and evaluating pupils' learning, including a recognition of the effects on that learning of teachers' expectations';
5. 'a readiness to promote the moral and spiritual well-being of pupils'.

We defy anyone to detect a principle for coherently clustering these items together. Some in the category, such as 1 and 3, appear to represent the vestigial traces of educational theory. Others appear to be included because they don't fit into other categories while some are included here when they appear to belong to other categories. For example, 3 is necessary for the effective management of learning, and 4 is surely a dimension of being competent at assessing pupils' progress.

Knowledge and competence

In discriminating elements related to subject knowledge from those involved in their application and use in classrooms the framework might seem to imply two distinct learning processes and forms of assessment:

knowledge versus performance based. Such an implication reinforces a division of labour between higher education lecturers and on-the-job trainers in schools and a split site organisation of learning experiences for trainee teachers. It also reinforces a dual assessment system. Moreover, given the fact that the framework lists less 'knowledge' than 'practical' components, its use as a basis for curriculum planning and assessment implies that higher education lecturers are the lesser partners in the training enterprise. In our view such a use pre-empts a number of important issues which can be raised about the relationship between knowledge and performance.

In a recent study of knowledge issues in competency based education MacLure and Norris (1990) outline three different accounts of knowledge and its relationship to performance:

1. *Knowledge as content in the form of information, facts, subject matter, concepts, theories and principles.* It is a static and stable set of attributes that a person can be said to have or lack, and which can once acquired be subsequently applied to create certain effects in situations. The skills in applying and using knowledge are quite separate attributes. The framework outlined in Circular 9/92 appears to be grounded in this sort of account of knowledge and its relationship to competence.

2. *Knowledge as a capacity for doing things; understanding, reasoning, reflecting, judging, deciding, problem-solving, analysing, predicting.* On this account knowledge is a set of abilities involved in the organisation of thinking. They might be called 'cognitive competences'. It is an account which refuses to differentiate between knowledge and competence, sanctioning only a distinction between the different competences involved in different kinds of mental activity.

3. *Knowledge as practice in the form of assumptions and beliefs embedded in practice; sometimes described as tacit or intuitive craft knowledge.* On this account knowledge is inherent in practice and further developed through it. Teaching competences on this account are not skills in applying practical principles learned outside the practice context, but abilities to develop the pedagogical knowledge already embedded in practice.

If we follow the second account and talk about a teacher's understanding of the subject rather than simply their knowledge of it, then we are not talking about something which underpins competent teaching but an intrinsic dimension of such competence; namely, the ability to perform certain mental operations on the subject matter. Of course, such abilities need to be highly developed prior to professional training, but in training they need to be further developed and assessed in the context of teaching situations. We can conclude that the separation of subject knowledge from its application in performance only serves to distort the professional development process and the procedures by which it is assessed. When subject knowledge is construed as the ability to think about subject matter in appropriate ways then it can be fully integrated into a competency framework which avoids dissociating knowledge from performance, and the need to assess it independently.

What are the implications of the third account for the development of knowledge about teaching and how does it relate to the implications we have drawn from the second account?

Recent attempts to identify the generic competences of professional practitioners can be interpreted as a quest to discover the structure of abilities involved in the generation of 'knowledge-in-action'. McBer & Co (Klemp, 1977), for example, categorise the generic attributes of competent professionals in terms of three major dimensions: the cognitive, interpersonal, and motivational. Elliott (1992, 1993) has employed this competence framework to elucidate the structure of competences involved in developing teachers as reflective practitioners and action researchers. He argues that the basic categories of competence for each dimension are 'situational understanding', 'empathy', and 'cognitive initiative' respectively, and that each has a bearing on the other in enabling practitioners to generate knowledge in action.

Elliott introduces a fourth category of generic competence into his account of what is involved in developing knowledge-in-action; namely, that of self-monitoring cognitions, communications, and interventions based on cognitive initiative. Although the practitioner may develop knowledge-in-action by intuitively and unselfconsciously processing information, exercising empathy in inter-personal communications, and monitoring his or her interventions, there will be times when intelligent practice requires a level of self-conscious reflection about cognitions, communications, and interventions. The category of self-monitoring picks out a cluster of meta-competences which are involved in developing knowledge-in-action, and introduces action research as a dimension of professional practice. Such competences do not negate the role of intuition in knowledge construction but complement it. The reflective practitioner or action researcher is both competent and 'meta-competent' in constructing knowledge-in-action.

The items listed under Further Professional Development in the 9/92 framework include 'a self-critical approach to diagnosing and evaluating pupils' learning'. It appears as a functional competence – a responsibility intrinsic to the role of a teacher but it contains a generic dimension which is applicable to good social practice more generally; namely, a capacity for self-criticism, which is a meta-competency.

Let's now look at the relationship between the second and third accounts of the relationship between knowledge and performance and its implications for competent teaching. Although abilities to perform certain mental operations in relation to a subject in a teaching context are constitutive elements of 'situational understanding' they are not context specific. In other words they can largely be developed independently of the teaching context in which they need to be demonstrated, although there are good reasons for fostering that development within the teaching context. Other elements of situational understanding are context-dependent. Thus the ability to 'discern patterns' of events in classroom situations which are pedagogically significant can only be developed through experience of teaching. For example, a teacher can only discern the phenomenon of the 'guessing game' – a risk-reducing strategy employed by pupils to avoid thinking about the subject too deeply – with experience. But this doesn't mean that 'pattern discerning' can only be developed through direct experience of teaching. Observational and vicarious experience are also relevant. Classroom observation, the analysis of case studies of teaching, role plays and simulation exercises can all contribute to the development of the competences involved in situational understanding. Such development in initial training is not the exclusive province of on-the-job trainers in schools. Capacities for situational understanding can be collaboratively developed through a combination of on-the-job training and off-the-job training based on higher education.

The relationship between 'subject understanding' and an important aspect of 'pedagogical competence' sketched out above on the basis of the second and third accounts of the knowledge-performance relation, has profound implications for the roles of schools and higher education institutions in competency-based teacher training. The development of 'subject understanding' need not be the exclusive province of higher education, despite the fact that it is not necessarily dependent on the experience of teaching situations. There are good practical reasons for integrating the further development of 'subject understanding' with the development of pedagogical competence once the foundations of the former have been laid; if only because classrooms can provide a context in which students' understanding can be challenged and thus supply the motivation necessary for further extending it. Conversely, the development of pedagogical competence can be fostered in higher education settings through a curriculum which involves student teachers in the analysis of case data and debriefing their experience of role-plays and simulations. Such activities can accelerate the development of pedagogical competence for a number of reasons. Firstly, they provide a safe environment freed from pressures of accountability pressures which enable novice teachers to more easily learn from their mistakes than they would in a context of direct experience. Secondly, support for in-depth reflection can be more easily created in the higher education context than in the school context where the need to distribute scarce human resources to support pupil learning necessarily has priority.

The second and third accounts of the relation between knowledge and performance provide a basis for conceptualising a competency-based framework which avoids the temptation to evolve a dual curriculum and assessment system; one operating exclusively in higher education and focused on the acquisition of subject knowledge and the other operating exclusively in the schools focused on the acquisition of pedagogical competence. The second and third accounts also provide us with a basis for understanding the contribution of educational theory to the development of pedagogical competence. In developing a capacity to improve practice through reflective self-monitoring student teachers are learning to theorise about educational problems and issues. In this context the sensitive introduction of relevant ideas and concepts selected from various forms of disciplined educational inquiry can foster a capacity for self-monitoring. The use of theoretical resources in teacher training needs to be contextualised through learning activities which require students to reflect about the experience of teaching. Although much of this contextualisation of theory through reflection on experience will be the responsibility of higher education staff it need not rule out many on-the-job trainers in schools who have a sound understanding of how theory can be employed as a resource for reflectively improving the quality of teaching.

Validity and reliability

Validity refers to the 'warrant we have for making inferences or judgements on the basis of evidence' (Norris, 1990). The criterial statements in Circular 9/92 are generally specified in terms that are open to ambiguous interpretations. For example, the ability to 'assess and record systematically the progress of individual pupils' raises questions about the meanings of 'systematically' and 'progress in learning'. Underpinning these questions are theoretical issues about the relationship between pedagogy and the assessment of learning – does 'systematic' imply that the latter is a procedurally discrete process? – and about the nature and process of human cognitive development – e.g. is progression understood as a predefined hierarchical sequence of knowledge, understanding, or skills or as an organic and dynamic process in which what constitutes development progressively unfolds? Any clarification of such ambiguous criterial statements will necessitate making the theoretical perspectives which underpin them explicit and open to critique and discussion. Their use as 'warrants' for validating judgements and inferences will depend on how their underlying theoretical perspectives shape up to critique and discussion. Circular 9/92 neither makes the theoretical assumptions which underpin its competency statements explicit nor makes any attempt to justify them in the light of possible critiques of them. One might therefore conclude that the 9/92 framework is quite inadequate as a basis for validating the judgements and inferences of those involved in assessing teaching competence.

However, we would argue that there is a great deal of virtue in the specification of competency statements that convey ambiguous meanings. This resides in their potential for fostering reflection and discussion amongst assessors at the grass-roots – teacher mentors, university supervisors, and the student teachers involved in peer and self-assessment as part of the overall assessment process – about the validity of their judgements and inferences. The problem with a precisely defined and theoretically justified framework is that grass-roots assessors will tend not to use it when the theoretical perspectives which inform it contradict the tacit and unexplicated assumptions which inform their own judgements and inferences. They may pay lip-service to it while constructing their judgements on the basis of 'hidden' mental constructs and assumptions. Such frameworks encourage a form of corruption in which the evidential basis of assessment acts is, with varying degrees of self-consciousness, misrepresented to fit the framework. We would argue that the function of an ambiguous framework of competency statements is to frame a reflective discourse amongst assessors about the warrant for their actual judgements and inferences. The framework itself should be formulated in a way which indicates and supports this reflective and discursive function. Later we shall indicate how we have tried to accomplish this in formulating our own competency framework at UEA.

Circular 9/92 not only fails to address the question of 'validity' but also that of 'reliability'. Reliability refers to consistency in judgements and consistency is normally considered to be a necessary condition of establishing validity but not sufficient. Thus the specification of competences in terms of precise and measurable behavioural outcomes of performance may ensure consistency in judgements between assessors and over time, but in as much as they distort the meaning of competence they cannot provide a basis for rendering such judgements valid. In as much as Circular 9/92 does not specify competency elements with sufficient precision to ensure consistency in judgements and inferences one can be grateful to it. In our view the problem should be addressed alongside that of validity in the context of a reflective discourse between those involved in the assessment process. Rather than imposing a consensus about the meaning of teaching competence and procedures for securing the reliability of judgements a competency framework should primarily serve the educative function of enabling the assessors to participate in the reflective and discursive process through which shared understandings of teaching competence, and agreed procedures for gathering and evaluating evidence of performance, are constructed.

Developing a Competence-Based Assessment Framework in Partnership with Schools: The Approach at UEA

The UEA joint working party on competency-based assessment consisted of two deputy headteachers representing our partnership schools and three faculty members (which included the authors). The deputy heads are 'link teachers' and have overall responsibility for the supervision of all the student teachers attached to their schools. The working party members used a small collection of background material in addition to Circular 9/92 (e.g. Elliott, 1993; Scriven, 1991).

The working group found itself confronted with the task of steering its way through the demands for a theoretically coherent framework grounded in research (such as the one provided by Scriven), for something which met DfE accreditation requirements, and from the schools for simple and workable advice. It was felt that although the framework finally produced would need to accommodate the 9/92 criteria they did not constitute a suitable basis on which to begin the creation of an assessment framework. It was generally felt that the DfE criteria were lacking in coherence and very uneven; some statements being very specific in their reference/meaning while others covered a large area of performance and were very vaguely articulated. The working party decided to begin with an attempt to define the basic principles they felt should underpin the assessment framework and procedures. This allowed the group to concentrate on what they felt was required for 'their' assessment process; external requirements could be incorporated at a later stage. After a great deal of debate, which continued into the process of constructing the framework itself, the following principles were identified. The assessment system should:

- differentiate between school experiences A and B;
- be a unitary one with no sharp division between university and school-based work;
- involve teachers (especially the student's subject mentor and link teacher), university tutors, peers and pupils;
- provide a basis for formative as well as summative assessment;
- be manageable since it will be used by a large number of people;
- use a common criterial framework to guide and support judgements, gather common types of evidence and operate common procedures for recording evidence, judgements and decisions.

Each of these will now be described in further detail.

A unitary system with no sharp division between university- and school-based work

If a partnership system is to work in practice all elements of the course should be complementary and the students should not be able to distinguish between the demands being made in different elements of their work. Therefore the criteria for assessment should be consistent with each other and to an extent be common to both school and university-based work. In the early days of the partnership we anticipated that this aspiration would be difficult to realise but that the competences framework should reflect it and support the development of a seamless curriculum as a context in which it could be realised in due course.

Differentiation between school experiences A and B

The course will involve pairs of students having two periods of school-based training in different schools during the year. The expectations placed on students during these two periods will clearly differ in many respects. The assessment framework clearly needs to take this into account and include criteria: (a) that may be more applicable to the second period of school experience than the first and vice versa; and (b) that may be applicable to both but in the second period to a broader range of contexts. Students need to develop a sense of progression during the course and this implies they should be aware of expectations at different stages of their training.

Involving teachers

It is important for the professional development of the teacher in training that they receive feedback from as wide a range of people as possible. Assessment can take a variety of forms of feedback: the provision of observational data as a basis for an assessment dialogue with the student, an analysis of the student's performance, giving advice, instructing the student to do something. The central figures in this process at the level of formal assessment will be teachers and university tutors. But since we wish to produce teachers who are capable of self-evaluating their own performance on a continuous basis throughout their careers the assessment context which may considerably strengthen this capability will be less formal opportunities to obtain feedback from peers and pupils.

Since all students will be paired with another student training to teach the same subject there should be ample opportunities for peer assessment. Pairs will be able to observe each other teach, team teach together, or observe an experienced teacher's lesson together. Such events can be used to generate evidence for discussion and analysis. Obtaining pupil feedback is a problematic process for pupils with respect to predicting a teacher's response and a threatening one for teachers. However, a student teacher who is able to cope with a process of peer feedback is in a good position to begin handling pupil feedback constructively.

The competences framework should provide a focus for reflection and discussion between students and their mentors, tutors, peers, and pupils and a structure for analysing the feedback they provide.

Providing a basis for formative as well as summative assessment

One aspect of the assessment is to decide whether students are to pass or fail the course. Careful thought has to be given to the support systems introduced for students who are experiencing particular difficulties. However, since the vast majority of students pass the PGCE course the main role of the assessment system is to assist in their professional development as a teacher. Therefore a key feature of the system should be to use the assessment to identify strengths and weaknesses so that assistance can be provided where it is required. This will be particularly appropriate in the assessment of classroom performance. It is vital for the assessor to find an appropriate balance between pointing out weaknesses and supporting the growth in confidence of students.

Being manageable since it will be used by a large number of people

Assessment information will need to be exchanged between a variety of interested parties, e.g. from school to tutor for report writing, and between the two school attachments to inform the next period of school-based training. Clearly it is important that the assessment system is easy to operate while at the same time meeting the information needs of all the parties involved.

Using a common criterial framework to guide and support judgements, gather common types of evidence, and operate common procedures for recording evidence, judgements and decisions

Schools differ in their organisational and professional cultures and therefore the demands placed on students will tend to vary accordingly. In the past university tutors visited all their students on a systematic basis and were able to put the individual school into a broader context and adjust their expectations of students accordingly. This will not now be possible to the same extent since schools will have much more power over student assessment. It is therefore vital that common assessment criteria are established to inform and educate judgement rather than to impose a strait-jacket which renders judgement the prisoner of fixed and immutable standards.

The way criteria are interpreted and applied will inevitably vary to a degree, particularly at the beginning, but as the partnership evolves it is hoped that teacher assessors will have opportunities to observe assessment practices in schools other than their own, discuss variations in each other's judgements, and share different interpretations and applications of criteria. By maximising opportunities for school assessors and university tutors to participate in discussions about their assessment practices in relation to the criterial framework, we anticipate that increasing degrees of consensus in interpretations and applications will emerge and become encapsulated in a continuously evolving framework and set of recording procedures. In this way we intend that all those involved in the assessment process will not simply reproduce a common criterial framework but actively reconstruct it in a form which gives them a sense of ownership over it.

Areas of responsibility

Having made a measure of progress in establishing these basic principles of assessment (further progress was made as we proceeded) the working party decided that the competences framework should be largely constructed around a normative analysis of the teacher's role in terms of their core responsibilities for classroom processes. Like Scriven (1991) the group rejected an approach based on a description and analysis of the jobs teachers actually perform in classrooms and adopted one which emphasised the professional duties of teachers. It was therefore very much governed by a collective commitment to certain professional values which teachers have a responsibility to realise in their performances. Although Scriven's 'Duties Analysis' influenced the decision to construct a coherent framework around the idea of role responsibilities, the details of that analysis were never referred to in the construction of the core categories, and indeed while the product displayed certain similarities, it also revealed some differences. Six core areas of responsibility were defined as a basic structure for the assessment framework; namely:

1. *Understanding of the subject and the National Curriculum requirements related to it.* The term 'understanding' here was deliberately selected in preference to knowledge, since it suggests a more dynamic and active grasp of the subject matter than that commonly attributed to knowledge as a rather passive appreciation of inert facts. It is highly consistent with the second account of the knowledge/competence relationship we cited earlier: namely, that knowledge consists of abilities to organise thinking in relation to the subject matter. Moreover, such cognitive competences can be developed to a degree within as well as outside the teaching situation and therefore, in accordance with one of our assessment principles,

negate the view that one requires different assessment criteria for school-based and university-based training.

2. *Construct effective schemes of work and lesson plans to support classroom practice.* Some might argue that planning is not a core responsibility because one cannot assume that effective teaching is always a product of detailed deliberation in advance. The working party felt that although this might be true with very experienced teachers it is far less likely to be the case with student and beginning teachers.

This area of responsibility doesn't simply imply an obligation to plan schemes of work and lessons but to construct plans which effectively support good classroom practice. Again the competences involved can be developed in the context of both the school and the university. For example, case scenarios and simulation exercises can provide a context for generating schemes of work and lesson plans which can be critiqued by tutors in terms of their consistency with the educational principles by which they define good classroom practice. Such a context provides a safe learning environment for experimenting with different planning frameworks and developing those powers of discernment, discrimination, and imagination which characterise effective planning. The university context frees students from the pressure in the school context to 'plan for real': a pressure which encourages the inexperienced to play it safe and lower their sights with respect to their aims and aspirations in the classroom. The quality of students' school based planning may be considerably enhanced by opportunities to engage in off-site simulated planning exercises.

3. *Communicate content to pupils in ways which promote meaningful learning.* Teachers have a responsibility to represent their subject matter in forms which are meaningful to pupils, i.e. engage their powers of understanding and promote authentic thinking. Representing content involves communication but not always in the sense of 'telling'. In asking a question, demonstrating a procedure or illustrating a way of thinking about a problem/issue a teacher is communicating content as something which poses questions, involves procedures, and which can be thought about in certain ways, etc.

There is a sense in which the competences involved in the meaningful communication of a subject within the teaching role can be categorised in terms of knowledge application. But this would encourage a somewhat misleading account of the relationship between subject knowledge and pedagogical competence in communicating it. What we have here are two categories of competences in which the latter is partly constituted by the former. In representing their subject to pupils in classrooms teachers demonstrate their competence to think about it. The additional dimension of competence is provided by the teacher's responsibility to communicate content in forms which foster the development of the same competence in their pupils.

Again the development and assessment of these communicative competences does not have to be confined to school-based settings. In recent interviews for a tutorial position as a teacher trainer at our university candidates from the teaching profession were asked how they would help teachers handle questions about the phenomenon of magnetism which young children had been known to ask their teachers. None of the candidates provided any answer other than suggesting that such questions need not be addressed at this stage of education, in spite of the fact that they were asked by the children. The candidates demonstrated an inability to represent the concept of magnetic force in a meaningful way to these children. This was partly because of their own limited understanding of the concept and partly because of their limited understanding of young children's cognitive capacities. Much can be done in the university setting to promote, through the discussion and analysis of observational and interview data, awareness of children's cognitive potential.

4. *Create and maintain effective classroom management.* This refers to a teacher's responsibility to establish a classroom environment which is conducive to learning. Again it may be felt that competences in this category are best developed in school-based settings. But it is always a mistake to confuse the context in which competences have to be ultimately demonstrated and the contexts which contribute to their development. For example, effective classroom management will involve the ability to discriminate events that are disruptive to children's learning. Such an ability develops through experience but it doesn't always have to be direct experience. The vicarious experience achieved through the discussion and analysis of classroom research data represented in the form of case studies can do much to accelerate the development of an ability to discriminate events in terms of their significance and salience for classroom management decisions.

5. *Assess and record pupil learning activities and outcomes.* This responsibility is not viewed as additional to the responsibilities of teaching pupils. Rather it is viewed as an aspect of the teaching role. As such the assessment practices will be shaped by the intention to improve the quality of learning in the classroom. Again much can be done in the university setting to foster the development of the competences necessary in good formative assessment to support teaching decisions.

6. *Reflect on one's own actions and pupils' responses in order to improve teaching*. Competence in discharging this responsibility in a teaching context involves the ability to self-monitor one's competence in discharging responsibilities (1)–(5). In other words it is what we described earlier as 'meta-competence'. Some would argue that as such it is not a category of teaching competence. Competence at evaluating one's teaching competence is not a necessary condition of good teaching. The advocates of this position often point out the many good teachers whose practice is spontaneous, intuitively based, and largely unselfconscious. Such a position makes sense when the competences necessary in discharging the responsibilities outlined are viewed as essentially non-problematic and commonly understood. But it does not make sense in a situation where what counts as good teaching is a controversial issue both inside and outside the teaching profession and no longer viewed as taken-for-granted common-sense knowledge. This is the situation in the UK. Given this situation it can be argued that teachers have an obligation as part of their teaching role to reflect continuously about the extent to which their performance of it constitutes 'good teaching'.

Given this it becomes clear why student teachers should make a significant contribution to the process of assessing the development of their teaching competence.

Having established six core areas of responsibility the working party at UEA took the view that the next step was to brainstorm and discuss the criteria we would use to judge how well these areas of responsibility were performed. A list of criteria was compiled for each category and revised in the light of discussion about their meaning, significance, and the principles of education which underpinned them.

After the development of an agreed list we discussed issues relating to its interpretation and use by faculty and teachers. We wanted to provide guidance and support to assessors without making them feel we were being over-prescriptive and diminishing their responsibility for professional judgement. From our experience of discussion within the group we were very aware that despite the achievement of a degree of consensus our interpretations of the criteria differed to some extent and that we would tend in practice to vary with respect to the weight we placed on some rather than others. We felt there was a danger in the list being interpreted as a check-list of competences carrying equal weight which had to be worked through systematically on a one-to-one basis rather than as a basis for fostering reflection and discussion amongst assessors about the basis of their judgements and the reasons for differences between them. We neither believed it practical or desirable to specify competences in a form which removed all ambiguity in interpretation and application. We wanted the framework to serve an essentially educative function and to be open to continuing reconstruction on the basis of the reflective dialogue we hoped it would stimulate amongst assessors.

In the light of these issues we decided to turn the criteria into questions worth reflecting about and discussing in the assessment process. We also hoped that this format would support self-reflection by students and foster their understanding of the links between professional responsibilities and certain elements of competence in a way that supported rather than constrained their own critical reflection about these links.

The framework was circulated to faculty for comment with a covering statement aimed at clarifying its use as a basis for a unified assessment system and its function as a support for reflective judgement and discussion within the assessment process. In spite of this some faculty interpreted the framework as applying only to school-based learning, and as a fixed check-list specification to be worked through item by item. It was therefore not surprising to find criticism of the number of criteria listed in some categories. The working party felt that it could go some way to addressing this criticism without endorsing the assumption that underpinned it. The questions' criteria, specifying potentially significant elements of competence worth considering and collecting evidence around within the assessment process, were re-examined with a view to eliminating those whose meaning clearly overlapped with other items to a considerable degree. We were also forced to reassess the significance we were prepared to bestow on some elements by including them in the framework. In these ways we significantly reduced the number of elements in the framework, at the possible cost of over-tightening the parameters of judgement in ways which excluded aspects of competence which assessors in the field consider relevant. This could however be redressed by clearly articulating the developmental nature of the framework.

The revised framework was discussed at meetings with headteachers and participating staff of our partner schools. In these meetings we had an opportunity to clarify its aims and functions and to point out that there was no requirement for assessors to use all the criteria or to restrict assessment only to those on the list. The meetings with representatives from our partnership schools revealed a very positive response in general to the proposed framework, but raised two particularly interesting issues. At one meeting the view was expressed that the criteria for category (3) (see above) were biased in favour of a didactic style of teaching and negated a pupil-directed learning process. Others in the group disagreed and the discussion which emerged began to focus on fundamental questions about the nature of teaching and learning in classrooms. Later in the same meeting one senior teacher expressed concern that the assessment framework was too pragmatic in its assumptions and that a theoretical framework needed to be generated by the faculty as something mentors in the schools could use to help students reflect about their practice in a theoretically rigorous manner.

In our view the competences framework we have generated embodies a wide range of theoretical issues about the nature and processes of education. Its potential to do this resides in the fact that the criteria are open to discussions about their meaning and significance for classroom practice; discussions which reveal and open to theoretical inquiry the assumptions which underpin the judgements of assessors, including those of the students themselves. In as much as students are involved in a self-assessment process involving genuine dialogue with peers, mentors and tutors, the framework will generate plenty of theoretical themes and issues for students to examine in relation to their practice.

In an attempt to anticipate some of the theoretical issues that the UEA framework might stimulate debates about, we carried out a thematic analysis of the framework in the hope that it would prove useful to both tutors and mentors in schools. Restrictions on space prevent us from presenting both the UEA criterial framework and the analysis of its underlying theoretical themes in detail. However, the example in Table 2.1 may suffice to illustrate both and the links between them.

We have made no reference in this section to our previous discussion of the place of generic competences within any assessment framework. In as much as the self-monitoring competences are meta-abilities exercised in all aspects of competent performance in the teaching role they can be described as generic.

However, there are other abilities which may be generic to the teaching role in general rather than specific to a particular area of responsibility within that role. And one might well be able to classify them in terms of 'situational understanding', 'interpersonal qualities', and desired 'motivations' connected with practical achievement and influence as the work of McBer Associates has indicated. Reviewing the framework to date we can see many generic dimensions which underpin the functionally specific criteria cited in some of our categories. For example, the question (3d) asks whether the manner of communication engenders regard and respect for pupils' values and powers of understanding. Underlying the ability referred to, which relates to responsibility for meaningfully communicative content in teaching, is a capacity to grasp the way individuals think and feel about situations and events which is significant for the exercise of the teaching role in classrooms more generally. It is as significant in lesson preparation (2), assessing and reporting learning (5), and managing the classroom environment (4) as in communicating meaningful content to pupils (3).

What is now required as a stage in further developing the framework is to identify competency elements which are generic across our

> 3. Communicate content to pupils in ways that promote meaningful learning
>
> *For example:*
> (a) Has the voice clarity and a variety of tone and pitch?
> (b) Can the student arouse the interest of pupils?
> (c) Is the language used appropriate to ensure understanding across the whole range of ability?
> (d) Does the manner of communication engender regard and respect for pupils' values and powers of understanding?
> (e) Are pupils' responses encouraged and reinforced?
> (f) Are pupils encouraged to ask critical questions and discuss issues?
> (g) Does the student utilise a variety of questioning techniques?
> (h) Is the student able to respond to group dynamics and alter planned content appropriately?
> (i) Is Information Technology effectively used to motivate pupils and enhance understanding?
> (j) Does the student employ a variety of teaching strategies and styles within a lesson and across a sequence of lessons?
>
> Theoretical themes:
> - pupils' 'interests' and the development of 'understanding';
> - teacher–pupils communication: uses of language to represent the relationship between knowledge, teacher and learners;
> - the teacher's uses of language in classrooms and the theories of knowledge implicit in it;
> - moral obligations implicit in the teacher's role.

Table 2.1

responsibility domains. And a good starting point for this will be the analysis of the generic elements already presupposed by the criteria we have specified. This is important if the claim made by McBer Associates is correct; namely, that it is the generic elements of competence which essentially explain the difference between superior and average performance in a professional role.

How Can Theory Relate to Practice After Circular 9/92?

We would contend that many 'partnership schemes' devised in response to 9/92 contain two fairly discrete components which are assessed independently; namely, the practicum in the school assessed against competency criteria, and the university-based studies assessed against fairly traditional academic criteria.

If we are right, then we have a dual curriculum evolving in initial teacher education which does not differ significantly from the old logic of *learning theoretical principles* and then *putting principles into practice*. The major difference probably resides in the fact that we have reduced the amount of time devoted to the former in order to devote more time to the latter.

We want to argue that a competency-based practicum need not exclude an in-depth consideration of theoretical issues and, therefore, there is no good reason for perpetuating practices which involve a dual curriculum and assume professional learning moves *from theory into practice*. Competency-based frameworks can be conceptualised as supports for a pedagogical process shaped by a dialogic and triangular form of assessment which is developmental in its aspiration. In this triangulation process – involving the school-based mentor, the university tutor and the student teacher – the theoretical issues emerge within the practicum, as assumptions which underpin the concrete practical judgements of assessors, and which are rendered controversial in the context of the assessment discourse between the parties involved.

Competency-based assessment provides a context in which one moves from practice into theory and where the student is invited to reflect on his or her practice in the light of theoretical issues which have emerged from an assessment dialogue with a mentor and tutor. For example, he or she might be invited to reflect on the conception of 'progression in learning' embedded in his or her teaching strategies as a result of different evaluations of these strategies which emerged from the assessments of mentors, tutor and the student himself or herself. In the context of the placement in schools, such reflection might focus on data gathered about those teaching strategies by the student under the guidance of the mentor. In the context of university-based work such reflection might continue to focus on the data gathered in the course of the practice placement but utilise the theoretical literature to deepen understanding and insight into the theoretical issues which underpin practice. However, the point is that the whole of the PGCE year becomes 'the practicum' in as much as the focus throughout is on data assembled about the students' practice in schools. The theoretical resources which are utilised are selected to help the student examine issues of a theoretical kind which have emerged from self-assessment and others' assessments of his or her developing competence.

References

Department For Education (1992) *Circular 9/92 on Initial Teacher Training (Secondary Phase)*. London: DfE.

Elliott, J. (1992) *Action Research for Educational Change*. Milton Keynes: Open University Press, Ch. 8.

Elliott, J. (1993) *Reconstructing Teacher Education*, Lewes: The Falmer Press, Ch. 6.

Klemp, G.O. (1977) *Three Factors of Success in the World of Work: Implications for Curriculum in Higher Education*. Boston: McBer & Co.

MacLure, M. and Norris, N. (1990) *Knowledge Issues and Implications for the Standards Programme at Professional Levels of Competence: Final Report to the Training Agency*. Norwich, CARE, University of East Anglia. Mimeo.

Norris, N. (1990) *Understanding Educational Evaluation*. London: Kogan Page.

Scriven, Michael (1991) 'Duties of the teacher' published originally (in a revised form) as 'Evaluating teachers as professionals: the duties-based approach', in Popham, J. and Popham, S. (Eds) (1988) *Practical Approaches to Teacher Evaluation*. Association for Supervision and Curriculum Development.

3

Profiling in Practice: The Goldsmiths' Experience

Pat Mahony and Vee Harris

The Rationale for Creating a 'Profiling Scheme'

Competence-based approaches to teacher education have become the subject of considerable debate, particularly in relation to the government's political agenda for education. In 1988 when the Postgraduate Secondary course team at Goldsmiths first began work in this area, however, our prime concern was to unpack and make explicit to students our assumptions in relation to 'good practice'. Our initial discussions were therefore not framed in the language of 'competence', nor were our preoccupations solely with developing a more coherent system for assessing students. As the introduction to the first draft of what we then called 'The Profiling Scheme' explained, our intentions were to:

- make explicit to students, tutors' assumptions and criteria for good practice;
- facilitate the involvement of students in monitoring their own progress and make it easier for them to engage in the debate about what constitutes good practice in teaching;
- enable students to experience for themselves the kinds of records of achievement being developed in school;
- begin to develop exit profiles for employers.

In short, we wanted to be more open, more democratic and more supportive of students' professional development.

Any general debate about teacher competences or any discussion of a particular institution's scheme has to be set in the context of a number of wider issues concerning how teaching is to be understood, what kind of teachers are to be 'produced' and the purposes to be achieved by using a profile of teacher competences (as we later called it, for obvious reasons).

As a course team we felt strongly that our beliefs about the nature of teaching were best represented by the following account:

> Teaching is not reducible to a set of technical operations nor to the simple transmission of subject knowledge: teachers are not robots and learners are not machines. Teaching is a complex and dynamic process which involves exploration, choice, decisions, creative thinking and the making of value judgements. (Hextall *et al.*, 1991:15)

We felt equally strongly that this view of teaching should be declared so that our starting point was made as explicit (and contestable) as the detail which we would go on to elaborate. In this respect, our initiative differed markedly from what was subsequently to emerge from some official guidance. For example, whereas we wanted to open up these wider questions as a matter of concern and relevance to students, there is nothing in recent circulars (DfE, 1992, 1993; TTA, 1994) which remotely suggests that the nature of teaching is problematic or that there are issues about what kinds of people are suitable to become teachers. Instead the models of teaching represented render the learner virtually invisible, present a highly laundered account of teaching as simply a matter of delivering and assessing the National Curriculum and thereby avoid entirely the ways in which teaching and learning are social activities and as such, unpredictable and messy. A more realistic view is that:

> Teaching takes place in a communal world with shared meanings. This world is held together by commitments to certain values which neophytes (or novices) have to learn. Teaching is a moral enterprise not only defined by skill or craft in the production or the winning of things, but also by the worth of what is learned and the manner of its learning. (Olson, 1992:22)

The Development of the Account of Teacher Competence

After a number of general discussions, the course team realised that the enterprise was much more difficult than we had envisaged. As was our wont, when faced with difficult issues, we set up a small working group whose task it was to produce a first draft of the framework for discussion by the rest of the course team.

The first issue was how to write a document which did justice to what we believed were the complexities of teaching. It was clearly not an option for us to produce a checklist of observable behaviours since our concern was as much with students' underpinning knowledge, understanding and values as it was with their performance in the classroom. That is, it was as important that students could give a thoughtful and informed account of *why* they had chosen to work with a class in a particular way and to be able to propose alternatives if necessary, as it was for them to be able to achieve a threshold of performance against pre-specified criteria for success. Without this kind of evidence it is difficult to see how the inference could be made from 'a teacher competent in a particular school' to 'a competent teacher'. Having rejected a behavioural check-list model of competence, we adopted an alternative approach, namely:

> ... to assign much greater importance played by knowledge, understanding and attitudes as central to the whole process of developing professional competence and to view them as permeating and affecting practice in an integrative and holistic way.... One advantage of applying this perspective to teaching is that it can accommodate the strong dimension of values which is present in professional activities of this nature. It can thereby provide the basis for elaborating a fully developed concept of the reflective practitioner. (Whitty, 1994:6)

In the event, we found it easier to draw pictures or describe three-dimensional models of this integration than we did to produce a draft which really captured what we wanted to express about the relationship between knowledge and skill. Without the benefit of the valuable work undertaken by colleagues in other institutions we did not manage to avoid the 'atomization of professional knowledge, judgement and skill into discrete competences' (Whitty, 1994:10).

With hindsight it is easy to see how the specification of 'generic competences' (see Chapter 4), 'core criteria' (Winter and Maisch, 1991) or the matrix figure produced by the group set up by the Department of Education for Northern Ireland (DENI, 1993) would have solved our difficulties. In the event, we did discuss the possibility of introducing what we called 'metacriteria' but the prospect of distinguishing these and mapping them on to other elements of the framework defeated us.

When the Working Group presented this first draft there was, predictably, much disagreement about what should and should not be included. This lack of consensus seemed to represent not only different views of 'good practice' but also genuine concerns arising from the varied nature of the subject areas. After many heated discussions, a decision was made that each subject tutor would also 'exemplify' the general statements in terms of their own specific subject area. This done, most of us agreed that as an account of what it might take a life-time to achieve, the framework represented the beginnings of a helpful tool to support students' development, though we also noted that if applied to ourselves as criteria for summative assessment, we the tutors would probably 'fail' – an observation which contained elements which were subsequently to plague us.

It would be easy to dismiss this early work which lasted for many months, as an inefficient use of valuable time. Yet in retrospect it was naive not to have predicted the strength of feeling which would inevitably be provoked once tutors really began to share their deeply held convictions about such a value-laden activity as teaching. In addition, it could be argued that given the state of understanding about competences at that time, it represented a considerable achievement on the part of the course team to have created a framework which was rich, compared to others produced more recently with the benefit of insights developed nationally and internationally. With or without these, our experience would suggest that developing a framework of teacher competence is an extremely complicated process which could be summed up as one in which 'the practical has become shrouded in theoretical confusion and the apparently simple has become profoundly complicated' (Norris, 1991:332).

Issues Arising from the Framework

Since these early days the 'Goldsmiths Profile of Teacher Competence', has undergone a number of changes. Some of these are undoubtedly for the better, having been initiated by students, new staff and more recently by school-based tutors in partnership with college-based tutors.

However one issue (rooted in an interest in survival) has been whether the revisions ought to incorporate the language of the official accounts of competence and whether this is compatible with the continued expression of our own beliefs about the nature of teaching.

A second issue has arisen from our attempts to extend the framework to the primary courses, replacing subject-specific 'translations' with those which are age specific. This has produced some interesting debates about the extent to which good primary and secondary practice really do differ, either in general conception or in the finer detail and the extent to which the differences are the artificial products of the National Curriculum or the structure of the school day.

Third, the tension between the framework as a document intended to empower students in their professional development and one against which students would be assessed, continues to present dilemmas. On the one hand it is important in our view that new teachers understand right from the start, what kind of activity teaching is:

> Teaching is not just a technical business. It is a moral one .... There are two senses in which this is true. First, teachers are among the most important influences on the life and development of many young children. They play a key role in creating the generations of the future.
>
> There is also a second sense in which teaching is deeply moral .... This has to do with the nature of teachers' decisions and judgements .... As Schon (1987) puts it, professional action involves making discretionary judgements in situations of unavoidable uncertainty.
> (Fullan and Hargreaves, 1992:28)

Looked at in this way it is difficult to avoid the conclusion that new teachers need to understand their own development needs as a matter of lifelong commitment. However those of us with a responsibility to issue 'a licence to teach' do not have a lifetime in which to do it. The temptation therefore is to limit the framework to what might be achievable in 1 or 4 years and this may well focus on matters of technique and skill. In this case there is a danger that what is left out could drop permanently off the agenda.

The difficulties of creating the framework and the dilemmas over the tensions in the purposes it could serve were taxing enough. When it came to developing the process of using the framework (profiling), the issues were to surface again along with some new questions and new concerns. It appeared that decisions as to the nature and the purposes of the framework itself had important repercussions for the process of using it. The following is an account selected from one subject area, namely Modern Languages, and includes discussion of its attempts to reconcile the formative and the summative purposes of the profile and to do justice to the original values that had guided us in drawing up the framework. The evidence used is based on questionnaires to students and school-based tutors, taped discussions of course evaluation meetings for both groups and field notes.

Using the Framework, Beginning to Profile

The issue was not just about using the profile to assess students' performance in the classroom. From what we have argued about the nature of teaching and the role of the modern teacher it is obvious that for us 'competence cannot be assessed from performance alone' (Durrant, 1992); it is also located in the accounts used to explain, justify or evaluate classroom practice. Often these accounts formed part of the students' written assignments and it would not have made sense to maintain an out-moded theory/practice split separating 'two fairly discrete components which are assessed independently; namely the practicum in the schools which is assessed against competency criteria, and the university-based studies assessed against fairly traditional academic criteria' (Elliott, 1994:1).

Some strategies were fairly obvious from the outset and indeed the framework has served as a useful bridge between what has traditionally been conceived of as 'theory' and 'practice'. For their written assignments, students are directed to appropriate statements from the framework as criteria by which each assignment will be assessed. In addition, many of the college-based sessions are concluded by inviting students to look through the relevant sections of the profile and to discuss how they relate to the content of the session, or to their own particular anxieties or development needs in schools. By making explicit what they are learning when, students gain a sense of gradually building up their understanding and expertise and feel that 'we're really getting somewhere'.

However, by no means have all the problems been resolved. The major issues have arisen largely in the assessment process – both in relation to summative assessment by school and college-based tutors and to students' formative self-assessment.

The Use of the Profile for Summative Assessment

In our initial discussions, students were quick to grasp the difficulties of striking the balance between using the profile to support their development and using it to assess them. Some felt that using the profile for assessment purposes was 'dangerous because of the potential effect of imprisoning us'. They also pointed out the 'dangers of becoming preoccupied with getting through the profile rather than with thinking about teaching children'. This language of 'danger' is perhaps indicative of the vulnerability experienced by people learning to teach and possibly underestimated by policy makers responsible for the organisation and administration of training arrangements.

Other students argued on the other hand that the profile had to be related to assessment. If it represented criteria for good practice, as we claimed, then whether or not students successfully completed the course had to be based on these criteria. If other criteria were being used for assessment then the profile was inadequate in not making explicit what these were. In the event, the advent of partnership arrangements with schools provided the final argument for using the framework for summative purposes, since we believed that it could provide a common basis for assessment by college and school-based tutors and ensure that students received complementary and not contradictory messages about their practice in the classroom. What we did not foresee, however, was that our original decisions about the nature of the framework would face us with a number of dilemmas, when we came to use it for the purposes of summative assessment.

We have already described why we rejected a framework that would be confined to the PGCE year. For the same reasons, the competence descriptors were not arranged in any temporal or hierarchical order, with some identified as priorities for the PGCE year and others for further professional development. However, the resulting length of the document and the lack of any indication of basic minimum requirements to achieve 'a licence to teach' presented us with a number of problems.

Many students found it 'daunting and off-putting' and despite reassurance to the contrary, clearly felt a pressure to achieve, in one year, a state of near perfection in relation to competence: 'I felt I could never possibly fulfil all those criteria in a year'. As for the school-based tutors, although the length and detail of the document avoided misinterpretations, it also presented them with an unwieldy and cumbersome burden of paperwork; there was 'too much to comment on and it was time-consuming at first'. Furthermore, it did not always provide the clear guidelines we needed in terms of final decisions as to passing or failing the weaker students. For example, it is debatable whether all the competences are of equal importance in decisions relating to the award of PGCE. Furthermore, in the context of assessment it is impossible to avoid the pressures to quantify how much competence or how many ways of 'motivating pupils' need to be developed. As one student at risk of failing commented, 'there are no bottom lines, so I can't tell if I am nearly there or still have a long way to go'. Her school-based tutor commented that the framework 'is not always the quick indicator they would like and we are all conditioned towards the marks out of 10 idea'.

The Modern Languages team believed, however, that grading competence was undesirable since it would focus attention on performance irrespective of the teaching context. On the other hand, a way had to be found of giving clearer guidance about the criteria for passing the course. Therefore the team of school-based tutors have selected 20 statements from the framework which in their view are the most important in determining whether a student should be awarded the PGCE. They have also begun to write more detailed indicative achievement criteria, stating for example what is expected with classes of motivated pupils and what with more disaffected ones. What all these difficulties raise is 'the massive mismatch between the appealing language of precision that surrounds competency or performance-based programmes and the imprecise, approximate and often arbitrary character of testing when applied to human capabilities' (Norris, 1991:336). The attempts to integrate knowledge and understanding have further increased our difficulties since how much one knows or how deeply one understands cannot be determined by tape measures or plumb lines (Borst, 1970).

The Use of the Profile for Formative Purposes

We intended that the framework should serve not only as a bridge between college and schools for summative purposes but for formative ones also. Some strategies to achieve this were obvious from the outset. The team believed that it was important to make explicit the links between the students' performance in the classroom and the profile framework. We therefore agreed on a common format for our written lesson observation notes which would end by indicating areas of progress and those for future development, linked to the profile statements. What was less clear, however, was the process by which we would ask students to evaluate their own progress and the forms of writing and dialogue that would best support them.

The Use of Writing in Self-Assessment

Journal writing is a popular way of encouraging students to reflect on their practice. We doubted, however, whether a journal was the best way to enable busy school-based tutors to engage in regular productive dialogue with the students about their progress. We were keen to ensure that in the course of the year, there should be what Richert (1990) calls 'structured reflection opportunities', where the students could review their progress together with both the school and college-based tutor and it was therefore decided that profile tutorials would be held in school at the end of each term with the profile serving as the basis for dialogue. Having rejected journal writing, it was decided that the student and tutors would prepare for these tutorials by completing a pro forma indicating under each of the major categories of the framework, the progress made so far and some priorities for the future. In this way, we hoped to encourage a three-way systematic analysis of progress on all aspects of the framework, and not just those that were of immediate pressing concern. In retrospect, it is clear that our agenda was simply to support the students in identifying what they had they grasped so far and what remained to be achieved. What we failed to provide was a structure which would also support them in coming to terms with other important aspects of the process of learning to be a teacher.

The limitations of our approach were evident in the students' mixed responses to the pro formas. For some, it clearly fulfilled a useful purpose in provoking them to go beyond their immediate feelings and concerns and to consider other aspects of their development on which they needed to focus. One student remarked, for example that, 'it made me adopt a rigorous and systematic approach to self-evaluation.' Another was honest enough to admit that, 'it's good to make us focus on areas we might not naturally feel inclined towards, e.g. IT!'. Another comment, typical of the more confident students was that, 'I had reached a sort of plateau by the middle of my teaching practice, where things were ticking over OK and I really wasn't clear where to go next. Reading through the profile reminded me of issues I'd somehow forgotten and helped me set myself a new agenda'.

The comments of other students, however, suggested the limitations of just using a simple pro forma. They pointed towards the need for a different form of writing to develop a different kind of reflection, if the nature of the original framework was to be respected. They 'found the subdivision or sections too constricting and you tended to make your comments fit the categories rather than writing down your feelings/ needs'. The comment is revealing in two respects. We had already been concerned in drawing up the framework that we were fragmenting teaching into a set of discrete, tidy compartments. For this student, at least, the process of using it seems to have been equally artificial and failed to represent in any useful way the emotional experiences of her life in the classroom. The reason may in part relate to Leat's (1993:505) criticism that the inadequacy of an approach to competence, based solely on cognitive development 'is the failure to recognise the salience of feelings to competence, in teaching, as in other domains'. He describes in some detail a student who was:

struggling though a period of conflict between cognition (knowing how she behaved and how she wanted to behave), her existing, dominant behaviour pattern and her feelings (her discomfort with her new target). She was trying on new clothes, feeling uncomfortable but gradually growing accustomed. She was adamant that sharing tension with others was vital in supporting the change. (Leat, 1993:506)

Clearly then a simple pro forma cannot provide the space necessary to acknowledge the affective dimensions of changing familiar patterns and the internal conflicts created. Nor does it allow students to explore 'the strong dimension of values' (Whitty, 1994) which are inherent in the teaching process.

Useful though the pro forma is, therefore, as a tool for charting the students' progress, we have come to feel that a different form of writing may be essential to complement it. Keeping a journal may be important if we are to do justice to the central role played by knowledge, understanding and attitudes in the process of developing professional competence. Not only does it acknowledge the need for teachers to deal with the affective aspects of teaching, it also enables them to question the fundamental assumptions underlying their practice. Whilst warning us that 'diaries and journals may suit only the more literary and introspective among us...', Fullan and Hargreaves (1992:92) also recognise them as one of a number of ways in which teachers can 'review the purposes and principles that underpin our classroom judgements...' and thus move beyond a simple analysis of 'what works and what doesn't' (Fullan and Hargreaves, 1992:91).

The Use of Evidence in Self-Assessment

As a way of encouraging the students to assess themselves realistically and honestly, we also asked them to provide evidence for any claims they made about their practice in school. In the event, this apparently straightforward request merely set up a whole chain of issues which we still have not resolved. These include what is to be counted as evidence (and how we decide when there is enough of it) and whether everything is amenable to the provision of evidence. There are obvious implications here for the initial definition of the framework of competences itself but simply because there may be areas which are not readily open to clear indicators or 'evidence', this should not mean that they are excluded from the framework. In this we agree with Leat who rightly warns against defining competence, 'solely through what is easy to assess' (Leat, 1993:507).

It was not just the process of how the students would use the profile, however, that raised problems; there were further issues to be addressed in terms of how we responded to the students' self-evaluations.

Providing Feedback on Students' Self-Assessment

Our initial and somewhat naive assumption was that the process of self-evaluation would be relatively straightforward and students would find little difficulty in charting their own development with the support of the clear and explicit criteria which the framework offered.

When students' profile entries were analysed, however, the variety of ways in which they engaged in the self-evaluation process became apparent. Although the sample was small, there appeared to be some correlation between the quality of reflection and the quality of their practice. However even within the group of strong students, women tended to talk about their practice most critically. Social class is also significant for this student: 'to be asked to judge yourself for yourself, when you've spent your life already being judged by middle-class standards (and trying to beat them) is just too much'.

Some of the weaker students experienced difficulties both in forming a realistic view of their own progress and in moving beyond a preoccupation with their own performance towards what would make for a useful learning experience for their pupils (Fuller, 1970). Other weak students wrote clearly and articulately about their problems and the effects on their pupils but seemed unable to move forward in practice to resolve them.

Given the variation in students' competence to monitor their own practice, it is clear that they need the kind of thoughtful feedback to which Copeland (1986) refers. Profile tutorials would seem to provide the ideal context for such feedback since as Eraut (1994:69) points out, 'teaching is primarily an oral culture...'. The reality so far, however, has been that it is difficult enough for both college and school-based tutors to provide time for the basic negotiation of progress and priorities during the joint profile tutorials, let alone for a full discussion about the quality of their self-evaluations. The alternative could be to review regularly students' written self-evaluations, although we would not want to arrive at a situation where 'provided you keep within acceptable limits, it's not what you think or do but the way you write about it that counts' (Eraut, 1994). Nor would we want to threaten the ethos of trust which students need if they are really to be honest about admitting their difficulties. This is an issue which will become acute, if proposals to develop a career-entry profile are implemented since who 'owns' the profile and who has the right to pass on what to whom is a source of much concern to students and again raises the tension between its formative and summative purposes.

Conclusion

Much has happened since the development of the original framework, perhaps most critically the extension and formalisation of partnership with schools. Our original aims in establishing the framework have to some extent been met and students, college and school-based tutors have all been generally enthusiastic about its benefits (Harris, 1994). Perhaps one of the most significant comments in favour of profiling teacher competence came from a student:

> It is very easy when you start teaching practice to evaluate your own performance by how you feel at the end of the lesson – 'that went really well' or 'that was terrible'. I think the profile has played a crucial role in moving me beyond these gut reactions to analyse in a more rigorous way what has actually happened in a lesson. I came to a point somewhere in the middle of the teaching practice when I realised that I could teach a lesson and I didn't need any feedback from my tutors because I had a clear picture myself of what had been good and what bad and what I would do differently next time.

However, we have become more aware of the intricate relationship between how the original framework is defined, how it is used in practice, and the models of teaching and learning to teach implied by both. It becomes clear that the profile alone cannot resolve all the tensions within ITE. Anybody who believes that simply placing a profile document in the hands of beginning teachers will enable them to achieve a high quality of practice is severely misguided. The profile can support their development but not replace the need for wise, well-informed and experienced staff who work with them. No matter how detailed the framework, the process of using it will always generate the need for interpretation, professional judgement and for ongoing discussion. Given this, profiles of teacher competence can never guarantee uniformity of standards. This is a matter of increasing concern as routes into teaching proliferate and more people become involved in the training process. As Broadfoot (1994:1) points out:

> there are no panaceas within education. No quick fix, magic tape solutions to improving the quality of education any more than there are instant remedies for the besetting social ills of unemployment, injustice, prejudice and poverty.

She goes on to suggest that:

> if profiling is to be the beginning rather than the end, of the learning process: if it is to encourage the maximum rather than reinforcing the minimum: if it is to be empowering rather than punitive, it must become the language of 'diagnostic discourse' not the 'dead data' of records, reports, and certificates. (Broadfoot, 1994:5)

For this to become a reality, not only must the framework itself take account of the complexity of teaching, not only must the process by which it is used acknowledge the challenge of learning to teach, but students, school and college-based tutors need time; time to come to grips with the profile framework, time for profile tutorials and time to provide proper feedback on the students' self-evaluations. Time is needed for other purposes too. If we are seriously interested in 'good practice' in terms of teaching pupils and students, then the profile should serve as a focus for a number of other debates through which HEI and schools can reach shared understandings. If the profile framework constitutes a definition of professional competence, then we need to agree on the kinds of opportunities students need to achieve that competence: this involves discussing the content and methods of the course as well as issues about which elements of the course are best 'delivered' where. Depending on the model of teaching embedded in the initial framework, so the answers will vary. In other words, the profile should serve as a trigger for a wider debate about what it means to educate teachers.

Having argued that for profiles to support the development of learning to teach, *time* needs to be available for proper professional conversations to occur, we have to recognise that time is what no one has. We live in a world shaped by market relations in which teacher education has to be delivered as (cost) efficiently as possible. If we suppress our excitement at the potential of profiles to empower beginning teachers, it is possible to understand the current enthusiasm for competence-based teacher education as a more cynical move towards specifying the product for the employer (Sidgwick, Mahony and Hextall, 1994). The more explicit these product specifications, the easier it is to 'tick them off' once acquired and to transfer the bearers of these skills (people) from one employment context to another. In addition, the more simplistic the product specification, the more cheaply it can be produced; it does after all take longer to get students to understand *why* than *how*.

Furthermore, if teaching can be defined according to common-sense definitions and then split up or broken down into its component parts, then training or education as we know them could completely disappear – much could be learnt on the job and since the emphasis would have shifted from input (education) to outcome (competence) it would be very easy to move financial responsibility from the state to the individual or employer. If we are already some way down this path then it becomes a matter of urgency to insist on the importance of developing profiling systems which do justice to the nature and purposes of teaching. This means clarifying what is involved in learning to teach well and being prepared to assert collectively that quality cannot be achieved 'on the cheap'. The question should not be 'Can we afford to educate our teachers well'? but rather 'Can we afford not to'?

Acknowledgement

This chapter is written in acknowledgement of the PGCE Modern Languages students whose constructive and insightful contributions helped to shape our thinking.

References

Borst, C. V. (1970) *The Mind-Brain Identity Theory*. London: Macmillan.

Broadfoot, P. (1994) *Profiling and the Professional Development of Teachers: Process, Product and Practice*, Conference Paper, Anglia Polytechnic University, 24 November.

Copeland, W. D. (1986) 'The RITE framework for teacher education: preservice applications', in Hoffman, J. V. and Edwards, S. A. (eds) *Reality and Reform in Teacher Education*. New York: Random House, pp. 25–44.

DENI (Department of Education Northern Ireland) (1993) *Review of Initial Teacher Training (ITT) in Northern Ireland: Report of the Development Group*. Belfast: DENI. (See also Chapter 7, this book.)

DfE (1992) *Initial Teacher Training (Secondary Phase)* (Circular 9/92). London: DfE.

DfE (1993) *The Initial Training of Primary School Teachers* (Circular 14/93). London: DfE.

Durrant, A. (1992) Speech given at the National Conference of Enterprise Awareness in Teacher Education (EATE), July 1992, Huddersfield.

Elliott, J. (1994) 'How does theory relate to practice post circular 9/92' Unpublished Observations.

Eraut, M. (1994) *Developing Professional Knowledge and Competence*. Lewes: The Falmer Press.

Fullan, M. and Hargreaves, A. (1992) *What's Worth Fighting For In Your School*. Buckingham: Open University Press.

Fuller, F. (1970) *Personalised Education for Teachers: One Application of the Teacher Concerns Model*. Austin, Tx: University of Texas, R and D Centre for Teacher Education.

Harris, V. (1994) *Partnership in Practice: What do Students Make of it? Links No. 11*. London: Centre for Language Teaching and Research.

Hextall, I., Lawn, M., Menter, I., Sidgwick, S. and Walker, S. (1991) *Imaginative Projects: Arguments for a New Teacher Education*. London: Goldsmiths College.

Leat, D. J. K. (1993) 'Competence, teaching, thinking and feeling', *Oxford Review of Education*, **19** (4), 499–510.

Norris, N. (1991) 'The trouble with competence', *Cambridge Journal of Education*, **21** (**23**), 331–341.

Olson, J. (1992) *Understanding Teaching*. Milton Keynes: Open University Press.

Richert, A. E. (1990) 'Teaching teachers to reflect: a consideration of programme structure', *Journal of Curriculum Studies*, **22** (6), 509–527.

Schon, D. (1987) *Educating the Reflective Practitioner*. London: Jossey-Bass.

Sidgwick, S., Mahony, P. and Hextall, I. (1994) 'A gap in the market?' *British Journal of Sociology of Education*, **15** (4), 467–479.

TTA (1994) *Profiles of Teacher Competences – Consultation on Draft Guidance*. London: Teacher Training Agency.

Whitty, G. (1994) 'The use of competences in teacher education'. Unpublished Observations.

Winter, R. and Maisch, M. (1991) *The Asset Programme*, Vols 1 and 2. Chelmsford: Anglia Polytechnic/Essex Social Services Department.

4

Diversity, Change and Continuity: Developing Institutional Policy at the Manchester Metropolitan University

Jack Hogbin, Pat Cockett and David Hustler

Introduction

The Didsbury School of Education at The Manchester Metropolitan University, is one of the largest Teacher Education units in the UK, with initial teacher education courses for intending secondary teachers (mainly 1-year Post Graduate Certificate in Education) involving 642 students in 1995 (across 13 subjects) and for primary involving 675 4-year BEd students and 86 PGCE students. In addition, there are over 1,000 students registered for various continuous professional development awards. There are 115 full-time academic staff.

Size of institution and variety of courses, age-phases, and subjects are not presented here as minor background. They are central to the nature of the case study in this chapter. As Andy Hargreaves notes 'it is easy to ... over-homogenize the cultures and perspectives of those who work within (faculties of education). ... Students often belong to different sub-cultures organized around the subject or age-phase ... the faculty also frequently divides into "methods" and "disciplines" people, etc.' (Hargreaves, 1995:4). This chapter overviews a process through which the staff at Didsbury together with teachers moved towards a policy for the professional development of teachers, in the context of dramatic national shifts in teacher education and more specifically in the context of government requirements concerning competences. Competency requirements became a powerful engine for opening up those different cultures, for explicating fundamental arguments regarding teacher eduction, for pointing up different histories and unrecognised commitments. There is a parallel here with the point made by amongst others Barton and Elliott, in Chapter 2 of this book, that competency-based approaches might be viewed as a major asset in so far as they are used explicitly to provide a framework for continuing discourse, amongst intending teachers, tutors and teachers: a discourse concerned with what it is to be a teacher and what teacher development could and should be about.

We start with an overview of traditions associated with differing routes into teaching and how those traditions resonate with the competency debate. Those differing traditions and associated cultures are all visible within the School of Education and the chapter discusses some of the differing tensions or polarities which became apparent in the process of moving towards an overall policy statement. This section touches briefly on some of the relevant literature on the management of change, before moving into a presentation of selections from the policy document which emerged. The last section, linked in with our concluding comments, touches on some areas associated with the policy document which are currently exercising our minds.

Routes, Competences and Socio-Historical Context

Decision-making in institutions offering teacher education within the UK has always taken place in the context of a balance between reactive processes and proactive development. The former has derived from long-standing government involvement and the latter from traditions of academic autonomy and collegiality. In 1995, the issue is one of relating quality (academic and professional standards) to funding (teacher supply and the political interests in education). One current link between proactive and reactive processes is the issue of competences. Competences are seen by some as a means of providing a key element of measuring quality and thereby providing a basis for raising standards and rewarding excellence. The context is one of a declining unit of resource and competition between institutions for funding and students.

The political significance of competences sits uneasily with a controversial and varied approach to them which derives from the traditions of academic and professional autonomy (Barnett, 1994; Hodkinson, 1995b). A key point of critical history is that of the difference between the liberal intellectual traditions associated with the arts and science first degrees offered by universities, and the craft traditions of the professions and industry which have long felt undervalued. Competences have their origins in this craft tradition and several formulations derive from an analysis of what is involved in performing a task or job efficiently. Competences viewed from the perspective of certain liberal intellectual traditions are often regarded as a travesty of what 'standards' are taken to be. The values of liberal education viewed from the craft traditions are often perceived as woolly theorising, lacking in practical relevance (see Chapter 8). Teacher education can be caught between these two perspectives.

This wider context has received a variety of expressions within the ethos, histories and particular organisational structures of institutions. Such is the case with the Didsbury School of Education. Historically, the merger in 1977 of the former Didsbury College with Manchester Polytechnic itself signalled the interaction between the vocational ethos and origins of the Polytechnic and the liberal aspirations of a higher education college. The complexities of such a merger were heightened by the size and growth of teacher education provision in the institution. Pragmatically determined institutional organisation resulted in responsibilities for PGCE developments being allocated to one head of department and BEd (Hons) development being allocated to another. The strong, independent traditions associated with departments and the location of the 'liberal subject' dimension within the BEd(Hons) resulted in a decade of largely 'separate development'. The PGCE tradition – influenced strongly by movements such as Enterprise in Higher Education and The Technical and Vocational Education Initiative – strengthened the vocational focus of the PGCE and the interest in learning contracts and competences found a field ready for development. By contrast, the BEd(Hons) remained relatively untouched by these developments and strongly influenced by a distinctive blend of the liberal subject based traditions and a constructivist ideology derived from the former Polytechnic Education Department (Pearce and Pickard, 1987). Staff provision was for many years sufficiently generous for many tutors to develop roles and identities in either the PGCE or BEd(Hons) traditions. Institutional structures reinforced different ideologies expressed in diverse languages. The eventual reduction and turnover in staff, further mergers and the emergence of an emphasis on enhanced partnership with schools eventually brought about widespread recognition of a need for change in this local context.

The local tradition of 'separate development' was, however, for the better part of two decades from 1970 caught up within the larger structure of routes within the teacher education system at national level. The major route for secondary teachers has been a conventional first degree followed by a post-graduate certificate. The major route for primary teachers has been a BEd or BA(QTS) and for more than a decade a distinction has been drawn by national bodies (CATE and HMI) between subject studies and subject application. Hence, the conceptualisation and structural developments have identified the two traditions: the liberal tradition embodied in a degree or subject, the craft tradition embodied in the PGCE or subject applications. Other aspects of the preparation of teachers have followed a similar crude division between Education Studies (theory) and curriculum studies/school experience (practical). The challenges to these conceptual and structural divisions have not been widely heard and have been reinforced by political debate which has blamed teacher education for poor standards of teaching in schools. These traditional patterns have been reinforced by the government quangos which have sought to mediate between political intervention and institutional academic autonomy. The Council for National Academic Awards reinforced the conventions with two committees: the Post-Graduate Initial Training Board (PGIT) and the Under-Graduate Initial Training Board (UGIT). These boards set a national framework of policy to which the different courses gave allegiance. The ethos and frameworks they developed presented significantly different rationales for the understanding of teaching. PGIT focused on the skills in teaching competence; UGIT focused on the skills of the reflective practitioner.

Courses in institutions reacted to these different approaches by developing different philosophies, expectations, modes of delivery and assessment. In general, secondary ITT was associated with the degree/PGCE route and the primary with the undergraduate BEd/ BA(QTS) route, though at Didsbury there also exists a growing Primary PGCE and a BEd secondary route. Declining resources, the rationalisation of institutions, the growth of INSET, the disappearance of CNAA and CATE and other factors have led to a new situation. Not least, teachers have been confused by working on courses in the same institution with markedly different philosophies and styles: hardly a powerful basis for coherent partnership. The desire for a more coherent approach has steadily grown, together with a key question: whether the 'thinking' and 'doing' aspects of teaching can be united on the basis of a new view of competence in teaching.

We recognise the simplistic nature of some of these distinctions, certainly when contrasted with the arguments marshalled elsewhere in this book. In addition, we have not addressed here issues to do with becoming a 'secondary teacher' *vis-à-vis* becoming a 'primary teacher'. However, the differing structural bases for differing routes into teaching and the substructures within routes have carried with them differing cultural histories and professional identities and commitments both with the Didsbury School of Education and across the broader range of partnership and alliances concerned with teacher education. We shift now to an overview of the more immediate context at Didsbury, a somewhat fragmented context with various parties addressing, or very deliberately not addressing, competency issues.

Towards a Policy

By June 1992, various developments were underway. One-year, 2-year and 4-year secondary courses had to be rewritten to meet the requirements of Circular 9/92. Postgraduate courses, primary and secondary, had included competences from Circular 24/89 into their assessment processes in the form of Learning Contracts. The Primary BEd course had not explicitly included competences in the course design. School of Education tutors in collaboration with LEAs through projects for newly qualified teachers were working on competence-based profiles. Tutors from the School of Education were also involved in: ESRC research into competence-based teacher education; designing competence-based courses for FE teachers; NVQ developments in further and higher education; school management competency profiles, etc.

Two things were clear. The first was that there was a need for greater coordination of, and coherence between, these developments and the second was that all primary courses would have to respond to competence-based criteria. Although there had been a move in the School of Education to more cross-institution and cross-course policies, the main lines of decision making were still through largely autonomous course committees. The word competence was being used in many contexts but it was quite clear that very different and even mutually contradictory meanings were being given to the term, as has been noted elsewhere (Hodkinson, 1995a; Tuxworth, 1989).

Whilst it was clear that something needed to be done, it was not clear what that was. In the end, more by accident than by design, a cross School of Education working group was formed with the brief to devise a School of Education policy on profiling and competences. The group was made up not of 'experts' on competence-based course design, nor of course leaders, but of people who had vested interests because they would have to put the results into practice. It was necessary to avoid getting locked into a battle between competing views of competences or a battle between courses. It was important that the outcomes of the debate would be intelligible and acceptable to the vast majority of tutors. The parallel developments to move teacher education further into schools made it imperative that the outcomes were not only accessible to teachers, but also could provide a meaningful framework for discourse. The group began by sharing information about current practice in relation to competences in the various courses and projects. The second stage was to explore models and developments from elsewhere. To do this, sub-groups were formed to research and report back. The sub-groups drew in extra participants so that a wide cross-section of the School of Education, schools and LEAs became involved. This research confirmed what had been intellectually understood from the beginning, that there was no answer waiting to be discovered. If progress was to be made it would be through sharing practical experience and knowledge and constructing a solution in our own context.

By December 1992, a report was circulated which formed the basis of a series of seminars and whole-school staff development sessions including teachers. At the end of these processes, in summer 1993, no statement of policy had emerged but a wide range of possibilities and their implications for course design had been explored. People had begun to recognise the legitimate concerns behind frequently contradictory opinions and beliefs. There was also an emerging consensus about the direction which the School of Education should be taking which will be described later in this chapter. The last stage of this phase involved the actual writing of the policy. In retrospect we have been led to revisit some of our understandings of the management of change.

Early research into the effective management of educational change concentrated on common factors which seemed to be always present in effective organisations. Studies of education institutions gave rise to lists of conditions which had a structure and logic: strong leadership, common aims, good communications. The attempts to manage change in institutions which followed from this had a parallel logic: train the leaders to lead, agree a mission statement, set common goals, change the system to meet those goals and monitor progress. Louis (1994), amongst others, challenges these notions. Her work is based on studies, not of schools which are seen to be successful but of schools which are seen to have changed significantly. What she found defied the logic of managed change:

- The most effective schools took action before they planned;
- the vision of what they were doing emerged after taking action rather than before;
- there was an opportunistic use of external pressures and available programmes;
- changes were constantly being scanned for problems and unexpected outcomes.

Other characteristics included risk taking, embracing conflict, story telling to give meaning and significance to action and so on. To explain these unanticipated results from her studies she turned to theories of 'organisational learning'. This she defines as learning:

> ... which involves the creation of socially constructed interpretations of facts and knowledge that enter the organisation from the environment, or are generated from within. This emphasis distinguishes the organisational learning literature ... from studies and theories that are derived from the individual cognition tradition. (Louis, 1994:9)

We would not claim that the process at Didsbury was modelled on theories of organisational learning. However, we see the organisational learning model as a frame for revealing some of those hidden complexities of the process that are disguised by the simple historical description given above.

The accepted way of managing change within the institution had been through the writing of papers and their review and acceptance through a hierarchy of committees, a prime example of the 'individual cognition tradition'. It is a process which works well enough when it is not necessary to question underlying assumptions and when the general culture of the institution is not being challenged. The introduction of competences into teacher education, however, was itself a challenge to aspects of the prevailing culture and the conflicts engendered would not be solved by someone doing some work on them and coming up with a 'solution'. The whole institution had to come to terms with a fundamental challenge. The process uncovered complex and deeply-rooted issues best described as a series of polarities:

1. Liberal arts – craft approach;
2. Undergraduate – post graduate traditions;
3. Common policies – autonomy/philosophy of courses;
4. External – internal;
5. Progression – learning.

Polarities (1), (2) and (3) we have already discussed. The fourth 'polarity' has two strands to it. First, the external pressure to produce measures of competence was a pressure to move at speed, structures to be in place for the new 'partnership' courses running from 1994. Internally, it was recognised that there must be an ownership of these developments and that takes time. Second, one of the purposes of competences is to describe learning outcomes in a way which communicates within and outside the institution. It must make the complex and even mysterious process of learning to teach as transparent as possible and yet that same description must work internally. It is a legitimate criticism that in the past there has been an unnecessary use of jargon, a sort of mystification of the processes of teacher education. There is, however, the contrary problem of over-simplification and the loss of a necessary professional language and perhaps much more. A key issue here was to provide a framework which was itself a usable and *accessible* basis for discussion amongst tutors, teachers and students.

The fifth 'polarity' is not quite a polarity in the same sense though there is a tension between the need to describe courses in terms of how a student makes progress through the course and the complex nature of learning. We return to this at the end of the chapter.

To an extent, engaging in a process of explicating these polarities was itself an action through which a different vision of course organisation, collaboration between courses and a School of Education structure began to emerge. The new structure must necessarily be less rigid than the old which had some of the characteristics of 'Balkanisation' as described by Hargreaves (1994) in which courses could operate as quasi-independent city states. The competences working group with its cross-school structure and floating membership would also appear to meet Hargreaves' call for temporary structures, cutting across existing organisation, which are set up to meet particular needs.

All meaningful change must be based on what is valued and 'you can't mandate what matters' (Fullan, 1993:21). The imposition of competences, whether by government decree or by 'expert' paper, could only have had a negative influence on practice. Though the process actually followed may have been a long one, emerging policy can allow both a restatement of what is valued and recognition of legitimate external demands.

The policy contains no list of competences but instead a list of questions to be raised in the next phase, which is to translate the policy into workable course structures. The process does not end in a revelation of exactly what it is that makes a teacher competent. Instead, questions lead to more questions as the organisation continues to learn, by trying things out, about the complexities and paradoxes of teaching, learning and learning to teach (Fullan, 1993).

The policy statement is much too long to include in its entirety here, though copies of it are available on request. What follows is the beginning to the document and after this we characterise and discuss the rest of the policy.

Policy for Professional Preparation of Teachers

Preamble

This policy offers a principled statement of the position of the School of Education with regard to the professional preparation of teachers. It is the outcome of a long process of discussion, consultation and debate across the School of Education and with colleagues in school. The policy is intended to provide a framework for all teaching programmes within the School of Education and addresses the key issues of:

- the understanding of the effective teacher;
- its basis in a view of knowledge;
- and the embodiment of these in a wide variety of course structures.

The policy is viewed as one that will evolve further over time and will, therefore, be subject to regular review and amendment as appropriate. Courses should include reference to this process in their development plans and annual monitoring and evaluation.

Introduction

Our view is eclectic, drawing on a range of perspectives and may be stated briefly as follows: professional preparation is grounded in experience and practice. Our students come with knowledge at a variety of levels that embodies facts, theories and procedures. They also come with a variety of experiences of schools, teachers and the processes of learning, whether implicitly or explicitly recognised by them. The courses we provide build upon knowledge, experience and practice in interactive processes. Experience and practice are analysed, knowledge is assimilated, developed and created, in an explicitly professional understanding. This understanding informs and influences practice.

Competences do not stand alone in the professional preparation of teachers. Competences are related to a view of knowledge and professional practice. Each is grounded in a range of values which are by their nature pluralistic or controversial. It is within this overarching concept of the process of professional development that competences are acquired, extended and used at a variety of levels. Although competences can be identified, they will be used in ways that cannot be predetermined. They will be used in different educational circumstances and within a wider educational perspective than a simple use of common sense or consensual application. In particular, their use in crude check-lists is rejected. The use of competences within a wider perspective of professional understanding is, however, fully endorsed. That wider understanding is embodied in our view of teaching:

> Our understanding of the effective teacher is that of a professional communicator who can think analytically and creatively, who can make decisions and solve problems, who can manage and not just survive change, and who can be a significant influence in a democratic and ethical society. Such a view rejects any suggestion that a teacher is a mere educational technocrat without wider responsibilities.

The understanding of an effective teacher entails three major perspectives as follows:

1. *A range of professional values.* These will include an explicit concern for the learner (at whatever age or stage or circumstance) as both an individual and a member of the community both in school and elsewhere. There will be explicit recognition of the need to promote equal opportunities and social justice for all in matters of race, religion, gender, class and disability. Policies and practices will be fostered which are non-discriminatory and anti-racist. Recognition of the need to respect the professional beliefs and values of others and commitment to the management of ethical responsibilities and value conflicts is fundamental.

2. *A breadth and depth of knowledge.* Courses and teaching programmes will promote the intellectual and imaginative powers of learners, will foster understanding, judgement, and the ability to engage in enquiring, analytical and creative activities, including the justification

and conceptualisation of knowledge in terms of its professional relevance and application. Learning of all kinds in the context of teaching in both the university and schools will foster independent judgement, critical awareness and the skills of communication.

3. *A variety of professional self-awareness and practice.* Knowledge and professional values will underpin professional self-awareness and practice. They will inform and contribute to the acquisition and development of professional skills and be manifest in learning outcomes, amongst which will be statements of competence, including those required by the Secretary of State. Professional awareness involves open and critical dialogue which in turn characterises all forms of communication between children, parents, teachers and others. Such dialogue based on mutual trust and respect will be sensitive to the nature and quality of all forms of personal interaction. Responsible judgement exercised by beginning teachers will take account of a variety of occasions, situations and circumstances in which the skills of teaching will be used.

The process of development included then the generation of a vision (Louis and Miles, 1992) which was captured in a short statement offering a consensus on what the group regarded as the 'effective teacher', (see quote, page 50).

This statement, while providing a vision, was sufficiently broad and open to have the capacity for adaptation by a wide variety of courses (both PGCE and BEd) while at the same time taking account of wider governmental mandates and the need for local use by schools. As such, the policy also emphasised that any policy statement should, 'be expressed in language which offers a coherent view of professional preparation and is accessible to all those engaged in educating students and teachers'.

The policy sought to draw up principles that would inform all course programmes, identify strategies for implementation and student entitlements and offer explicit guidance through a series of key questions which all courses could use in their development procedures. Key principles covered teaching and learning, competences and learning outcomes, profiling and assessment. A typical statement of principles on assessment embodies the kind of balance the policy sought to achieve:

> All assessment activities will offer students opportunities to engage in relevant professional activities, will be worthwhile learning experiences in themselves and will enable students to demonstrate competences together with higher order and analytical skills. (Part A, no 7)

The strategies described related to course development procedures, quality assurance and familiar elements of these, but gave special prominence to the concept of student entitlement as a foundation of professional progression:

> Provision of the entitlements in a variety of ways but by means of progression which will take account of the range, pace and depth of students' professional needs. More detailed descriptions will be provided in relation to particular components throughout the course. (Part B, 2b)

Professional progression was linked to earlier principles, for example, the statement on assessment was followed up in a range of strategies for the use of different courses:

> Course mechanisms which facilitate the interaction of values, knowledge, professional self-awareness and professional practice on a continuing and developmental basis, e.g. journals, learning contracts, reviews. (Part B, 2c)

The policy paper set out a series of questions which were action-orientated but had two clearly stated major purposes:

> To guide course/programme development (including those in partnership contexts); to embody a perspective on development in relation to quality. (Part C, 1a, 1b)

The questions covered:

- the framework of courses, for example course aims, roles and responsibilities and resources;
- the structures of courses, for example, the interaction of theory and practice;
- use of oral and written dialogue;
- the use of course mechanisms, for example, the opportunities for individual creative interpretation, formulation of professional goals;
- use of evidence to support the analysis of professional development;
- issues relating to assessment, recording achievement and profiles.

Once the draft policy had been prepared, opportunity was provided by widespread dissemination for all staff to comment and respond and for official responses to be gathered from formal committee consideration. A joint management group, having received a report of this process, endorsed a final version which became official policy by January, 1994. At this stage, however, the detailed development of the policy had in reality only just begun and particular courses or course programmes (primary or secondary) began to turn policy into practice. As always, that transition is not a tidy and logical process; nor does implementation mean that policy development ceases. The two aspects of development went on simultaneously, if not always hand-in-hand. This account offers some confirmation that Louis' description of school restructuring has a wider relevance in educational organisations:

> The image of an effective change process focuses on the ambiguity of practice and knowledge, the need for 'doing' and 'discussing' as the means to learning,

the importance of interpretation in the context of the school's history and not segregating information or people in ways that impede decentralised learning. Above all, there is a need to ground thinking about change in a clear value system. (Louis, 1994)

Current Developments and Closing Comments

We have described an attempt to overcome a variety of polarisations and tensions, including in particular the polarisation of the liberal and vocational approaches to teaching in a view of the 'effective teacher'. In this effort, the principles of students exercising professional autonomy and engaging in processes of reflection upon their experience, can be said to underpin both perspectives; it is the means by which these values are implemented that has given rise to controversy. A key concept is that of professional development. Interestingly, Circular 24/89 linked professional development with exit competences from courses of ITE. Both PGCE and BEd courses have been assumed to share identical exit competences and the notion that these could provide a basis for a profile of student achievement continues to exercise current professional thinking.

PGCE courses lasting 1 year and BEd(Hons) courses lasting 4 years may present some superficially different perspectives. However, whatever the length of the course and from whatever background the students, the nature of professional development is unlikely to be different fundamentally. Key issues are that in government thinking, no significant developmental concepts have been built into the descriptions of competences and that the view of competences suggested is inadequate. Key weaknesses have been identified by Elliott (1991):

> For the reflective practitioner, the acquisition of relevant and useful knowledge cannot be separated from the development of competence conceived as capacities for intelligent action in unpredictable and complex social situations.

The importance of critical reflection, the analysis of practice, the perception of theory and practice interpenetrating, the recognition of context with which competences are used, the ways they are interpreted and the need for underpinning competences in a process of professional progression and development are all issues which have been largely ignored in the Secretary of State's circulars.

Current Didsbury thinking identifies two fundamental but related concepts: structured professional progression and personal professional development. Structured professional progression is that sequence or pattern of knowledge and skill which a student is expected to acquire or extend, leading to a level of competence demonstrated in learning outcomes. Knowledge and skills are acquired, used and developed in relation to specific perspectives. Three perspectives are identified: the technical, the contextual and the interpretative. The technical perspective relates to the mechanics of teaching, learning, planning, managing, implementing, resourcing and evaluating, the basic knowledge skills and processes which are commonly practised in the act of teaching. The contextual perspective seeks to place technical matters in the context of school situations and individual professional values and beliefs. Assumptions found in teaching situations are analysed and problems identified and addressed. The interpretative perspective incorporates the technical and contextual perspective in a wider approach to the social and ethical framework within which a teacher works. A thread running throughout each perspective is a broad grouping of competences under headings related to children's learnings: the curriculum, professional skills; assessment, recording and reporting, and confirming professional understanding. In short, this represents a more sophisticated approach to the competences model and deals with those matters that are predictable and that can be used to shape the sequence of course provision, whatever the length of the course of ITE. It is a matter of debate how far the perspectives may have a linear character.

Personal professional development is that sequence of personal professional awareness which each individual constructs and changes in the light of his or her own individual experience. Personal professional development relates to the starting point of experience particular to individuals firstly, at the start of a course and subsequently to the priorities and interests they determine or discover during a course, how they justify their professional approach and decisions and construct their own vision of the kind of teacher they wish to be. Personal professional development may also be seen to progress through three phases: role construction, role development and role evaluation. Role construction includes such things as those experiences, knowledge and resources which an individual brings to a course and an attempt to articulate current assumptions about teaching. Role development involves a more systematic articulation of being a teacher and includes professional dialogue and debate in which alternative possibilities in personal style, priorities and practices are affirmed, subject to critical analysis and extended in different situations. Role evaluation expects students to justify their practice of teaching in relation to both context and their own professional values, located in a wide, social and theoretical framework.

The three perspectives on structured professional progression and the three phases of personal professional development can be interrelated as follows:

- Technical perspective/role construction phase.
- Contextual perspective/role development phase.
- Interpretative perspective/role evaluation phase.

The goal of the process is the achievement of the role of the effective teacher as identified by the ITE programme but assimilated to the personal belief system of the individual.

This approach has, we feel, some potential to address some of the issues identified earlier in this chapter. The liberal and vocational concerns can be synthesised in the relationship between structured professional progression and personal professional development. A clear concept of professional development capable of relating to a systematic approach to a broad view of learning outcomes can be identified as a framework of ITE. Structured professional progression provides a framework for a broad approach to assessment of kinds familiar in higher education. Personal professional development provides a framework for individual self-assessment. The synthesis of the patterns of progression and development can provide a basis for profiling. The competences can be treated as a resource and stage descriptions derived, for students and tutors to engage in a dialogue which produces a slimline record of achievement. Quality is seen to reside in the processes of analysis and to be promoted by dialogue with others, whether teachers in school or tutors in higher education.

Of course, each and every one of these assertions, regarding the potential of this approach, is currently involving tutors and teachers in revisiting certain dilemmas and professional values and opening up new challenges. The policy, in this context, does seem to be a living document, providing a framework for discourse and course development. In the absence of such debates, how can learning to be a teacher be 'presented' by tutors and teachers in such a way as to be perceived by students as both demanding in practice and rigorous in intellectual challenge, two hallmarks of what it means to be a professional?

References

Barnett, R. (1994) *The Limits of Competence*. Buckingham: SRHE and Open University Press.

CNAA (1992) *Competence-Based Approaches to Teacher Education: Viewpoints and Issues*. London: CNAA.

Elliott, J. (1991) 'A Model of professionalism and its implications for teacher education', *British Educational Research Journal*, **17 (4)**, 309–18.

Fullan, M. (1993) *Change Forces: Probing the Depths of Educational Reform*. Lewes: Falmer.

Hargreaves, A. (1994) *Changing Teachers, Changing Times, Teachers' Work and Culture in the Postmodern Age*. London: Cassell.

Hargreaves, A. (1995) 'Towards a social geography of teacher education', in Shimakara, N. K. and Holowinsky, I. Z. (eds), *Teacher Education in Industrialized Nations*. New York: Garland.

Hodkinson, P. (1995a) 'The challenge of competence for the caring professions: an overview', in Hodkinson, P. and Issitt, M. (eds), *The Challenge of Competence*. London: Cassell.

Hodkinson, P. (1995b) 'Professionalism and competence', in Hodkinson, P. and Issitt, M. (eds), *The Challenge of Competence*. London: Cassell.

Louis, S. K. (1994) 'Beyond "Managed Change": Rethinking How Schools Improve', *School Effectiveness and School Improvement*, 5 (1), 2–24.

Louis, S. K. and Miles, M. B. (1992) *Improving the Urban High School: What Works and How*. London: Cassell.

Pearce, J. and Pickard, A. (1987) 'Being a teacher: towards an epistemology of practical studies', in Smyth, J. (ed.), *Educating Teachers – Changing the Nature of Pedagogical Knowledge*. Lewes: Falmer Press.

Tuxworth, E. (1989) 'Competence based education and training: background and origins', in Burke, J. W. (ed.), *Competency Based Education and Training*. Lewes: Falmer.

5

Trying to Make Profiling Useful for Teacher Education: The Oxford Experience

Anna Pendry and Donald McIntyre

The attempt at Oxford University Department of Educational Studies to conceptualise, identify and articulate the competences and other qualities needed of beginning teachers began when the new 'internship' programme was being jointly planned by university and school staff in 1986-87. In 1989, building on this earlier work, the idea of 'profiling' was explicitly introduced. The profile that was first used, in 1991–92, and subsequent versions, were again the products of a working party of university tutors and school teachers. In each academic year since 1991 we have, to a greater or lesser extent, revised the profiling scheme in use. That we are not yet satisfied with it indicates that we have found it difficult to meet the diverse criteria that we believe a profiling framework needs to meet.

The criteria that we think are important include:

- The practical feasibility of using the profile.
- The subjective value of the profile to its users: the student teachers, their mentors, and their tutors.
- Its capacity to reflect continuity from admission to a PGCE to induction into a qualified teacher role.
- The theoretical coherence of the scheme in terms of the kinds of competence articulated, the assumptions embedded in it about the nature of professional expertise, and the beliefs about how that expertise may best be acquired.
- Most of all, the usefulness of the profiling system in promoting and supporting the kinds of learning which our teacher education programme has been planned to foster.

We seek here to address two questions which relate to the system of profiling that we have developed:

1. What beliefs about the nature of professional expertise, about the learning of that expertise, and about distinctions between different kinds of competence are embedded in our teacher education curriculum?
2. Why was it seen as necessary to develop an explicit profiling system, what problems have we experienced in trying to develop an appropriate one and why have these problems arisen?

Relevant Ideas Embedded in the Teacher Education Curriculum

General conception of the curriculum

Like many other 1-year PGCE courses for secondary teachers, the Oxford course can be represented as having three broad goals:

- enabling student teachers to become competent beginning classroom teachers;
- developing in student teachers the understandings, dispositions and skills necessary for them to become self-critical and self-developing professional teachers;
- helping student teachers to understand and to develop their classroom practice as embedded in a wider range of professional responsibilities and of whole-school and social concerns.

The Oxford course is more distinctive, however, or at least was in 1987, in its conception of the processes through which these goals could most effectively be attained. On the premise that in principle there is no knowledge about teaching which students should take on trust, they are asked to engage in a dialectical process whereby ideas from any source are subjected to critical questioning and examination. Important among these ideas, it is assumed, will be ideas that student teachers bring with them and which they will need to become aware of and to articulate. Equally, however, ideas from academic sources, especially those of which students' tutors are convinced, and ideas from school sources, especially those which are embedded in the taken-for-granted practices of the schools in which students are working, need to be subjected to critical examination.

The 'internship' structure of the course is designed to facilitate this process of critical questioning. Ideas acquired academically, from theory and research of different kinds, from reported practices elsewhere, or from personal theorising, need first with the help of tutors to be expressed in such terms that they can be examined in practice in the schools. There, through observation, discussion and often through their own teaching, students can explore the feasibility, acceptability and effectiveness-in-context of theoretically attractive ideas. Similarly, all ideas and perhaps especially those ideas acquired in the context of the school need to be questioned in terms of the assumptions they make, the values implicit in them, their theoretical coherence and their generalisable validity; and such questioning can often be best pursued through reading, writing and debate with tutors and peers at the university. The effectiveness of such a curriculum depends of course on shared understandings and detailed joint planning between the school mentors and the university tutors, so that the student teachers can experience continuity as well as tension as they move backwards and forwards between the two very different sites of their learning.

Two complementary but very different kinds of learning are used in this kind of curriculum. The 'practical theorising' discussed above is an unambiguously intellectual kind of learning, of a very demanding kind. In principle, there are no grounds for giving priority to any of the different kinds of criteria that this theorising should use. In practice, however, student teachers understandably give the highest priority to one criterion, that of whether they themselves can make effective use in their own practice of any particular idea. And, of course, whether they can use an idea effectively or not will depend not only on the usefulness of the idea, but also on their own skill. To engage adequately in the process of practical theorising, therefore, student teachers need to be engaged also in extending their practical and social skills of teaching; but equally, to decide which of these skills are worth developing, they need to engage in practical theorising.

It should be clear that an important principle of this curriculum is that every step of student teachers' development should be dependent on their rational consideration of their practice and of the ideas informing it. It follows that the conditions within which student teachers are asked to learn, and the tasks which they are set, in the schools as in the university, must allow them to engage in such rational deliberation. A further important principle therefore is that of the graduated progression of practical teaching and other tasks so that student teachers should always find their tasks challenging but never so complex or stressful as to discourage rational analysis. Perhaps the most important task of mentors, as managers of student teachers' school-based learning, is that of putting this principle into practice.

One very important implication of that general principle, established during the piloting of the new PGCE in 1986–87, was the need to divide the course into two main phases. This was needed to take account of tensions between the two goals of preparing competent beginning teachers and of helping student teachers to become self-developing teachers. Student teachers found the task of articulating and exploring the implications of their own criteria for their teaching too complex and stressful while they were still at a stage of feeling dependent on their mentors and tutors for judgements about their basic competence. Mentors too found it difficult to deal with the two goals at the same time.

The resolution of this problem by introducing two phases depended on our eventual clarification of how basic teaching competence was to be understood. Studies of experienced teachers (e.g. Brown and McIntyre, 1988) suggested that they typically evaluate their day-to-day teaching in terms of their attainment of short-term goals such as 'getting and maintaining the pupils' attention' and 'ensuring that the pupils understand what they are supposed to be doing and how to do it'. Experienced teachers seemed to rely on a limited number of such criteria for evaluating their teaching, although they had extensive repertoires of activities for achieving these short-term goals, and selected activities from their repertoires according to the circumstances.

This seemed to provide a helpful way of thinking about the basic competence which student teachers needed to acquire, during a first phase of their course. For a start, it proved possible to establish a reasonable consensus among teachers and tutors about the aspects of teaching in which it was most important for beginning teachers to become competent (Aplin, 1987). Student teachers during this first phase would have the task of finding ways of achieving the given short-term goals, of judging the appropriateness of these ways against the diverse academic and practical criteria we have already discussed, and of gradually extending their repertoires so as to be able to attain reliably the given goals where appropriate in a variety of circumstances. They would be working, however, within the given explicit framework of short-term goals and in relation to the standards applied by their mentors and tutors. During the second phase of the course, when they could be confident that in their mentors' and tutors' eyes they were competent beginning teachers, student teachers could be asked to concentrate on the more open task of identifying aspects of their teaching of particular concern to them, and investigating ways of developing their expertise in these areas.

The curriculum thinking which has very briefly been outlined above provided the framework for the development of a profiling system for the Oxford PGCE course. To make the links clear, we need to highlight three distinctions which relate the above outline to wider debates about the nature of professional expertise in teaching.

Generic qualities and specific competences

Should teachers' expertise be understood in terms of their practical competence to carry out many specific identifiable aspects of a classroom teaching role? Or should it be understood rather in terms of much more generic personal qualities? Elliott (1989) is one of the many who rejects the former in favour of the latter. He suggests that the 'deep structure' of professional competence may be identifiable as a small number of very general personal qualities, with other more job-specific qualities being dependent on these general qualities. Teachers' professional development, Elliott argues, necessarily involves their development as people, including their emotional and motivational tendencies, the beliefs that underpin these, and their powers of self-determination.

We would argue, in contrast, that the nature of teachers' expertise cannot be reduced either to generic personal qualities or to specific competences: both are essential elements in any satisfactory account of professional expertise. Empirical evidence suggests both that the two ways of describing expertise do reflect rather different abilities and also that both these aspects of expertise are valued by teachers' employers. Cameron-Jones and O'Hara (1990), analysing two sets of over 1200 ratings of student teachers on an 18-item profiling system derived from the objectives and content of a teacher education programme, found that the items were grouped into two clearly distinct dimensions: one of *competence as practitioners*, concerned with various aspects of the planning and teaching of lessons; the other of *professionality*, concerned with more general qualities. Cameron-Jones and O'Hara also found that prospective employers were concerned both with the practical competence of teachers and also with their professional qualities – 'a carer, a giver, a well-read intelligent committed individual and so on' (1990:77).

We are in no doubt about the importance of personal qualities as a major aspect of teachers' expertise. Subject teachers surely need to believe that their subjects are worth learning and can be learned. They have to be committed to their students' learning, irrespective of the students' social class, race, gender, physical characteristics or attractiveness to the teacher. They need to be able to communicate clearly, to organise activities, to empathise with others, to listen, to assert themselves, to show enthusiasm and to show caring for the people with whom they work. They need such qualities as robustness and tact in order to work in a modern secondary school. And in order to learn to be good teachers, student teachers need to recognise the complexity and difficulty of the task of teaching, to believe in the learnability of teaching expertise, and to have respect for the sophistication, subtlety and commitment implicit in the teaching of most experienced teachers.

We are less persuaded of the possibility of enabling people to develop such qualities in the context of a 1-year PGCE course. These are qualities which are of major importance in selecting student teachers for entry to the course; they are qualities to be fostered and encouraged; and they are certainly qualities which need to be assessed throughout the course before awarding qualified teacher status. Our curriculum, however, is not planned with the aim of imbuing such general qualities into student teachers. It is much more focused on various kinds of more specific abilities.

Professional practice and educational thinking

We have already drawn attention to the two very different but complementary kinds of learning involved in the curriculum: the practical theorising about the strengths and limitations of different ideas for practice; and the development of practical and social skills necessary for using and trying out these ideas. Although closely complementary, these two kinds of learning and the kinds of competences to be learned are very different. The distinction relates closely to the well-established one between *preactive* aspects of teaching and *interactive* aspects of teaching. It is a distinction between *competence in doing* those aspects of teacher work with overt action (largely social interaction) and *competence in thinking* when not engaged in such overt action, for example when planning and evaluating one's teaching, but also in seminars and in writing activities. Of course teachers do think while engaged in interactive teaching, but the thinking required for competence in doing is of a very different kind from the considered thinking which is possible while not engaged in teaching (Brown and McIntyre, 1988; Jackson, 1968; Lortie, 1975).

There are of course many different qualities which can usefully be sought in educational thinking and many distinctions which can be made between types of educational thinking. In the context of a PGCE curriculum, and in relation to all components of our curriculum, we would highlight three perspectives. First, while many graduate student teachers have learned to be fluent as critical thinkers, many of them need to learn for teaching to be constructive and creative thinkers, generating ideas and plans for teaching. Second, as critical thinkers in relation to their own work as teachers, they need to learn to apply the wide range of generic criteria needed for practical theorising. Third (cutting across and usefully complementing the second), they need to think systematically about their work as teachers in terms of all three of Habermas's 'knowledge-constitutive interests' – the 'technical', the 'practical' and the 'emancipatory' (Carr and Kemmis, 1986).

Common standards and self-directed professionality

We have already explained the two phases of the PGCE course and why they were seen to be necessary: the first phase, in which student teachers could explore ways of being competent in relation to a consensual framework of criteria and to standards set by their mentors and tutors; and the second phase, in which they could explore ways of realising in practice aspects of their own personal educational visions. During the first phase, practical competence is to be understood in terms of student teachers' abilities to attain the kinds of short-term classroom goals which all teachers regularly have to attain. In the second phase, however, competence has to be conceived in more generic and abstract terms of linking general educational ideas to the practicalities of one's own classroom, collecting valid evidence about one's practices, diagnosing problems in realising one's aspirations, and generating imaginative and sensitive solutions to these problems.

We do not subscribe to the hierarchical views advanced by some writers (e.g. Wise *et al.*, 1984), according to which a higher level of expertise is associated with greater individuality in the making of professional judgements. Our concern is a more pragmatic one of achieving the two equally important goals of ensuring that beginning teachers are competent according to consensual professional criteria and of helping them to develop the skills and dispositions necessary for their own continuing professional development.

In this first main section of the chapter we have attempted to map out the concerns and beliefs about professional expertise and learning which shaped our PGCE curriculum. In the next section, we shall seek to explain why a profiling system was seen to be desirable to support this curriculum, and also to consider some of the problems which we experienced in developing and implementing such a system.

Profiling, its Uses and its Problems

The need for profiling

In one sense, the need for profiling was apparent from the start of the new course. Effective working of a partnership between schools and university, involving around 100 mentors, 20 co-ordinating professional tutors, 20 university tutors and 200 student teachers, depended crucially on explicitness about mutual expectations. Nowhere was this need for explicitness felt more strongly than in the assessment aspect of the work, and especially that part of the assessment work for which mentors had a major responsibility, the assessment of student teachers' classroom teaching. Individual mentors felt the need for an explicit set of consensual criteria if they were to avoid making idiosyncratic judgements; it was challenging enough for them to have to interpret these criteria and to judge appropriate standards to set, even with the help of university tutors in moderating roles. For the system as a whole, there was a need to ensure that all assessments of competence in classroom teaching were being made on the basis of similar criteria.

With the passage of time, this need for explicitness and shared understandings has come to seem more not less important. It has become increasingly apparent that one of the major problems for partnerships like ours is that of achieving 'quality assurance' across the whole system (Rothwell *et al.*, 1994). Student teachers have a right to expect that both the management of their learning opportunities and the assessment of their developing competence will be conducted within a common framework and will not vary widely according to the idiosyncrasies of their tutors or mentors. Explicit and specific assessment criteria can provide one important contribution towards such quality assurance.

Profiling, however, means more than making explicit the criteria in terms of which students are to be assessed. What precisely profiling does mean is less clear, an issue to which we shall return. A further element of it on which there would seem to be general agreement, however, is the active involvement of students. It was this that motivated the move in 1989 to an explicit profiling system. A curriculum conceived, as this one is, primarily in terms of the intended learning *processes* depends very heavily for its success on students' understanding of, and willing engagement in, these processes. Student teachers come to PGCE courses with widely varied ideas about how they will learn to teach, and rarely with an expectation that it will be an intellectually demanding activity; and one of the things which we had initially failed to do at Oxford (and still do not do adequately) was to devote sufficient time and energy to educating our student teachers into our practical theorising conception of the curriculum process. One way of doing this was through engaging them in a profiling system through which they would articulate, for example, their successes in achieving specific short-term teaching goals, the means they had used to achieve these goals, and the judgements they had made in relation to other criteria about these means to success. Profiling was thus seen primarily as a means of engaging student teachers in consciously directing the processes through which they were learning to be teachers.

A related purpose which the introduction of profiling was designed to serve was the involvement of student teachers in their own assessment. If an important aim of the whole programme was to be that student teachers should learn to be self-evaluating, self-developing teachers, then it was important that their self-assessments in relation to all aspects of the curriculum should be taken seriously as an integral part of the processes by which we assessed them. Given a profiling system which articulated the criteria in terms of which student teachers were to be assessed by their mentors and tutors, it was intended that formal and summative assessments would normally involve nothing more than the rubber-stamping of conclusions already reached by student teachers through their own self-assessment and through ongoing dialogues with their mentors and tutors relating to these self-assessments. Sometimes of course there would be disagreements between students and mentors and tutors; but, it was hoped, these disagreements should never surface for the first time at the stage where summative assessments were to be made, and indeed would often be resolved by that stage.

The profiling system

The profile as originally introduced and as currently in use has three sections, reflecting distinctions made earlier in this chapter: interactive teaching qualities; qualities of educational thinking; and general professional qualities (see appendix, page 70–1).

The interactive teaching qualities are concerned with competence in classroom teaching – they represent the common core in relation to the practical competence needed while engaged in classroom teaching. In accordance with the curriculum rationale explained earlier, they are expressed in terms of short-term effects to be achieved in classrooms. This list is used by both the student teachers themselves and those working most closely with them in the classroom: their school-based mentors, other teachers, and their university curriculum tutors. Given that this list represents a statement of basic competence, it is of greatest value during the first phase of the year.

The second section – qualities of educational thinking – is divided into two parts: those qualities that relate to student teachers' thinking about their teaching and their subject curricula, including in particular their planning and evaluation of their teaching; and thinking qualities that are concerned with their professional studies work – that part of the programme which is devoted to the policies and practices of schools which extend beyond individual subject classrooms, and to the relationship of schooling to the wider society. The first part is used by the student teachers principally in conjunction with their mentors and curriculum tutors, and the second with the school professional tutors and university general tutors who are jointly responsible for the non-subject-specific element in their programme.

A statement of general professional qualities makes up the third section of the profile. Here are included statements about qualities such as the ability to collaborate with colleagues, to manage time effectively and to learn from discussion, advice and observation. As the earlier discussion about personal qualities will have suggested, what are not included here are the essentially personal qualities which might be expected of a teacher: for example, sensitivity, a capacity to communicate and the ability to care for those with whom they work. Such qualities form part of our selection criteria; the attempt here is to highlight those qualities which are necessary for, but can only be apparent in, professional contexts.

The intention is that this profile should be used as a working log, with a formative function to enable student teachers and those working with them to direct and monitor their progress and to set targets for the future. Its use leads directly into the summative assessment process, in that it represents most of the assessment criteria for the course, and it is anticipated that the summative judgements reported jointly by school teachers and university tutors should be consistent with their discussions about profile qualities with individual student teachers. As will be explained below, for the first 4 years while the profiling system has been in use, this link with summative assessment was formalised through meetings at three points during the year of each individual student with his or her mentor and curriculum tutor, and parallel meetings with his or her professional and general tutors, to consider progress in terms of the profile.

Successes and problems with the profiling system

In this section we shall focus primarily on the problems which we have experienced with the profiling system. It would be wrong, however, to give the impression that it has not been successful at all. In particular, the Interactive Teaching Qualities section – which we have tended to see as the core of the system – provides, as we know from its widespread use, a coherent, comprehensible and valued statement of basic competence. The present version of this section has slowly evolved, with successive significant changes being made to overcome clumsiness in language and presentation and to make its use easier. With these improvements, it has increasingly been helpful to student teachers and their mentors for judging where progress is being made and for setting targets for future learning, without imposing arbitrary constraints on the range of approaches to teaching which they can explore. At the same time, it provides a demanding and consensual common set of criteria which all student teachers have to meet. Incidentally, it satisfactorily covers, with the rest of the profile, the set of competences specified by the Department for Education in Circular 9/92, though that has not been something which has influenced the development of the profile.

One of the major problems which we have experienced, however, relates as much to the Interactive Teaching Qualities section as to other parts of the profiling system. The problem is one of tensions between different reasons for introducing profiling. As we have noted, although the intention has always been that the profile should be used on a daily basis as a form of working log, until recently there were three times a year identified as formal 'profiling points', when all student teachers had to engage in discussions with those working with them about their progress in terms of the profile questions, and to write their own reflections on these discussions in their profiling documents. This system was originally introduced for two reasons. Firstly, it was to ensure that the formal summative assessments of students at these three points in the year were based on systematic discussion by all concerned of each student teacher's progress and achievements, and especially that the student teachers' self-assessments were treated as important. Secondly, it was an exercise in quality assurance, aimed at ensuring that all tutors and mentors did indeed explicitly use the agreed criteria, both in their discussions with students and in their summative assessments.

Although reactions to these profiling meetings varied widely, a widespread view developed that they were not a valuable way of using scarce staff time; and it was primarily for that reason that they were abandoned. An additional concern, however, was that the bureaucratic importance attached to these profiling points could make it appear that the profiling system was primarily intended to contribute to the summative assessment, not to provide a framework to guide and support the daily learning processes we wanted to encourage. From this perspective, abandoning the profiling points was intended to signal, with the help of accompanying rhetoric, that the primary function of the profiling system was to support daily learning. Of course tutors and student teachers were then under no pressure (except from each other on an individual basis) to use the profiling system at all. The dilemma, which must be experienced by all school–university teacher education partnerships, is that of how to develop a coherent shared approach among a very large and spread out number of people engaged on the same programme.

A further main problem, however, and quite a different one, is that the profiling framework as so far developed is with the (possible) exception of the Interactive Teaching Qualities section, quite inadequate to provide support and guidance for student teachers' learning. Indeed, it does not even provide a coherent framework of criteria against which student teachers' attainments can be satisfactorily assessed.

This inadequacy can briefly be exemplified in a number of areas. First, while we have indicated relative satisfaction with the Interactive Teaching Qualities section concerned with basic classroom competence, the profiling framework offers virtually nothing to guide and structure students' efforts in Phase 2 to develop their classroom expertise further through a process of self-directed evaluation. In other course documents student teachers are given useful advice about procedures which they should follow in such development and evaluation of their teaching, but it is the profiling framework which should offer them guidance about the qualities they should seek to develop in doing such work. At the very least they could be offered such structuring questions as the following:

- On what grounds do you claim that the aspect of your teaching on which you are focusing is a significant one?
- How clearly have you formulated the problem you are seeking to

resolve or the goal you are seeking to attain?
- How well grounded (for example in research literature) are your reasons for believing that your proposed solution/strategy will be effective?
- What other criteria (e.g. of ethical, epistemological, practical or political kinds) have you used in choosing your strategy?
- On what grounds can you justify the evidence you have collected and the conclusions you have reached in your evaluation as being valid?

Such questions may well not be the most fruitful way of helping student teachers to direct their efforts to learn to be self-developing teachers. Our concern is that no focused help of any kind is given in our profiling framework.

A second example of the inadequate development of our framework is to be found in the section on Qualities of Educational Thinking, for example in relation to non-subject aspects of educational thinking. This outlines only the need for beginning teachers to make use of a range of perspectives in formulating their ideas, and the need to relate the topics dealt with in the programme to their own teaching as well as to schools as a whole. It offers nothing to challenge the readiness of many student teachers to be socialised into the existing practices of schools, which might be done through articulating such qualities as, for example, understanding the failure of the British school system to provide an adequate service for working-class people, and developing realistic strategies for countering social injustice in their own teaching.

A third target for criticism, in relation to our espoused principles, is the section on professional qualities. This section includes qualities which relate directly to *doing* in the beginning teachers' roles as form tutors ('engage in pastoral and tutorial commitments') and in classrooms more generally ('relate appropriately to (a) individual pupils (b) small groups and (c) whole classes'), but also qualities concerned with both *doing* and *thinking* such as 'treat all pupils fairly'. Here we seem to have a rag-bag of qualities which did not quite fit elsewhere. The contrast to, and indeed the failure to make use of, recent attempts to identify generic qualities of professional practitioners, using such general categories as 'situational understanding', 'empathy', 'cognitive initiative' and 'self-monitoring' (Elliott, 1993), is striking.

A fourth and general weakness of the profiling framework is its failure to incorporate any indications, except minimally in relation to Interactive Teaching Qualities, of the kinds of progression that might be expected in student teachers' thinking and other qualities in the course of the PGCE year. Are there not different criteria which the students should be attempting to meet at different stages of the year? And if so, should they not be reflected in the profiling framework?

Why then is our profiling framework so undeveloped and conceptually inadequate? At this point we as authors have to adopt a rather different stance, standing back from the committed perspective from which the rest of this chapter has been written and aiming now to present our own position as only one of those involved in the generation of the profiling framework. As is no doubt apparent, we both were heavily involved in the planning and conceptualisation of the Oxford PGCE curriculum, and equally in the decision to develop profiling as a support system for the planned curriculum. From an early stage, however, the working party responsible for the development of the profiling system was dominated by school and university staff with very different concerns from our own. Having been uninhibited up to this point in presenting things from our own perspective, we must now try to give some indication of the viewpoint of the Profiling Working Party.

In our understanding, the Profiling Working Party have from the beginning attached a great deal of importance to the first two of the criteria which we outlined at the beginning of the chapter, those of the practical feasibility and the subjective value of the profile to its users. Accordingly, they have devoted a great deal of attention, very profitably, to issues of language and presentation. They have also attached great importance to ensuring the simplicity of the profiling document, in order to ensure its ease of use. They have been less concerned with criteria which are especially important to ourselves, those of theoretical coherence and support for theoretically conceived patterns of learning.

That has been one very important difference in perspective which helps to explain our dissatisfaction with what the Profiling Working Party produced. It is not however the only difference, nor perhaps the most important one. Those members of university and school staff who were most interested to join the Profiling Working Party not surprisingly included several who had previously been actively and enthusiastically involved in profiling or records of achievement initiatives in secondary schools. They wanted to bring to teacher education benefits from profiling similar to those which they had witnessed in schools. Among the most widely valued of these benefits at the secondary school level has been the opportunity which profiling offered students to articulate and receive recognition for achievements of kinds other than those derived from the official agenda of teachers and schools; and in order that students should be encouraged to formulate and reveal these achievements, very open frameworks were developed. It may therefore not be surprising that the profiling framework developed by the Profiling Working Party was one which used very simple, open and unconstraining categories. If that is a correct interpretation, the divergence between what we wanted from the profiling system and the system which was actually devised is due not so much to differences about the criteria to be emphasised as to differences in conceptions of what profiling is and what it is for.

We certainly should not wish to claim that our conception of profiling is superior to, or more correct than, the conception which we think the Profiling Working Party were using. It is very clear to us, on the other hand, that the system they have generated – for whatever reason – is not well geared to the functions which we wanted a profiling system for. Debate will no doubt continue within the Oxford partnership about how the profiling system needs to develop; but if we are to learn from our experience so far, we need to be much clearer about what we mean by profiling and what we want it to do for us and our students. And again, a problem for us and for all teacher education partnerships is how we can maintain coherent shared understandings of what we are doing in a non-hierarchical system involving a lot of people spread over many institutions.

References

Aplin, R. (1987) 'The assessment of interns for qualified teacher status', *SDES Dissertation*, Department of Educational Studies, University of Oxford.

Brown, S. and McIntyre, D. (1988) 'The professional craft knowledge of teachers', *Scottish Educational Review: Special Issue on the Quality of Teaching*, 39–47.

Cameron-Jones, M. and O'Hara, P. (1990) *Improving Training*. Edinburgh: Moray House College.

Carr, W. and Kemmis, S. (1986) *Becoming Critical: Education, Knowledge and Action Research*. Lewes: Falmer.

Elliott, J. (1989) 'Appraisal of performance or appraisal of persons', in Simons, H. and Elliott, J. (eds) *Rethinking Appraisal and Assessment*. Milton Keynes: Open University Press, pp.80–99.

Elliott, J. (1993) *Reconstructing Teacher Education*. Lewes: Falmer Press, Ch. 6.

Jackson, P.W. (1968) *Life in Classrooms*. New York: Holt, Reinhart and Winston.

Lortie, D. (1975) *School Teacher: A Sociological Study*. Chicago: University of Chicago Press.

Rothwell, S., Nardi, E. and McIntyre, D. (1994) 'The perceived values of the role activities of mentors and curricular, professional and general tutors', in Reid, I., Constable, H. and Griffiths, R. (eds) *Teacher Education Reform: Current Research*. London: Paul Chapman, pp.19–39.

Wise, A.E., Darling-Hammond, L., McLaughlin, M. and Bernstein, H. (1984) *Teacher Evaluation – A Study of Effective Practice*. Santa Monica: Cal.: The Rand Corporation for the National Institute of Education.

Appendix: Profile Qualities

The qualities listed here are both a means of directing the interns' learning and the criteria by which they are assessed on the PGCE course. These qualities should, therefore, be used on a daily basis to guide, monitor and set targets for the interns' learning, as well as to make formal assessment decisions about them.

Section 1: Interactive Teaching Qualities

Interactions

Does the intern:

1.1 Ensure that the pupils' levels of talk and movement are appropriate to the learning activity?

1.2 Gain and maintain pupils' attention?

1.3 Ensure that pupils work co-operatively with each other and with themselves as the teacher?

1.4 Manage oral work among pupils and with themselves as the teacher?

Transitions

Does the intern:

1.5 Manage the beginnings and endings of lessons in an orderly and effective way?

1.6 Manage changes of activity during the lesson in an orderly and effective way?

Understanding

Does the intern:

1.7 Help pupils understand what they are supposed to be doing and how to do it?

1.8 Help pupils understand the subject matter of the lesson?

1.9 Manage resources to help pupils' understanding of the subject matter?

1.10 Ensure that the pupils are positively involved in the lesson?

1.11 Ensure that the pupils are making progress?

1.12 Monitor pupils' progress?

1.13 Ensure that pupils are aware of their progress?

Safety

1.14 Does the intern make sure that the pupils are working in a safe environment?

Section 2 : Qualities of Educational Thinking

(a) Curriculum work

Does the intern:

2.1 Take account of a range of factors when planning their lessons (e.g. subject matter, including National Curriculum Programmes of Study and Attainment

targets; pupil needs; time and place of the lesson)?
2.2 Make balanced judgements about their own and other teachers' lessons?
2.3 Take account of the following in their thinking and classroom practice:
    (a) the perspectives of your school department
    (b) national perspectives (i.e. national policies including the National Curriculum and practice in other schools)
    (c) theoretical perspectives (i.e. literature and research)?

(b)   Professional development work
Does the intern:
2.4 Take account of the following perspectives in their thinking about topics in the Professional Development programme:
    (a) school perspectives (i.e. policy and practice in your school)
    (b) national perspectives (i.e. national policies including the National Curriculum and practice in other schools)
    (c theoretical perspectives (i.e. literature and research)?
2.5 Consider the Professional Development programme topics in relation to:
    (a) their own teaching
    (b) their understanding of their role as a teacher
    (c) their understanding of the role of schools?

Section 3 : Professional Qualities
Does the intern:
3.1 Collaborate with colleagues on a professional basis?
3.2 Collaborate with school colleagues in meeting the statutory requirements of the National Curriculum?
3.3 Learn from (a) observations of (b) discussions with, and (c) advice from you and your colleagues?
3.4 Manage their own time?
3.5 Engage in pastoral and tutorial commitments?
3.6 Treat all pupils fairly?
3.7 Relate appropriately to (a) individual pupils (b) small groups (c) whole classes?
3.8 Is the intern's attendance satisfactory, as defined in the Course Handbook?

Part Two
Case Studies of National Initiatives

6

'Competence' Guidelines in Scotland for Initial Teacher Training: 'Supercontrol' or 'Superperformance'?[1]

Ian Stronach, Peter Cope, Bill Inglis, Jim McNally

In 1992–93 The Scottish Office undertook a 'revision, updating and consolidation' of teacher training guidelines (SOED, 1993:1), producing a competence-based account of required skills and attitudes, following the production and discussion of draft guidelines for comment in July 1992. The period of consultation provoked some debate at the time, with one lecturer arguing in the *Times Educational Supplement (Scotland)* (TESS) that the 'competences' represented a half-baked attempt at what ought to have been a more rigorous specification of objectives:

> to judge what constitutes a minimum level of competence, the performance indicators of competence must be couched in terms of criterial standards and the range/constraints of context(s) in which the performance will be displayed. (McClellan, 1993)

On the other hand, others saw the competences as already intrusively technicist, threatening the autonomy of the profession and even the 'democratic life of this country' (Carr, 1993a). Walter Humes commented:

> The marginalising of the conceptual aspects of training and their systematic replacement by narrowly conceived skills-based courses will lead to the de-professionalisation of the teachers and their adoption of a reduced role as 'functionaries' – perhaps even, in the end, their 'proletarianisation'. (Humes, 1992)

Finally, there were those such as Gordon Kirk who argued that 'more sharply defined competences' were no more than the consolidation of good practice and a matter of 'professional consensus' (Kirk, 1992).

The debate was curiously polarised: was it the end of civilisation or business as usual? Common sense or technical nonsense? State coercion or professional consensus? This chapter aims to examine these themes of technical analysis, professional autonomy, and political regulation as they are expressed in the SOED *Guidelines*, or the ensuing Committee of Scottish Higher Education Principals (COSHEP) competence-based profile, and also to relate the Guidelines to the experiences of student teachers and probationers. The themes will be interpreted from three different orientations. The first concerns the critique of 'competence' offered by Jones and Moore (1993), in which they view the competency movement as a new and more coercive mechanism for state regulation of the professions (see Carr and Humes above). The central notion we will address here is the notion of competence as an instance of what Giddens calls socially 'disembedded' knowledge (Giddens, 1991:18).

The second perspective examines the construction of the draft and final *Guidelines* themselves. It draws on an insider account of their development (although no doubt there are other accounts that can be told), as well as looking at the differences between draft and final *Guidelines*. Our intention here is to argue that the *Guidelines* emerge as a form of compromise between widely different conceptualisations of the profession and then to contrast that 'socially embodied' account of competency building with the 'disembedded' critique offered by Jones and Moore.

The third perspective is a more empirical one. The *Guidelines* prescribe competences which new teachers in Scotland ought to exhibit. It follows that an empirical examination of the experiences and perceptions of teachers in training, and of probationers, should tell us something about the match or mismatch between the 'competence' specification and reality – at least as perceived by those taking part in the training. In addition, it should be possible to say something about whether the SOED 'competence' statements are a useful pedagogic or assessment device. Do they help learning, or its valid assessment? Is the profile based on the *Guidelines* a sensible prescription? Similarly, such data can be used to evaluate the adequacy of Jones and Moore's account of competence. Will the data support Kirk's notion of competence as a consolidation of good practice, or Carr's and Hume's suspicions?

First Perspective: The Coercive State

Jones and Moore offer a penetrating sociological critique of 'competence'. Drawing on Giddens and Bernstein (Bernstein 1990; Giddens, 1991) they argue that competency movements in general involve the 'disembedding' of knowledge. Such a process decontextualises knowledge in ways that are simplistic and contradicted by 'actual cultural practices' (Jones and Moore

1993:389). In addition such decontextualisation and subsequent recontextualisation (the SOED Guidelines are a 'decontextualisation'; their implementation a 'recontextualisation') is atheoretical – since 'competence' involves a denial of theory in favour of the alleged transparency of performances which can be prescribed, defined, and assessed. Competence-based professionalism, therefore, removes the mystique of professional knowledge, and is a form of de-skilling.

Such changes have consequences for power as well as knowledge. By making explicit and public the criteria for professional competence, Jones and Moore argue, the state 'progressively extend[s] its direct control over the sphere of professional expertise' (1993: 390). Lists of competences can be altered to redefine the professional task by management, or to hold professionals accountable through audit measures. The profession loses the autonomy to define and police its own practices, professionals are redefined as technicians, and such attacks reflect a much more general phenomenon noted by Bernstein – 'the state's hostility to its professional base' (Bernstein, 1990:154–55; cited by Jones and Moore, 1993:389).

We have written at length elsewhere about the nature of such critiques of 'competence' (Stronach *et al.*, 1994), and concluded that such analyses ended in a suspiciously clear dichotomy: it was not hard to separate the Goodies from the Baddies (Table 6.1).

Professional	*Technician*
liberal humanism	coercive state
professional autonomy	state control
craft 'conscience'	managerialism
'reason value' (Davis, 1991)	'trade value'
high trust	low trust
high 'indetermination' (Jamous and Peloille, 1970)	high rationality
Professional practice	
critical	procedural
reflexive	conformative
embedded	disembedded
contextualised	decontextualised
cultural/collective	technical/individual

Table 6.1

Of what should we be suspicious? Perhaps the presence of an heroic emplotment of the professional, an ideological and rather one-dimensional portrait. Such binary and polarised thinking may obscure messier realities. Perhaps also the neatly nested nature of the analysis, especially as articulated by Jones and Moore: from 'competence' to mode of control to political ideology to 'coercive state' to the spirit of the age of 'late modernity': the giddy ascent of 'competence' as an essence of contemporary power.

And there are absences as well as presences to consider in the competence critique. The critique pays little attention to the 'information asymmetry' in professional work (Buchanan, 1988), that is, to the implications of who has knowledge and therefore power in the professional/client relationship, and seems unwilling to regard professions as at least possibly oligarchic, monopolistic or repressive in tendency. Instead there is an insistent and characteristic idealisation of the profession (Stronach, 1992). The notion of teaching as part of an 'ideological state apparatus' (Althusser, 1971) which was common in critiques in the 1970s has vanished without trace from the debate.

With these reservations in mind, our next task is to review critically the SOED competence *Guidelines*, considering both those elements of the *Guidelines* that seem to fit with the general thrust of the above critique, and noting those which appear discrepant or ambivalent.

The case for 'disembedded knowledge'

It is clear that the Guidelines can be interpreted as reducing the autonomy of the profession in several ways. First, they introduce the principle of 'externality' in relation to the validation of initial teaching courses, external examiners being subject to the approval of the Secretary of State (SOED, 1993:2). The monitoring of standards, then, may be conducted from outside the profession.

Second, the *Guidelines* lay down a series of 'core competences' which constitute a national curriculum for initial teacher training, removing autonomy from the training colleges. These competences are expected to act as a basis for course assessment as well, and to inform external accountability.

Third, the core competences imply a redefinition of professionalism as 'performance in teaching' (SOED, 1993:2), and reflect a desire for more school-based learning for beginning teachers. They also specify appropriate competences for subject teaching, classroom management, classroom competences, assessment and so on. While these are vague in relation to standards and precise meaning (as McClellan observes), they nevertheless point towards an instrumental and technical specification of the role.

The recent translation of the *Guidelines* into a COSHEP profile (1993a, b, c) which insists on a national prescription of competence categories, and specifies levels of grading, epitomises this trend towards decontextualising professional knowledge, and then injecting a forced 'recontextualisation' in terms of an assessment of each individual student teacher's competences against sets of vague categories and grades. Such a process is philosophically confused (Carr, 1993b, c), politically coercive (Jones and Moore, 1993), comparatively invalid and unreliable (Cameron-Jones and O'Hara, 1990), and practically unrealisable.

Finally, the competence *Guidelines* are most problematic in that they give the state a mechanism with which to generate tighter control of teacher training and professionalism in future. Despite their current vagueness, they provide a slippery slope towards the reduction of professionalism to an inventory of classroom and school behaviours.

Some counter-critical readings

If we now try to read the SOED *Guidelines* against the criteria for the 'professional' rather than the 'technician' model, however, we find that we can plausibly construct a very different interpretation.

Commentators on 'professionalism' stress values such as reflexivity and professional discretion (Davis, 1991; Jamous and Peloille, 1970; Jones and Moore, 1993). 'Essentially it is critical reflexivity which is at issue' (Jones and Moore, 1993:395).

In the *Guidelines*, there are numerous references to what might be taken to be a critical reflexivity. Beginning teachers have to be able to 'justify' what is taught, to have knowledge that 'goes beyond' the demands of the school curriculum, and so on. In addition, the document certainly talks of 'core' competences but it also talks of them as 'mere' competences, and goes on to stress a series of six commitments that teachers must make. Clearly, these are vocational commitments in that they are kinds of dedication held to be necessary for the proper performance of the job.

A review of the professional definition of the beginning teacher role implied in the SOED *Guidelines*, then, might well argue that what is so striking about the competence guidelines is their *idealisation* of the job, and of the sorts of abilities beginning teachers are supposed to have: 'justify what is taught from knowledge and understanding of the learning process, curriculum issues, child development in general and the needs of his or her pupils in particular' (SOED, 1993:3).

Far from offering a restricted version of professionalism, we might well choose to argue that the guidelines offer an hopelessly over-extended view of professional achievement in relation to the beginning teacher. We should not accuse the SOED of coercive technicism, but of seductive utopianism.

As in the case of 'disembedded knowledge' we could go on, but the point is already clear. It is possible to make both arguments. The document is much more politically ambivalent than the critique of Jones and Moore would have predicted, and so we need to understand why it contains such a mixture of procedural, conformist, reductive, critical, and utopian features; why it seems to offer the promise of autonomy with one hand, and greater state control with the other. That takes us to the second perspective that we wish to discuss.

Second Perspective: 'Embodied Knowledge'

First, a story. It is an insider story, although of course we have no way of knowing whether it really happened, or whether it represents an institutional myth. No matter, it is relevant as a possible story concerning the construction of the competences. The minister with the Scottish education portfolio decides – in the light of radical moves in England and Wales, and in the darkness of his New Right thinking – to summon one of his top officials and demand 'root and branch' reform of teacher education. The senior civil servant summons his staff and ironically translates the instruction as 'We must reform the guidelines' (This is a 'Yes Minister' story).

We note that first translation, that first domestication of the proposed policy change. A process of consultation is then started, a draft produced, more discussion, and then a final version. The consultation, we may assume, picks up shades of the concerns that are expressed in the TESS debate with which we began. We do not know the precise process (more insider information would be welcome), but the *Guidelines* emerge as a series of suggestions and counter-suggestions mediated through the Inspectorate. The technical enthusiasts presumably argue for greater specificity; the liberals for a more open document capable of wide interpretation; the radicals for an abandonment of the whole project. The result is a series of translations or domestications of the original project, based on a consultative process that is as much part of Scottish tradition as is teacher education itself (the latter being the oldest tradition in Europe). We can reasonably assume that the result is designed to attract a measure of support from teacher education, or at least to blunt some of the criticism.

The point we wish to make here is that such a process does not simply involve an elaboration of a 'technical' specification of competences (such as McClellan wanted to see). Instead there is a certain amount of horse-trading; the competences represent a series of political compromises. So, for example, the liberals try to insist on getting 'critical' and 'reflexive' elements into the specification, and there is a push to identify 'commitments' that ought to accompany and go beyond 'mere' competences. These install a broad and vocational definition of the job, and incorporate various appeals to social justice.

On the other hand, there are pressures to tighten up the language of the competences. To some extent, at least, we would argue – on the admittedly limited data available to us – that an overall process of 'liberal recapture' is at work in this process. But whether it is or it isn't, it is clear that we cannot understand the production of these 'competences' without taking into account 'the actual circumstances of their production' (Fuller 1988) and the ways in which the meanings of words like 'competence' change under those sorts of political pressure – the 'domestication' of the key vocabulary (Rouse, 1993). As Woolgar (1988) and others have shown, even supposedly 'hard' scientific knowledge is shot through with the influences of its social construction. In the case of such 'soft' social technologies as 'competences', the social and political fluidity of their definition and construction is vivid. They show little technical sophistication, but much political sleight of hand in creating an amalgam of form and function that can be quite widely accepted, and given a range of different but still plausible meanings.

What are we to make of that fluidity of meaning, of the shifting relation of form and function? We can probably assume that the political imperative to have 'core competences' was irresistible. That was the deal with the Minister that would yield 'root and branch' reform. It would (or would appear to) offer the opportunity to standardise and control the curriculum of Initial Teacher Education in Scotland. It would give outsiders (the 'externality') a purchase for accountability. Thus the 'form' of the innovation was a given, but within that 'form' we can see that there were much more fluid possibilities concerning 'function', and indeed that the specification of functions could begin to contradict the form itself. Thus the 'core' competences are also 'mere' competences, and the 'commitments' are prominent even although they are inherently incapable of any sort of specific criterial specification that a competency system might be assumed to demand.

Or perhaps we should interpret the situation as surreal, rather than containing conflicting versions of reality. Magritte offers us a picture of a pipe. Underneath, a caption: 'this is not a pipe'. We are invited to think about the picture as a representation that cannot be the thing it represents. Why not? Perhaps because the picture represents the form of a pipe, but not its function (Stake, 1994). The SOED, in contrast, offers us a caption. It reads: 'this is a competence system', but the picture above seems to represent something that looks (whether suspiciously or reassuringly) like a liberal humanist ideology, little different from its predecessors although dressed up as a system of 'core competences'. In that case we confront liberal humanism in competence drag – a carefully engineered simulacrum of control. (We do not mean to imply, however, that attempts could not subsequently be made to 'realise' that form in terms of more congruent and coercive possibilities – such an anticipation is located in the text, as we have seen, and partly realised in the COSHEP competence profile. The problem for COSHEP, of course, is that they are trying to smoke a picture of a pipe.)

In terms of trying to determine what kind of a beastie these 'Competence' *Guidelines* are, where does that now take us? First, we can explain the ideological eclecticism, logical confusion, and strategic imprecision of the *Guidelines*: they have much to accommodate.

Second, we cannot give the competences a definitive reading. We can plausibly offer the 'liberal recapture' story: these *Guidelines* (see Kirk in the TESS debate) are business-as-usual. They encapsulate liberal principles in a pseudo-technicist frame. Or we can conclude that they represent a 'slippery slope': having sold the form of 'core competences' to the education profession in Scotland, the government will make further attempts to tighten control over the focus of the curriculum, the assessment criteria, and their monitoring. Or we can conclude that even if such attempts are made, they will come to nothing because what managers take to be a 'technical' problem is in fact a political problem incapable of technical solution.

Third, we can begin to understand why the competences are so idealised in their nature, overloading the poor beginning teacher with enough competences and commitments to see her or him through several careers with greater distinction than most experienced teachers, rather than simply indicating what it is realistic to expect in relation to a 1-year training for a job. They are an idealised expression of professionalism, lodged within and against a technicist specification.

Fourth, it allows us to argue that Jones and Moore are mistaken in their interpretation of competences – at least in this instance. Their rather one-dimensional account (see also Humes and Carr) tells only one side of the story. The other side is carried by the 'socially embodied' way in which these competences are created and negotiated.

Thus far we have argued that the notion of the effectivity of 'competences' is strung out between two fantasies. The first is the fantasy of *superperformance*, by which we mean these utopian characteristics, as well as the belief that 'standards' can be determined by a weak instrument in the face of a powerful occupational culture, and the curious indifference to the actual transitions that student and beginning teachers make. The second is the fantasy of *supercontrol* – exaggerated notions about the impact of innovations, deprofessionalisation, an increasingly coercive state, and the end of democracy. That takes us to our third perspective, an attempt to understand something of the actual transitions that Scottish teachers currently make, and to relate those experiences and perceptions to the notions of competence expressed in the *Guidelines*, and to wonder why 'competences' in ITE neglect such realities so strenuously.

Third Perspective: Actual Transitions

Our research into the experiences of beginning teachers (McNally *et al.*, 1994a,b) suggests that what they mostly experience is their own incompetence, rather than competence[2]. Their experiences do not reflect the multiple skills and abilities envisaged in the SOED's document. The nature of that 'incompetence' is worth spelling out from an anthropological perspective, because much of it is unavoidable and concerns their entry into the school both as novices and strangers:

> you're coming into the school for the first time. You've obviously got to fit into the way the school's running ... well, for the first year definitely there's very little room for any of your own ideas to come forward, the second year maybe a little more, and certainly after that you should be able to be in a position where you've got the respect of your colleagues ... and you can start to introduce your own ideas, teach things your own way.

As a stranger, the new teacher lacks a 'reputation' with the pupils, and has to negotiate his or her identity as a teacher. Different personae and tactics are tried out (like 'Mr Serious', or not-smiling-till-Xmas). Being novice members of a school community, they are in these senses fundamentally incompetent – and of course the common practice of allocating student teachers to a variety of placements adds to this phenomenon. As a result, beginning teachers have to try to create and establish a version of themselves that pupils will accept, as the following account suggests:

> I didn't blow up, I didn't go into a rage or anything. I just gave them my honest opinion, the opinions of the Germans I knew and that's that. Then I went back to what I was doing and he said, 'Miss, the lady before never let us talk about him, she always went into a rage and shouted at us and told us not to mention him'. I said 'Well, am I that person? 'No'. 'Well, there you go – different person, different reaction.'

Such negotiations are the commonplace of teacher initiation.

Teachers' accounts at this 'trial' stage of their initiation are often full of references to the 'deep end', 'the law of the jungle', and to a sense that they have at last confronted 'reality'. Reality means conflict not consensus, failure not success, a negative rather than a positive state of affairs:

> I said that third year class, I have really done them, done them wrong here. I haven't taught them anything. She said 'what do you mean?' So I explained and she said, 'Welcome to the real world'. Which I thought was quite good and cheered me up.

This reality is often felt to conflict with the version of teacher identity promoted in initial teacher training, and many of the teachers come to dismiss that training as 'idealised'. It is a 'vacuum', unconnected to the reality of survival in sometimes difficult schools:

> in college you know it's all that stuff, psychology, self-esteem, and all the rest of it and I used all that at first and it was completely useless [...] I've given it up, all the academic stuff [...] When I've said to the other teachers, 'Look how do you actually do that?' and the answer is basically, 'Bawl them out'.

From the point of view of a novice and a stranger coming to be accepted by the school community, 'competence' is a kind of experiential award, granted principally by the pupils to the teacher in terms of acceptance of the persona of the teacher, the end of initial challenges, the giving of positive feedback, and so on (see McNally *et al.*, 1994 for an elaboration of this argument). They experience their learning in holistic terms, not in terms of discrete competences which they believe they are or are not achieving. Our data suggest that there are three broad phases in the induction of beginning teachers. The first is a stage of *'idealised competences'*, wherein the values and ideals of the training course are inculcated. To some extent they are resisted during training, but the real breaking point comes with the need to cope with being a new teacher – a double stranger – both to other teachers and to the pupils. This provokes a sharp change in attitudes and values, and a series of *'coping competences'* are then developed as teachers learn to fit in, deal with confrontations, negotiate an acceptable identity with pupils and other teachers, and so on. The learning process is often a fairly solitary one, achieved mainly through 'trial and error'. In this coping stage there seems to be a lot of transitory behaviours, particularly relating to discipline and the need to establish an acceptable 'reputation'.

It is striking that the SOED 'core competences' resemble the 'idealised competences' stage, and hardly at all the stage of 'coping competences'. This is ironic when one considers that the ideological point of 'core competence' lists is their supposed relevance, their sense of reality, their common-sense and systematic analysis of actual job functions. Yet in this instance, the competences seem very distant from the real experiences of beginning teachers.

We would rather argue, on the basis of our data on how beginning teachers are inducted into secondary school teaching, that what they first acquire are a series of *'vernacular competences'*, acquired mainly through a fairly solitary process of trial and error, although also assisted by the advice of teachers in their subject department. These vernacular competences may be temporary or permanent features of a developing teaching 'style' and 'persona'. Most of them refer to relationships rather than to learning outcomes, and there is an emphasis on disciplinary competence. The coping stage (if successful) gives way to a third stage of *'realised competences'*, where relationships become more settled and discipline issues recede in importance:

> it's the case of the chicken and the egg. You know, which comes first? I'm not quite sure but because I'm getting to know them better it's easier to manage them, or because I'm managing them better, I'm getting to know them.

The third stage involves more stable relationships with most classes, and quite often the emergence of surprisingly firm sets of belief about the nature of teaching, what kids are like, and why standards are as they are.

Familiar arguments emerge – about school uniform, 'these kids', children knowing their rights these days, too many things being done for them, inability to concentrate – 'all those flickering images they watch'. We concluded that there was an intense sense on the one hand of how much these novice teachers had learned (become teachers, learned routines that work, decided what teacher 'personalities' to have, experimented with their effectiveness), and on the other hand of how quickly they had grown old in their knowledge. Such teachers seemed to move from the stress and uncertainty of becoming a teacher, to a plateau of certainties with which to fortify their practice and identity. It seemed that the kind of 'reflective practitioner' implicit in parts of the SOED competences and commitments was quite frequently caught and extinguished between the Scylla of initiation and the Charybdis of routine.

Conclusions

Our first conclusion is that the debate aroused by the issue of SOED competence guidelines has been over-polarised. The processes of 'social disembedding' noted by Jones and Moore are a feature of this particular case of competence, but they are not its only feature. It is plausible that such competency systems could be used in the future to undermine the professionalism of teaching, especially by giving managers and politicians an apparently direct purchase on redefining and policing the profession through the accountability offered by 'core competence' statements. But such an interpretation fails to do justice to the complex processes of negotiation and domestication involved in the construction of the SOED competences themselves. Our interim conclusion would be that it is necessary to understand these 'actual cultural practices' (as Jones and Moore call them) if a less one-sided and more complex view of the competence *Guidelines* is to emerge. We argue that the absence of this double perspective on knowledge – as both 'disembedded' and 'embodied' – makes their argument self-contradictory in an important sense.

Secondly, we are sceptical of the sorts of direction proposed by McClellan in the TESS debate. Attempts to treat teacher competences as a 'technical' problem run into the same sands as earlier attempts to specify job performance in industry (MBBO), to identify skills inventories for prevocational education, or to identify specific teaching skills in micro-teaching in the 1970s. If they were to 'succeed', they would remove just those elements of 'indetermination' that define teaching as a profession irreducible to specific and atomistic skills. The changes from draft to final *Guidelines* suggest that there is some support for this kind of attempt to make the competences more 'scientific', as seen in the tightening up of the language of the descriptors, and the mooted development of the competences into a more detailed specification of performance that would allow them to be used as assessment criteria. As the development of the

COSHEP profile indicates, such developments are likely to end up being technically impossible, politically unacceptable, and practically unworkable. They will lose credibility faster than they can gain control.

Thirdly, we reject, therefore, the notion of what we called 'supercontrol', as variously expressed by Jones and Moore, Carr, and Humes. At the same time, we reject the notion of 'superperformance', including the assumption that somehow such a competence-based reform is likely to have far-reaching consequences for the quality of Scottish teaching, the nature of initial teacher training, the autonomy of the profession, the cause of liberal humanism, and so on. We put most of these over-reactions down to the tendency of 'competence' to act as a focal and symbolic contest between state-sponsored managerialism and oligarchic professionalism.

Yet most innovations are characterised by failure, not success (Pressman and Wildavsky, 1979), or by the triumph of the unintended, and there is very little reason thus far to see these competence reforms in Scotland as much more than a series of diplomatic manoeuvres that offers consolation to the Right in the form of a simulacrum of control over the teaching profession, and a consolation to what might approximately be called the Centre–Left in terms of providing an opportunity to embed professional virtues in some kind of professional declaration. As we have tried to show, neither of these two strategies has much to do with how beginning teachers actually struggle with their role and the development of this expertise: it is once again the supreme irony of the 'competence movement' in general and in this particular that it never quite manages to address the reality on which it is so insistent, and we have tried to indicate how a research-based approach to the business of developing the 'competence' of beginning teachers might proceed.

We would only add as a final comment that the need to develop the critical reflexivity of teachers (meaning the continuing ability of teachers to improve their practice) ought to be confronted somewhere towards the end of the 'coping' phase. We have some evidence to suggest that many teachers succumb to occupational socialisation at this stage, and – more often than we might wish – to a premature and unambitious definition of the possibilities of their role. It is there that the developmental accent should fall, rather than in the initial period when 'coping' concerns are a dominant and necessary concern. And it is there that it most certainly does not:

> as a probationer suddenly I'm expected to monitor my own performance and evaluate my own performance and there's nobody waiting there to give you a pat on the head and say 'well that was really good, or that was mince' ... Suddenly, all of a sudden, nobody seems to care how you perform in front of a class.

Notes

1. This chapter summarises the critique of SOED 'Competence' guidelines published in the *Scottish Educational Review* (1994) **26(2)**, 118–133.
2. This research was initially supported by the University of Stirling, and later by an SOED grant directed towards research into probationer experiences.

References

Althusser, L. (1971) *Lenin and Philosophy and Other Works*. London: New Left Books.
Bernstein, B. (1990) *The structuring of pedagogic discourse, class, codes and control*, Vol. 4. London: Routledge.
Buchanan, A. (1988) 'Principal/agent theory and decision-making in health care', *Bioethics*, **2 (4)**, 317–333.
Cameron-Jones, M. and O'Hara, P. (1990) 'Getting the measure of new teachers in Scotland: does the system work?', *Scottish Educational Review*, **22 (1)**, 38–44.
Carr, D. (1993a) *Times Educational Supplement*, (Scotland) 26 February.
Carr, D. (1993b) 'Questions of competence', *British Journal of Educational Studies*, **41 (3)**, 253–271.
Carr, D. (1993c) 'Guidelines for teacher training: the competency model', *Scottish Educational Review*, **25 (1)**, 17–25.
COSHEP (1993a) *First Appointment of Teachers: Revision of Profile Forms*. Glasgow: COSHEP.
COSHEP (1993b) *First Appointment of Teachers: Revision of Profile Forms. A Report on the Conference*. Stepps: COSHEP.
COSHEP (1993c) *A Professional Report for Teachers Completing Initial Teacher Training*. Glasgow: COSHEP.
Davis, J. (1991) 'Professions, trades and the obligations to inform', *Journal of Applied Philosophy*, **8 (2)**, 167–176.
Fuller, S. (1988) *Social Epistemology*. Bloomington: Indiana University Press.
Giddens, A. (1991) *Modernity and Self-identity*. Cambridge: Polity Press.
Humes, W. (1992) *Times Educational Supplement (Scotland)* 18 December.
Jamous, H. and Peloille, B. (1970) 'Professions or self-perpetuating systems? Changes in the French university–hospital system', in Jackson (ed.), *Professions and Professionalization*. Cambridge: Cambridge University Press.
Jones, L. and Moore, R. (1993) 'Education, competence and the control of expertise', *British Journal of Sociology of Education*, **14 (4)**, 385–397.
Kirk, G. (1992) *Times Educational Supplement (Scotland)*, 11 December.
McClellan, E. (1993) *Times Educational Supplement (Scotland)*, 5 March.
McNally, J., Cope, P., Inglis, W. and Stronach, I. (1994a) *Project EASEL: Evaluation and Analysis of School-based Experiential Learning*, Final report. Department of Education, University of Stirling (for SOED), January.
McNally, J., Cope, P., Inglis, W. and Stronach, I. (1994b) 'Current realities in the student teaching experience: a preliminary inquiry', *Teaching and Teacher Education*, **10 (2)**, 219–230.
Pressman, J. and Wildavsky, A. (1979) *Implementation*, (2nd edn.) Berkeley: University of California Press.
Rouse, P. (1993) 'Policing knowledge: disembodied policy for embodied knowledge', *Inquiry*, **34**, 353–364.
SOED (1992) *Initial Teacher Training: Draft Revised Guidelines for Teacher Training Courses*. Edinburgh: Scottish Office.
SOED (1993) *Guidelines for Teacher Training Courses, a Paper by the SOED*. Edinburgh:

Scottish Office.
Stake, R. (1994) 'Program evaluation and promotionalism', paper delivered at the 5th International Cambridge Conference on Educational Evaluation, Hughes Hall, December.
Stronach, I. (1992) 'Signs of the times: understanding ideas of 'emancipation' in recent teacher education texts', *Scottish Educational Review*, **24 (1)**, 57–63.
Stronach, I. (1993) *Rough Notes on Competence*. ESRC seminar, Manchester.
Stronach, I., Cope, P., Inglis, B. and McNally, J. (1994) 'The SOED "Competence" Guidelines for Initial Teacher Training: issues of control, performance and relevance', *Scottish Educational Review*, **26 (2)**, 118–133.
Woolgar, S. (1988) *Knowledge and Reflexivity: New Frontiers in the Sociology of Knowledge*. London: Sage.

7

Professional Competences and Professional Characteristics: The Northern Ireland Approach to the Reform of Teacher Education

*Geoff Whitty**

Background

Teacher educators in many parts of the world are exploring ways of using competences to assist the professional development of teachers without undermining traditional professional values. I was recently involved in such an exercise in Northern Ireland, where I chaired a working party on competences which included representatives from the higher education institutions, education and library boards and teachers. The working party was established by the Department of Education for Northern Ireland (DENI) as part of a government-initiated review of teacher education in the province. Our terms of reference required us to define the competences which characterise the successful professional teacher and to consider their relative importance, their use and their assessment. We were also asked to consider how their development should be phased across initial teacher training, induction and further professional development, and suggest the balance between higher education institutions and schools in their development. This work on competences was intended to form the basis of work by further groups reviewing in more detail the curriculum of initial teacher education and the links between initial training, induction and the early years of professional development.

---

* This article is based on the report of the working group on 'Competences' established by the Department of Education in Northern Ireland (DENI) in connection with the review of initial teacher training in the province. Other members of the working group were: G. Colohan, C. Coxhead, S.I. Davidson, A.E.A. Lamb, D.G. McIntyre, A. Magee, P. Maguire, S. Marriott, M.G. Salters, R. Small, T. Stewart, M. Matchett and I. Hamilton.

While conscious of the unresolved debates about the definition of competences and their application (Whitty and Willmott, 1991), the working group was also aware that most people in teacher education did now recognise that there could be some benefits in using competences in certain aspects of teacher education. In the Northern Ireland context, where (as in England and Wales) teacher educators were required to work within the framework used by the then Council for the Accreditation of Teacher Education, we took the view that, if our proposals were to be workable, they would need to bear a recognisable relationship to the 'official' categories of competence listed, as follows, in the government Circulars:

- Secondary list:
– Subject knowledge
– Subject application
– Class management
– Assessment and recording of pupils' progress
– Further professional development
- Primary list:
– Curriculum content, planning and assessment:
  (a) Whole curriculum
  (b) Subject knowledge and application
  (c) Assessment and recording of pupils' progress
– Teaching strategies:
  (a) Pupils' learning
  (b) Teaching strategies and techniques
– Further professional development

However, we also felt that neither these broad categories nor the individual competences listed within them were adequate for our purposes. Although they were not intended to define the whole curriculum of initial teacher training, we considered that some omissions needed remedying. Indeed, on balance, the working group felt that the disadvantages of producing a longer list of competences were outweighed by the dangers of anything not on the list being relegated to second-class status and regarded as dispensable when resources were under pressure. With my colleagues on the Modes of Teacher Education project, I had already encountered widespread concern in England and Wales that not only traditional educational studies work, but also reflective practice, would be expunged from initial teacher education as a result of the limitations of the official lists. There was particular unease about the implication that such things as special educational needs and even critical awareness were hitherto to be concerns for further professional development rather than pre-service training.

Although we started with the CATE list of competences, the working group looked to other sources to elaborate – as our terms of reference required – a specification of the competences required of the successful professional teacher. Given its provenance in initial teacher training, the list of competences in Circular 9/92 was not particularly helpful in defining those to be developed during induction and further professional development. Neither time nor other resources were available for us to undertake the sort of task analysis, functional analysis or other research activities that have been used to develop competence-based education and training in other fields. We had to rely instead on secondary sources supplemented by the ideas and experience of the working group itself and of those whom it had an opportunity to consult.

Our terms of reference had drawn our attention to the work of the Scottish Office Education Department (SOED), and we found their notes of guidance helpful in refining and augmenting the list of competences to be developed within the phase of initial training. Like the SOED (1992), we took the view that the term 'professional competences' should be taken to refer to knowledge, understanding and attitudes as well as to practical skills. We agreed with their view that to teach satisfactorily certain craft skills have undoubtedly to be learnt. We agreed too that teachers must in addition to this have a knowledge and understanding both of the content of their teaching and of the processes which they are carrying out, and be able to evaluate and justify their actions. We added that they also need an appreciation of the broader context in which they are working.

We decided that a simple list of competences, no matter how comprehensive and well structured, could not convey the totality of what we wanted to say about the professional competence of a teacher. One of the criticisms often made of competence-based approaches to education and training, and to professional education and training in particular, is that the atomisation of professional knowledge, judgement and skill into discrete competences inevitably fails to capture the essence of professional competence. One way to meet the objection would be to specify some generic professional competences. This approach has been adopted in respect of police training by John Elliott and his colleagues working at the University of East Anglia (Elliott, 1992; and Chapter 14). For similar reasons, a project concerned with social work training run by Richard Winter at Anglia Polytechnic University has chosen to specify a number of core assessment criteria which bind together the individual competences which it has identified (Winter and Maisch 1991). The principles underlying such work were highly influential in our thinking, even though our detailed proposals diverged from it in significant ways. They are also similar to those being advocated by Jim Walker in Australia (Preston and Walker, 1993; Walker, 1992; and see Chapter 8).

One way to deal with the problem might have been to incorporate at the end of the list of specific knowledge and skills a section entitled 'professional attitudes' or 'competences related to professionalism'. This is essentially how the Scottish scheme deals with the problem. But the items under this heading are really of a different order from those under the other headings. In some ways, they are more in the nature of personal qualities or the general (and perhaps ideal) characteristics of successful teachers which permeate all their specific competences and enable them to apply these appropriately.

The Identification of Competences

We therefore ended up with two sets of qualities which we look for in a successful professional teacher – what we termed 'professional characteristics' and 'professional competences'. Professional characteristics were what we considered to be the underlying qualities of the teacher which enable him or her to pull the individual competences together and apply them in the professional context. In describing the characteristics in this way we were not, of course, suggesting that they are innate, and that 'good teachers are born and not made': these qualities too can be fostered and developed. Our suggested list related to the following aspects of professional activity.

Professional Characteristics of the Successful Teacher

- Professional values
- Professional development
- Personal development
- Communication and relationships
- Synthesis and application

This list had then to be read along with our list of specific competences, which we divided into professional knowledge and understanding and professional skills, as follows.

Professional Competences of the Successful Teacher

1   *Knowledge and understanding:*
    1.1 Knowledge of children and their learning
    1.2 Subject knowledge
    1.3 Knowledge of the curriculum
    1.4 Knowledge of the education system
    1.5 Knowledge of the teacher's role
2. *Skills:*
    2.1 Subject application
    2.2 Classroom methodology

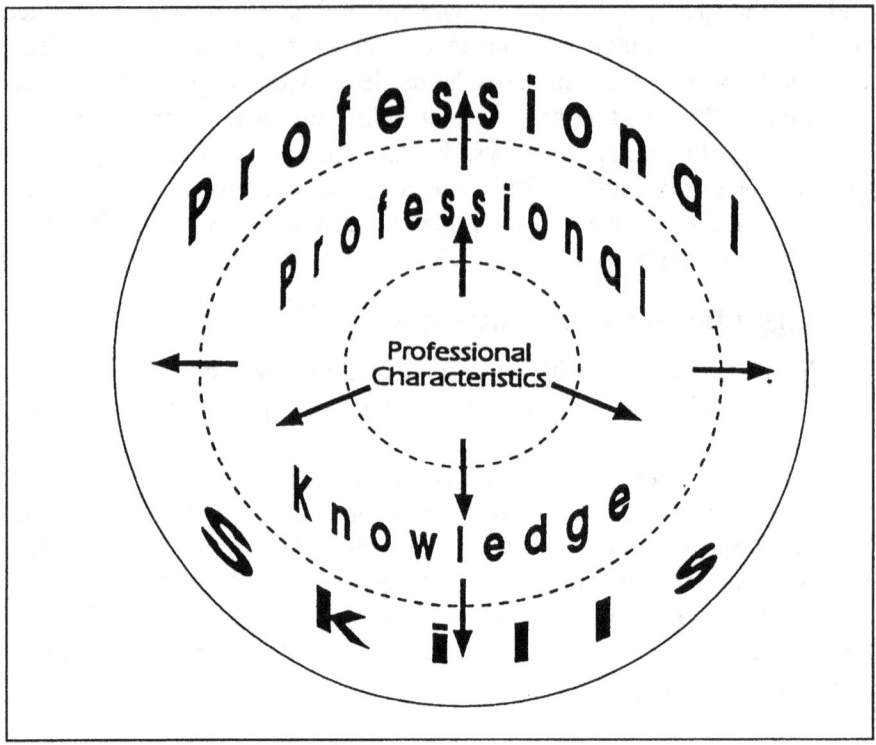

Figure 7.1

    2.3 Class management

    2.4 Assessment and recording

    2.5 Undertaking the wider role

We envisaged the two statements as interlocking with each other. This could either be seen as a matrix with professional characteristics permeating the performance of professional competences – or it might be represented graphically as in Figure 7.1. Either way, we were trying to indicate that the professional characteristics of the teacher ought to permeate the application of the specific competences identified under the headings of professional knowledge and professional skills. We wanted to insist to our political masters that a professional teacher requires both.

Phasing and Location

We also made some preliminary suggestions about which of the competences should receive particular attention during the successive phases of ITT, induction and the early years of in-service education. Some competence schemes have discrete lists of competences for ITT and INSET. But, given that the Northern Ireland group took a developmental view of competences rather than one expressed in terms of minimum thresholds, we did not see any of the competences as entirely disposed of at the end of ITT. Instead, we tried to indicate priorities for development at the respective stages rather than to imply that a competence should be entirely neglected in any of them. The competences were assigned letter codes to indicate the stages at which most attention should be given to their development. Letter 'A' indicates initial training, letter 'B' induction and letter 'C' the early years of further professional development. A capital letter is used to signify that a particular phase of training should have a principal responsibility for the competence in question, while a lower case letter suggests that the phase should have a significant but subsidiary role in its development.

A page from our report, shown in Figure 7.2, gives a flavour of our approach, though the specific codings suggested are, of course, open to debate. It should be noted that, since our remit referred to 'the early stages of in-service training', we did not make any recommendations about the development of school management competences, such as those specified in the work of the School Management Competences Project in England (Earley, 1992), nor did we refer to the role of teachers in the training of other teachers.

The Northern Ireland group also made suggestions about where the individual competences might best be developed, though these related to the particular conditions of Northern Ireland and do not reflect the extent of the move towards school-based training that is now taking place in England. They are anyway preliminary thoughts on the subject. As can be seen in Figure 7.2, we employed a five-point scale to indicate the amount of school experience that we believe is required to develop the respective competences. Those which are scored '1' require little or no school experience, while those scored '5' could be developed wholly in a school, with no explicit input from outside. Others require both a structured input (tutoring, guidance or support) and a greater or lesser degree of classroom experience or practice. Thus '2' may be taken to mean that a competence can be developed largely outside the classroom, but requires trainee teachers to have experience on which to draw in order to develop full understanding; '3' means that development requires roughly equal amounts of work inside and outside the classroom; and '4' that it requires substantial experience and practice in the classroom supplemented by appropriate guidance and support.

This sort of analysis, though often contentious in detail, can help clarify a division of labour in partnerships between higher education and schools. In practice, though, the Northern Ireland group took the view that the development of very few of the competences could be the *exclusive* preserve of either higher education institutions or schools.

Course Design

The Northern Ireland working group did not engage in course design. That

COMPETENCES		SCHOOL EXP	PHASE
1.4.5	awareness of contemporary debates about education;	2	Ac
1.4.6	understanding of schools as institutions and their place within the community;	1	Ac
1.4.7	knowledge of the part of the education system in which he or she is working and its relationship to other parts of that system;	1	aB
1.4.8	knowledge of the organisation and management of schools, and the place within these of school policies and development plans.	3	aBc
1.5	**Knowledge of the teacher's role**		
	Demonstrates:		
1.5.1	awareness of the importance of informed critical reflection in evaluating his or her professional practice;	2	Abc
1.5.2	understanding of how to draw upon sources of professional help and expertise;	3	aB
1.5.3	knowledge of his or her contractual, legal, pastoral and administrative responsibilities;	2	aBc
1.5.4	awareness of his or her role as a member of a professional team within the school;	5	abC
1.5.5	awareness of how to respond to current social problems which may manifest themselves in schools.	2	aC
2	**PROFESSIONAL SKILLS**		
2.1	**Subject application**		
2.1.1	Plans appropriate lessons within teaching programmes.	3	Ab
2.1.2	Demonstrates a knowledge of the particular methodologies and procedures necessary for effective teaching of the subject(s) forming the content of his or her teaching.	3	Ab
2.1.3	Is able to prepare appropriate learning materials for pupils.	3	Ab

Figure 7.2 Extract from list of competences

was a responsibility left to another group and to individual institutions and their partner schools. The specification of competences does not of itself imply that courses should take a particular form. Indeed, the philosophy underlying extreme versions of competence-based education suggests that, providing a student can demonstrate a competence he or she can gain credit for it without having followed a course at all. Such a strategy places the entire burden of assuring the attainment of the required standards on the assessment process. It has also been suggested that students might be permitted to leave a course of initial teacher education and enter teaching once they have reached a certain threshold of competence (Hargreaves, 1989). There are, though, legitimate concerns about the extent to which this approach can undermine the experience of a coherent programme of study, often seen as a necessary part of teacher education. However these issues are resolved, courses designed to help students develop particular competences will clearly need to make use of these competences as a vital tool in curriculum planning. Competences can usefully be grouped into modules for the purposes of curricular design and assessment, as has been done in the Anglia social work project to which reference was made earlier (Winter and Maisch, 1991).

The extent to which exit competences will inform course design in teacher education will vary. Prior to the requirements of Circular 9/92, most course teams used the approach only for parts of their courses and it is perhaps not surprising that the most extensive use of competences has been in relation to school experience. Indeed, some tutors believe that, in principle, the approach should be limited to this area, particularly where a narrow definition of competences is being used. Other course teams, usually working with a broader definition, have tried to adopt a competence-based approach to a whole course. School-based courses provide an obvious opportunity for trying to relate all elements of a course to the achievement of workplace competences.

At present, the specific competences used in course design can be derived from a variety of sources. In addition to the competences specified in government circulars, the various task analyses of teaching or attempts to specify the attributes of the teacher as professional might be one starting point. In other cases, they might be determined by the staff designing the courses, probably in consultation with teachers and LEA advisers. There is also considerable scope for students to negotiate the competences which they wish the course to help them develop and this is likely to be a central feature of INSET provision which is based on the use of competences.

Teaching, Learning and Assessment

Despite claims that competence-based approaches emphasise outcomes at the expense of processes, Jessup (1991:138) argues that the whole point of specifying outcomes is to promote learning. If competence-based approaches encourage teacher educators to be more explicit about the characteristics of skilled professionalism that they seek to encourage, this is likely to have implications for teaching and learning. In some cases, it will lead to whole-course policies on teaching and learning. In theory, courses designed with an emphasis on exit competences might be expected to be non-prescriptive about the methods used to encourage their attainment. Indeed, they should provide considerable scope for the negotiation of teaching and learning methods. In practice, teaching methods are likely to be influenced by the particular definition of competences adopted and by the actual competences being encouraged. The competences required of the reflective teacher are likely to require rather different methods of teaching and learning from those of the instructor.

The early association of competence-based approaches with vocational training, especially in some of the narrowly behavioural approaches adopted in the USA, has sometimes led to a view amongst teacher educators that competence-based education implies an instructional form of pedagogy. A narrowly skills-based definition of competence has, as in earlier courses based upon behavioural objectives, sometimes led to teaching that stresses performance at the expense of understanding. The early work of NCVQ was criticised for similar excesses, but it is now accepted that such an approach is inappropriate to the development of higher-level professional skills.

This has obvious implications for assessment. NCVQ now acknowledges that for levels four and above, it may be necessary to assess underpinning knowledge and understanding separately from workplace performance. It is certainly likely that in a field such as teacher education a range of assessment methods will need to be employed, even in courses based around the achievement of workplace competences. Definitions of competence that go beyond skills to include knowledge, values and attitudes raise particular problems for assessment. There is controversy over whether competence-based assessment raises any more problems of validity and reliability than more conventional academic approaches, but the arguments are by no means decisive (Gonczi, 1994; Jessup, 1991). Whatever approaches are adopted, we need to acknowledge that the attainment of competences requires inferences to be made on the basis of a range of evidence; the less specific the criteria enunciated, the higher the level of inference will be and the more informed the judgement that will be called for. One strategy for attempting to ensure that the competences being assessed are not based on too narrow an experiential context is to specify range indicators which describe the context within which a performance should take place; for example, a student-teacher may need to demonstrate practical ability in more than one type of school.

The competences specified in some courses are the minimum or threshold competences necessary to perform particular teaching activities and, in others, those characteristic of the 'good teacher'. There are also differing views about whether a competence is something that is either a specific achievement or, alternatively, a dimension of performance in terms of which one can perform at different levels. In the former case, one might expect distinct lists of competences of ITT and INSET courses, while the latter approach implies a similar (or overlapping) list of competences with different levels of attainment. This was the approach adopted in Northern Ireland.

A major issue for teacher education which leads to higher education awards and to qualified teacher status is how to decide how the assessment of individual competences relates to the criteria used in making the overall award. In hybrid courses the relationship of the assessment of competences to any other forms of assessment employed on a course also needs to be clarified. Here again, the social work courses developed at Anglia Polytechnic University provide a possible model (Winter and Maisch, 1991).

Profiling

Even though the Northern Ireland schedule of competences embodied a substantial number of individual items, some of which are clearly more specific than others, the list remains at a fairly high level of generality. We took the view that it was neither feasible nor desirable to sub-divide these competences into even narrower technical and behavioural components, even though our terms of reference required it. Although they are mainly expressed in behavioural terms, few if any of them amount to precise measurable statements of performance criteria. This is because professional competences tend not to be susceptible to discrete measurement and the form in which these might be assessed will depend to some extent on the locus of training.

Nevertheless, the specification of competences lends itself to relatively clear reporting of assessments for both students and potential employers. It is therefore highly compatible with current trends towards the use of profiles in teacher education courses. Like other approaches to profiling, the use of competences can be formative and/or summative and it raises similar concerns about ownership of the profile of achievement, an issue that could become particularly significant in the context of teacher appraisal.

The official view in Scotland appears to be that it is for institutions and their partner schools to decide how each competence should be assessed (SOED, 1992). The SOED also suggests that there may be a case for nationally defined performance criteria, but the lack of professional consensus about what these criteria might be makes such a task difficult to undertake at the present time. The Northern Ireland group was of the opinion that it would be better for any such generally agreed criteria to emerge out of work done at local level by partnerships between higher education institutions and schools as they attempt to operationalise and assess the competences. Similarly, we felt that student self-assessment schedules and profile statements might best be developed through a sharing of good practice amongst the various partners in the training process.

In England, though, it seems that there is to be a common national framework for such profiles (DfE, 1993b). But, whatever form this eventually takes, it is to be hoped that the profile statements will refer to what the Northern Ireland group defined as professional characteristics as well as to professional competences.

Conclusion

My experience of the exercise in Northern Ireland was that it was seen as an extremely fruitful one by the various parties involved, including some who were initially suspicious or sceptical about the use of competences in teacher education. It provided an important opportunity for partners to think through issues together and to develop a common framework for thinking about their roles. Most members of the group felt that the process of thinking through the issues had helped to demystify teacher education, provide clearer goals for students, point to a clearer definition of the roles of schools and institutions and provide a firmer base for induction and further professional development. And – despite widespread unease among teacher educators about narrow behaviourist approaches to the specification and assessment of competences – the approach adopted, by recognising the importance of generic professional competences as well as specific classroom skills, appears to have commanded widespread support in Northern Ireland. How it will actually be implemented is now a matter for government decision.

The government has established a Northern Ireland Teacher Education Committee (NITEC), under the chairmanship of Sir William Taylor, to implement its reforms. The Report of the 'Competences' working group is being used by this body as a basis for the development of a profiling system. Although I have not yet seen the results of this work, I understand that it has entailed the drawing together of some of the competences identified by the working group to make the profiling process as manageable as possible. The outcome of NITEC's work on this issue will be contained in a booklet which will shortly be issued to schools in the province to help them prepare for the whole range of teacher education reforms that will be introduced in September 1996.

References

Barrett, E., Barton, L., Furlong, J., Galvin, C., Miles, S. and Whitty, G. (1993) *Initial Teacher Education in England and Wales: A Topography*. London: Institute of

Education, University of London.
DES (1989) *Initial Teacher Training: Approval of Courses* (Circular 24/89). London: Department of Education and Science.
DfE (1992) *Initial Teacher Training (Secondary Phase)* (Circular 9/92). London: Department for Education.
DfE (1993a) *The Government's Proposals for the Reform of Initial Teacher Training*. London: Department for Education.
DfE (1993b) *The Initial Training of Primary School Teachers: New Criteria for Course Approval* (Draft Circular). London: Department for Education.
Earley, P. (1992) *The School Management Competences Project: Final Report*. Slough: School Management South.
Elliot, J. (1992) *The Role of a Small Scale Research Project in Developing a Competency-based Police Training Curriculum*. Mimeo. Norwich: University of East Anglia.
Gonczi, A. (1994) 'Competency based assessment in the professions in Australia', *Assessment in Education*, **1 (1)**, 27–45.
Hargreaves, D. (1989) 'PGCE assessment fails the test', *The Times Educational Supplement*, **3 November**.
Jessup, G. (1991) *Outcomes: NVQs and The Emerging Model of Education and Learning*. Lewes: Falmer Press.
McElvogue, M. and Salters, M. (1992) *Models of Competence and Teacher Training*. Belfast: Queen's University of Belfast.
NCVQ (1989) *National Vocational Qualifications: Criteria and Procedures*. London: National Council for Vocational Qualifications.
Preston, B. and Walker, J. C. (1993) 'Competence based standards in the professions and higher education', in C. Collins (ed.) *Competencies: The Competencies Debate in Australian Education and Training*. Canberra: Australian College of Education.
SOED (1992) *Initial Teacher Training: Draft Revised Guidelines for Teacher Training Courses*. Edinburgh: Scottish Office Education Department.
Walker, J. C. (1992) 'Competence-based Standards in Teaching: A General Rationale and Conceptual Approach', in Schools Council: *Agenda Papers*. Issues arising from *Australia's Teachers: An Agenda for the Next Decade*, Vol. 2. Canberra: Australian Government Publishing Service.
Whitty, G. and Willmott, E. (1991) 'Competence-based teacher education: approaches and issues', *Cambridge Journal of Education*, **21 (3)**, 309–318
Winter, R. and Maisch, M. (1991) *The ASSET Programme*, Vols. 1 and 2. Chelmsford: Anglia Polytechnic/Essex Social Services Department.

8

Professional Standards for Teachers in Australia

James Walker

Introduction

Recent reforms in teaching and teacher education in Australia have been stimulated more by government policy than by professional opinion and educational research. Proposals for competency based and other professional standards are clear examples of this, as are quality assurance schemes mounted by federal and state governments. Professional issues, however, have come to the fore in this context. Foremost among them have been questions about the nature of professional competence in teaching, what sorts of standards are appropriate and how they should be judged. Indeed, the recognition of the nature and importance of professional judgement in teaching has been one of the main reasons that the development of competency standards and their relation to quality assurance have taken the direction they have. Moreover, this has led to some creative thinking and research on professional competence.

In this chapter I will outline policy developments, discuss professionalism and professional competence in teaching and give some examples of standard setting at national and state levels.

The Policy Context

The Australian teaching profession is currently embroiled in responses to and collaboration with government in areas such as curriculum change and reform of relationships between the school and training sectors to boost efforts in vocational education. In the 1980s and early 1990s national collaboration in curriculum proceeded from mapping of the curriculum across state education systems to a statement of goals for Australian schools agreed by all governments, federal and state, to the development of an outcomes-based curriculum approach in national 'statements' and 'profiles' which are now being revised and implemented in the states and territories.

Preceding these issues, however, and persisting alongside them, has been national concern, spearheaded by John Dawkins – the controversial centralist and interventionist federal Minister for Employment, Education and Training – over the quality of teaching itself, and therefore over the quality of learning. This has been prompted as much by international discussion through forums such as the Organisation for Economic Cooperation and Development (OECD, 1989, 1990) as by Australian debate (Schools Council, 1989, 1990). This concern has at least two major sources: first, by the mid- to late 1980s there had been a decade and a half of criticism, some of it quite trenchant, of the standards of teachers and teaching in Australia; and second, the national microeconomic reform agenda had begun to include the professions, but especially teaching, as an object of reconstruction towards greater quality of outcomes. This economically oriented thrust was spearheaded by Dawkins through the new economically oriented mega-Department of Employment, Education and Training (DEET). Dawkins saw the quality of Australia's schools as critical to the country's economic future and forged a national consensus around this theme (Dawkins, 1988).

The buzzword through all this was 'quality'. Whatever else 'quality' meant, it meant standards; and in professional work this meant professional standards. With the shift from an emphasis on inputs and processes to an emphasis on outcomes, there was a shift in policy thinking about teaching towards asking what capacities and qualities a teacher needs to produce learning of the desired kind and quality. In short, a new context had developed in which to ask the old question: what makes a competent teacher?

In this way the new search for quality in teaching became linked with an older idea, the notion of competency-based standards. It was obvious to all that quality requires competence. What was controversial was whether competency based standards were appropriate measures of professional competence, and whether a competency based framework was appropriate for the design of teacher education courses. Given that a competences approach was desirable – and by no means all teachers or teacher educators accepted this – the next question was how it should be applied. Competency based standards can be applied in more than one way: in competency based assessment, in competency based curriculum design and in competency based pedagogy. It is possible to have competency based assessment without competency based curriculum and teaching methods, and vice versa. 'Competency based education and training' is usually taken to include all three.

The discussion of competency standards in teaching has been concentrated in the past 4 years and has taken place in three contexts: the professions generally and their relation to the professional education programmes of higher education institutions; the national microeconomic focus on teaching; and the political concerns of state governments to be seen by parents and employers to be doing something about the quality of teaching and teacher education.

Competency Standards in the Professions and Higher Education

I commented above that, so far as the Australian teaching profession is concerned, the origins of the current interest in competency standards lies in the politically motivated national microeconomic reform agenda and that professional involvement has followed in the wake of political and economic instigation. However, this has not been the case for other professions in Australia. Several professions had been developing competency standards for their own professional reasons since the mid 1980s: among them nursing, architecture, accountancy, dietetics, pharmacy and veterinary science. One of the major reasons for this was to achieve consistency and integrity in standards for registration of professional practitioners. For example, in 1986 the Australian Nurse Registering Authorities Conference determined that it was necessary to identify nationally agreed minimum competences for registered and enrolled nurses. This was 3 years before the federal government decided to encourage and assist professions to develop national competency standards and competency based assessment. The profession and the government concurred on certain objectives including the need to establish a rational basis for determining the eligibility of nurses trained overseas for registration in Australia and the need to provide a basis for assessing nurses wishing to re-enter the workforce after a period of absence. Additional professional reasons were to determine eligibility for initial registration of nurses prepared in Australia (where nurse education had just moved from a hospital-based to a university-based system) and to determine a basis for assessment of nurses who are required to demonstrate a minimum level of competence for the purposes of ongoing practice (Gonczi, Hager and Athanasou, 1993:87).

The development of competency standards for other professions was significant for teaching in that the philosophical and technical basis on which these standards were developed was an innovative and highly professional one, far away from the crude behaviourism of earlier competency-standards, including the competency-based teacher education movement of the 1960s and 1970s. Because of the link with recognition of overseas qualifications, these competency developments were sponsored and funded by the National Office for Overseas Skills Recognition (NOOSR) within DEET. This office commissioned researchers in the Faculty of Education at the University of Technology,

Sydney – Gonczi, Hager and their colleagues – to construct procedures for competency development. The 'integrated model' proposed by this team of researchers, joined by other scholars including the veterinary scientist Heywood of the University of Sydney (Gonczi, Hager and Oliver, 1990; Heywood, Gonczi and Hager, 1992) has been very influential and has been one of the reasons why competency development for the professions in Australia has not gone along the traditional behaviourist, reductionist route. Further developmental work was done by the Australian Council for Educational Research (Masters and McCurry, 1990). Proposals similar to the Australian 'integrated model' have been put forward in other countries including England (Whitty, 1994).

Unfortunately, although this sort of approach has been the case for the professions, the same cannot be said for the competency movement in vocational education, where the National Training Board, a body consisting of the federal and state ministers responsible for vocational education and training, supported by powerful sections of the trade union movement wanting skill specifications neatly tied down so that wage scales and training could be constructed to match, has developed a hierarchical, atomistic and behaviourist system within a 'National Standards Framework' (NTB, 1992). Because of the prominence in public reporting of this approach to competences where apprenticeships, trade training and indeed the whole vocational education system was being pushed towards behaviourism, it was behaviourism which the public mind identified with competency standards, rather than the innovative integrated model developed for the professions by Hager, Gonczi and their colleagues. As Hager (1994) has pointed out, this has led to considerable misunderstanding of the nature of more advanced and sophisticated work on competence and competency standards.

It was within this context that there arose a debate about whether competency standards should be introduced into higher education. Australian Vice-Chancellors caught up rather late with the competency movement, and when they saw it they did not like what they saw (AVCC, 1992; NOOSR 1992). They identified competences with narrow, workplace-related skills, and seemed almost innocent of the work already done by several of the professions whose professional education was occurring within their own institutions. They were worried that the specification of sets of competences could threaten the integrity of university education by giving 'undue weight and significance to attributes removed from the necessary, if less measurable, intellectual context in which they must be embedded'.

Another worry was that competency approaches could lead to outside agencies and professional bodies dictating what ought to be taught in university courses. Professor Brian Wilson, Vice Chancellor of the University of Queensland and Chair of the Committee for Quality

Assurance in Higher Education, asserted that the curricula and outcomes of university education must be concerned with issues broader than 'immediate professional competency – and should, therefore, be primarily informed by the judgement of academics in touch with advancements of knowledge on a worldwide basis' (Wilson 1992:58). As if to hose down this debate, DEET announced that it had no agenda for the introduction of competency based approaches into universities (Kelleher, 1992), and its Higher Education Division commissioned a survey of academic opinion which came up with the predictable finding that academics believed that although the competency movement was producing useful gains, it was doubtful that these were taking the form that some of the competency movement intended, and that it was unlikely that a 'full blown' competency approach to education would become dominant in university courses (Bowden and Masters, 1993:x).

National Microeconomic Focus on the Quality of Teaching and Teacher Education

The second context of competency standards, as stressed above, has been the specific microeconomic focus on teaching, as one profession among others, albeit a critical profession (Marginson, 1993: Chapter X), from government's (especially the federal government's) human capital view of education's contribution to national economic performance. It can be argued that the notion of competency is the most important conceptual link between Australian (micro-) economic policy and educational theory (Walker, 1992, 1993b). This economic context was most sharply defined in the National Project on the Quality of Teaching and Learning (NPQTL), in which the Commonwealth joined with representatives of teachers' employers (government and non-government) and representatives of teachers (through their unions).

Instigated by the federal government, the NPQTL was set up in 1990 to lead a process of national debate and negotiation aimed at improving the quality of teaching and learning in Australian schools. It had a life of 3 years. Its developmental work was conducted by three working parties, one investigating the organisation of teachers' work, a second national professional issues and a third teacher preparation and career development. A major agenda of this third working party was the development of national competency standards (NCS) for teachers.

The structure of the NPQTL reflected the corporatism which had become characteristic of Australian national political life under the Hawke Labor Government during the 1980s and has been continued through the 1990s by the Keating Government. National economic issues have been tackled by tripartite groups consisting of government, employers' representatives and employees' representatives – national corporatism. Where state issues were involved (as was the case in education, which is constitutionally a state responsibility) the state governments were represented – corporate federalism (Lingard, 1991). The NPQTL was a clear instance of both of these, in that state governments, through their Departments of Education, are the major employers of teachers in Australia. So the NPQTL governing board consisted of representatives of the federal government, employers (the state Education Departments and independent and catholic schools) and employees (the teachers unions). Its three working parties initially reflected this structure.

Given that one of the NPQTL's major agendas was teacher preparation and the possible application of competency standards in this domain, the lack of any representation of teacher educators or universities on NPQTL was regarded as a serious problem by these groups. Lobbying by the Australian Council of Deans of Education, a body formed in 1991 precisely to represent Education Faculties in the national corporatist context, resulted in its president (myself) being appointed to the Working Party on Teacher Preparation and Career Development as a representative of employers of teacher educators, the Australian Vice Chancellors' Committee, along with a representative of the universities' academic union as a representative of teacher educators as employees. Thus was another major interest group included while the principles of national corporatism continued to be observed. Later, at the time universities were expressing general consternation about the possible insinuation of competency standards into universities, another representative of the Vice-Chancellors was included.

The working party's first step on competency standards was to commission a background policy paper. This paper (later published as Walker, 1993a) set the framework within which subsequent development work occurred. Like Hager, Gonczi and others, the paper argued for a holistic approach which excluded the possibility of behaviourist reductionism being introduced into NCS for teachers. It had the support of teachers' and employers' representatives.

After a process of public tender, three separate consultants, representing alternative approaches, were appointed to develop draft sets of competency standards (Abbott-Chapman, Radford and Hughes, 1993; Eltis and Turney 1993; Louden, 1993). One of the three approaches (Louden's) was endorsed and the working party spent several months refining the approach while consulting with employers and the teaching profession. The result was a draft statement of national competency standards which was then 'validated' and 'field tested' by workshops with groups of teachers and teacher educators and consultants conducting further detailed inquiries into how the NCS would be useful in teacher education and areas of professional practice.

At the time of writing (May 1995), NPQTL has ceased to exist and another, caretaker, corporate body supported by DEET has the responsibility of recommending further action on NCS. It is unclear what such further action might be, or to whom, apart from DEET, the recommendations might be made. One possibility is that the newly founded national professional association for teachers, the Australian Teaching Council (itself an outcome of the work of NPQTL) might take over the carriage of NCS for teachers. Yet the Council is in its infancy, is numerically weak and is itself not yet clear whether it wishes to enter in a formal way into registration of teachers or accreditation of teacher education programs. Any bid to do so would almost certainly be opposed by more than one state government. What the Council might do with NCS is therefore unclear. Moreover, since the time of Dawkins, the initiatives in education policy, at least for primary and secondary education, have swung back to the states, who are jealous of their powers to decide who will teach in government schools and what characteristics, and forms of competence, they should have. It could be that the movement for NCS has become a spent force before the standards themselves are really in a form ready for implementation.

So far as teacher education is concerned, the consultants appointed to investigate the applicability of the draft NCS have recommended that the NCS be further periodically refined and developed and that the process by which this is done include the teacher unions, the Australian Teaching Council and the Australian Council of Deans of Education. Meantime they have considered and reported on eight possible uses of NCS in initial teacher education, including their application to the practicum, their use as a guide to course structure and coherence and to assessment, as a framework for collaboration and as a framework for student self-management of learning (Kennedy and Preston 1995, Preston and Kennedy 1995).

State Governments' Political Concerns about the Quality of Teaching and Teacher Education

The third context for the development of professional standards for Australia's teachers was formed from the concerns of state governments, and of state Ministers of Education in particular, to be seen to be doing something about the quality of teaching and teacher education. Indeed, in 1992 the then Minister for School Education in New South Wales set up a committee whose name embodied precisely this concept: the Ministerial Advisory Council on Teacher Education and Quality of Teaching (MACTEQT). One of the first tasks set this committee was to develop competency standards for teachers in New South Wales schools (Deer, 1993). The desired outcome was to show the public that the government was ensuring standards and therefore quality and therefore value for money. Since MACTEQT got under way and produced its statement,

Desirable Attributes of Beginning Teachers (1994), the state of Victoria has also embarked on its own pursuit of standards setting, establishing a governmentally appointed Standards Council of the Teaching Profession. This Council developed its own set of standards, making use of statements produced by NPQTL at the national level and MACTEQT in New South Wales. These two state bodies exist to assist the state governments' concerned to take a closer interest in teacher education and to influence its content and direction where this is considered appropriate, most obviously in relation to the abilities and qualities of the teachers graduating from the universities who will be employed in the schools of that state.

Purposes and Outcomes of Standards Setting

While work in each of these three contexts has overlapped to some extent with the others, the different origins and aims have produced slightly different outcomes. One crucial policy difference – which related to some critical professional issues including professional registration, initial training and professional development – concerns the point of the professional teacher's career to which the standards are applicable. For instance, do they apply to the new graduate, the neophyte, or do they apply to the more experienced teacher? Are they to be interpreted as a minimal baseline expectation of professional competence, or as expressing a statement of what it is to be a fully competent professional, something which is most unlikely to be the case with fresh graduates yet to have experienced their induction and probationary period. Answers to this question have differed, and have led to policy inconsistencies between state and commonwealth governments.

For example, the background work commissioned by the National Office for Overseas Skills Recognition, and reflected in DEET policies, suggests that competency based standards, because they concern competent performance in the workplace, do not apply in any direct way to new graduates in the sense of defining the abilities to be expected of them (Heywood, Gonczi and Hager, 1992:14, 18). This is prima facie inconsistent with the MACTEQT position and probably even with that of NPQTL, where the desired competences or attributes of beginning teachers are what is spelled out.

Nevertheless, in practice the position adopted will probably be an in-between one in both cases. The escape clause, or concept, which occurs frequently in both NPQTL and MACTEQT documents, is 'developing': students and new graduates are seen to be in the process of developing certain areas of competence, not to have already developed them, for example:

> All beginning teachers should be able to demonstrate that they ... show developing skills in adapting their teaching to suit the individual learning

needs of all their students in the context in which they are teaching ...; have developing knowledge and understanding of the nature, sources, and application of learning and information resources ....
(MACTEQT, 1994:3).

The purposes of competency standards conceived at the national level have been much wider in scope. The position adopted by NPQTL endorsed the following purposes, which reflect the microeconomic concerns with skill identification and recognition, work and workplace reorganisation and the mobility of professional labour:
Competency standards for teachers should:

- provide modes of recognition and achievement of competence;
- enhance deployment of competence through labour market efficiency and equity;
- enhance effective organisation of teachers' work;
- establish links between work, training and recognition;
- secure standards for the teaching profession;
- facilitate and enhance career path restructuring; and
- provide the basis for communication about the quality of teaching and learning.

(Walker, 1993a:96)

The teaching profession had no option to reject these purposes, even if it wanted to. Indeed, the President of the Australian Education Union (the national teachers' association) strongly supported both the standard setting project and the holistic and integrated approach:

> The challenge for the education community is thus to determine if it is time we established an agreed set of professional values against which we can define and assess competency standards. Are we mature enough as a profession to demystify the nature of our work, to define and promote its richness and complexity, and hence to establish the standards by which we can guarantee our students quality assurance? (Burrow, 1993:111)

In this spirit, the professional educators amongst those who made up the board and working parties of NPQTL successfully argued that a set of quality control standards be applied to competency statements and standards themselves, to ensure the integrity of professional work in teaching. These quality requirements strongly built in an insistence on the knowledge base of teaching, using the work of educational researchers such as Shulman (1987). They made it impossible that competency standards should merely reflect discrete, observable behaviours. They were as follows:
Competency statements and standards should:

- reflect the distinctiveness, richness and complexity of teaching as a profession;

- recognise the centrality of ethics in teaching and the essential role of personal relationships;
- reflect the substantial knowledge base of teaching, in particular:
  1. content knowledge;
  2. curriculum knowledge;
  3. general pedagogical knowledge;
  4. pedagogical content knowledge;
  5. knowledge of learners;
  6. knowledge of educational contexts;
  7. knowledge of workplace relationships; and
  8. knowledge of educational ends and purposes.
- recognise the interactive nature of teaching, including teacher-student interaction, and teachers' interactions among many members of school communities and the surrounding society;
- appreciate the effectiveness of a collective, collegial approach to teachers' work; and
- recognise the extension of teachers' work beyond the classroom and the direct teaching of students to encompass:
  1. the culture and organisation of the school;
  2. the relationship between the school and other schools;
  3. the relationship between the school and the community;
  4. the development of the teaching profession.

(Walker, 1993a: 96)

The NPQTL *Draft Competency Framework for Teaching* proposes five areas of competence:

- Using and developing knowledge and values.
- Developing relationships and working with others.
- Teaching.
- Monitoring and assessing.
- Reflecting, evaluating and planning for the future.

Each area has a general rationale statement and a set of generic competences with broad indicators which could be satisfied in a variety of ways reliant on context and professional judgement. For example, 'Using and developing knowledge and values' opens with these remarks:

> The teacher's capacity to apply both theoretical and practical knowledge underpins effective teaching practice. The teacher's professional knowledge combines:
> - well developed knowledge of the curriculum and fields of knowledge,
> - knowledge of learning, including understanding of theories of learning and personal understandings of students as learners and how they learn best,

- a wide repertoire of teaching approaches and an understanding of how to present content in ways that will motivate and engage learners.

The teacher demonstrates values and attitudes appropriate to responsible professional practice, and to the intellectual and social development of students.

The first element of competence and its indicators are as follows:

i. The teacher knows the content and its relationship to educational goals.

As indicators of effective practice in relation to this element, the teacher:
- demonstrates knowledge of the curriculum in appropriate key learning areas;
- understands the basis of the curriculum in human knowledge;
- appreciates and can convey the complexity of learning areas;
- understands how particular areas of content knowledge and modes of inquiry relate to overall educational goals;
- continues to acquire curriculum knowledge and understanding.

The depth and breadth of competence required by these indicators, their generic nature, and the cognitive grasp explicit in most of them and implicit in the others, demonstrates the holistic, contextual and genuinely professional character of the NCS developed by NPQTL for teachers. The same scope and flavour runs throughout the draft. It has been a considerable achievement for the teaching profession, teacher educators and policy makers.

A similar level of conceptualisation of competence was adopted in New South Wales by MACTEQT and endorsed by the Minister. The areas of competence (or 'desirable attributes') are:

- The ethics of teaching.
- The content of teaching.
- The practice of teaching.
- Management in schools/classrooms/centres.
- Interaction with parents and the school community.
- Professionalism and professional development.

Under the last of these, as an example, it is stated that beginning teachers should:

(a) understand the responsibilities and obligations of belonging to the profession of teaching
(b) acknowledge their responsibilities for their continuing professional development
(c) appreciate the collegial nature of teachers' work and be able to work

effectively as members of a team
(d) have knowledge of the framework of law and regulations that effect teachers' work
(e) have knowledge of current educational issues.
(Deer, 1993; MACTEQT, 1994).

Professionalism and Professional Competence

Essential to the NPQTL 'professionalised approach', and reflected in the above quotation from MACTEQT, is the notion of truly professional work as continuing professional growth for which the individual professional has to take personal responsibility for his or her development as a professional person, and which requires support from the profession as a whole and from the community through government and employers. Although this cannot always be spelled out in clear-cut competency statements, it does concentrate on the focus of the competency approach – performance. The notion has been best expressed by Nowlen (1988), who extends Houle's earlier (1980) characterisation of professional work as involving:

> unceasing movement to new levels of performance. In the achievement of these new levels, inadequacies of performance become clear and better levels of performance possible. This is an untidy but energising process with observable characteristics: concern with mission/function clarification, mastery of theoretical knowledge, capacity to solve problems, use of practical knowledge, self-enhancement, formal training, credentialling, creation of a subculture, legal reinforcement, public acceptance, ethical practice, penalties, relations to other vocations and relations to users of service.

On this account sound professional education and performance involve much more than the acquisition of an established knowledge base of a set of specified technical competences. They include the capacity to make sound professional judgements in a variety of educational contexts, which in turn entails a special form of understanding, 'situational understanding' (Elliott, 1990; Walker, 1992). To this can be added the need to be able to receive and monitor continuous feedback from the environment and to adjust performance accordingly, to display what Evans (1992:47) has called 'knowledge in action', the idea that 'as we perform our performance is continually changing our knowledge of the context and of the situation in which we are performing. We are continually regulating what we do on the basis of that feedback'.

Accomplishing this style of self-regulating and self-enhancing professional performance necessitates accepting responsibility for one's actions as a professional, where of course in the case of education and the so-called 'human service professions' this extends into the area of interpersonal relations between professional and client and raises ethical issues of a distinct kind. This has been recognised in such contemporary statements of professional competence and attributes for teachers as have been produced to date.

Within this holistic professional approach it has also been recognised that it is not really possible, at least if we want to maintain a coherent picture of professional work, to identify items of competence in isolation from each other, let alone to educate for them in this way. They develop and are exercised and exhibited in 'structures of competence' (Klemp, 1977) in which abilities are not isolated, discrete elements, but are linked together structurally:

> For example, cognitive abilities, interpersonal abilities and motivational attributes are unified in competent teachers' powers of practical understanding which underpin the complex professional judgements and actions characteristic of good teaching and essential for quality in teaching and learning.
> (Walker 1993a:95)

Contrasts with Other Approaches to Competence and Competency Standards

One reason why the government policy moves towards competency standards were greeted with scepticism, and even contempt and horror by many in the teaching profession and especially in teacher education, was that competency based approaches had been tried before and had, to put it mildly, been unpopular and widely regarded as a failure and unsuited to teaching. The behaviourist competency approaches of the late 1960s and early 1970s broke a teacher's performance down into discrete, observable items of behaviour, or 'behaviours' (Elam, 1971).

Despite the work of NPQTL and MACTEQT, and the evidence presented above, this history, combined with the approach being pushed in vocational education by the National Training Board, continues to lead many to identify any and all competency approaches as 'behaviourist' or 'reductionist'.

I shall not enter the discussion as to whether behaviourism is an appropriate approach to the analysis of competence in non-professional occupations. What needs notice, rather, is that both professional and non-professional occupations are included in the Australian Standards Framework endorsed and promoted by the National Training Board. Questions of articulation and recognition, intersectoral issues (especially between universities and Technical and Further Education) require some consideration of the relation between the two approaches. Moreover, employers of teachers, for reasons of accountability and quality control, might come to favour the kinds of neat, clear-cut and often quantifiable measures provided by the behaviourist approach. In the behaviourist approach quality can be ensured through system control over the individual and their work, because all skills are prespecified by employers and can be checked by standard observations. There is no room for variable professional judgement.

In the holistic, professional approach quality is assured through professional judgement and responsibility. The contrast between the two approaches can be seen in Table 8.1 (Preston and Walker, 1993:119). Development of professional standards for teachers in Australia, including national competency standards, has kept us so far firmly in the right-hand column. For the good of the profession and the quality of education it is important that we stay there.

	Behaviourist approaches	Holistic approach
Nature of competences and relations between competences	Individual, specific, discrete defined in terms of behaviour only.	Competences are complex combinations of personal attributes, enabling the performance of a variety of tasks. They form coherent 'structures of competence', and attributes have a distinct coherent structure.
Evidence of competences	Direct observation of performance of relevant activities – assumed to give direct and clear indication of whether or not the competency is held.	A range of evidence may be sought, in general none can give certainty that relevant competences are held. What evidence to use and what to make of it would be indicated by relevant theories.
Relation between knowledge and competences	Required knowledge is inferred directly from behaviourally defined competences.	Knowledge exists and can be understood separately from the exercise of competences. Knowledge and understanding can be understood as having a complex and coherent structure.
Relation between competency statements and the education or training programme	Competency statements indicate directly the content, structure and assessment criteria of education and training programmes. There can be little diversity, local flexibility, experimentation and development.	There is a broad coherence between structures of competence and education and training programmes, and programmes will generally have overall coherence. Programmes can, however, be diverse in their structure and involve experimentation and research.
Variation in specification of competency based standards according to purpose	There can be little variation in the way standards are specified.	The way standards are specified can vary significantly according to purpose. In particular, for 'summative' purposes standards can be explicit and public, and assessment procedures rigorous, valid and reliable; for 'formative' purposes a more flexible and open approach is possible.

Table 8.1 Characteristics of behaviourist and holistic approaches to competences: a summary (From Preston and Walker, 1993:119)

References

Abbott-Chapman, J., Radford, R. and Hughes, P. (1993) 'Researching teacher competences', *Unicorn* **19** (3), 3–48

AVVC (Australian Vice-Chancellor's Committee) (1992) *Competency-Based Education and Training: The AVCC Position*. Canberra: Australian Vice-Chancellor's Committee.

Bowden, J.A. and Masters, G.N. (1993) *Implications for Higher Education of a Competency-Based Approach to Education and Training* (National Office of Overseas Skills Recognition, DEET Higher Education Division, Evaluations and Investigations Program). Canberra: Australian Government Publishing Service.

Burrow, S. (1993) 'National competency standards for the teaching profession: A chance to define the future of schooling or a reaffirmation of the past?', in Collins, C. (ed.) *Competences: The Competences Debate in Australian Education and Training*. Canberra: The Australian College of Education.

Dawkins, J.S. (1988) *Strengthening Australia's Schools: A Consideration of the Focus and Content of Schooling*. Canberra: Australian Government Publishing Service.

Deer, C.E. (1993) 'Areas of competence for teachers: The New South Wales scene', in Collins, C. (ed.) *Competences: The Competences Debate in Australian Education and Training*. Canberra: The Australian College of Education.

Elam, S. (1971) *Performance-Based Teacher Education: What is the State of the Art?* Washington: American Association of Colleges of Teacher Education.

Elliott, J. (1990) *Competency-Based Training and the Education of the Professions: Is a Happy Marriage Possible?* Unpublished paper. Norwich: University of East Anglia Centre for Applied Research in Education.

Eltis, K. and Turney, C. (1993) 'Researching teacher competences', *Unicorn*, **19** (3), 24–36.

Evans, G. (1992) 'Alternative approaches to the development of competence', in *Competency and Professional Education: A Symposium* (Transcripts of Conference Proceedings). Canberra: University of Canberra Centre for Research in Professional Education.

Gonczi, A.P., Hager, P.J. and Oliver, L. (1990) *Establishing Competency-Based Standards for the Professions* (National Office for Overseas Skills Recognition Research Paper No. 1). Canberra: Australian Government Publishing Service.

Gonczi, A.P., Hager, P.J. and Althanasou, J.A. (1993) *The Development of Competency-Based Assessment Strategies for the Professions* (National Office for Overseas Skills Recognition Research Paper No. 8). Canberra: Australian Government Publishing Service.

Hager, P.J. (1994) 'Is there a cogent philosophical argument against competency standards?', Australian Journal of Education, **38** (1), 3–18.

Heywood, L., Gonczi, A.P. and Hager, P.J. (1992) *A Guide for the Development of Competency Standards for the Professions* (National Office for Overseas Skills Recognition Research Paper No. 7). Canberra: Australian Government Publishing Service.

Houle, C.O. (1980) *Continuing Learning in the Professions*. San Francisco: Jossey-Bass.

Kelleher, R. (1992) 'Policies of the Department of Employment, Education and Training', in *Competency and Professional Education: A Symposium*. Canberra: University of Canberra Centre for Research in Professional Education.

Kennedy, K.J. and Preston, B. (1995) *The Draft Competency Framework for Beginning Teaching and Initial Teacher Education Courses*. Report to the Working Party on Teacher Competences. Canberra: Department of Employment, Education and Training.

Klemp, G.O. (1977) *Three Factors of Success in the World of Work: Implications for Curriculum in Higher Education*. Boston: McBer & Co.

Lingard, R. (1991) 'Policy making in Australian schooling: The new corporate federalism', *Journal of Education Policy*, **6** (1), 85–90.

Louden, W. (1993) 'Researching teacher competences', *Unicorn* **19** (3), 13_23.
MACTEQT (Ministerial Advisory Council on Teacher Education and the Quality of Teaching) (New South Wales) (1994) *Desirable Attributes for Beginning Teachers in New South Wales*. Sydney: NSW Ministry of Education.
Marginson, S. (1993) *Education and Public Policy in Australia*. Cambridge: Cambridge University Press.
Masters, G.N. and McCurry, D. (1990) *Competency-Based Assessment in the Professions* (National Office for Overseas Skills Recognition Research Paper No. 2). Canberra: Australian Government Publishing Service.
NOOSR (National Office of Overseas Skills Recognition) (1992) *Competency Update No. 3*, (June/July). Canberra: Department of Employment, Education and Training.
NPQTL (National Project on the Quality of Teaching and Learning) (1993) *Draft Competency Framework for Teaching*. Canberra: Department of Employment, Education and Training.
NTB (National Training Board) (1992) *National Competency Standards: Policy and Guidelines*, 2nd edn. Canberra: National Training Board.
Nowlen, P.W. (1988) *Continuing Education for Business and the Professions: The Performance Model*. New York: Macmillan.
Organisation for Economic and Cooperation and Development (OECD) (1989) *Schools and Quality*. Paris: OECD.
Organisation for Economic Cooperation and Development (OECD) (1990) *The Teacher Today*. Paris: OECD.
Preston, B. and Kennedy, K.J. (1995) *Issues and Principles for the Application of the Draft Competency Framework for Beginning Teachers to Teacher Education*. Report to the Working Party on Teacher Competences. Canberra: Department of Employment, Education and Training.
Preston, B. and Walker, J.C. (1993) 'Competency-based standards in the professions and higher education: A holistic approach', in Collins, C. (ed.) *Competences: The Competences Debate in Australian Education and Training*. Canberra: Australian College of Education.
Schools Council (National Board of Employment, Education and Training) (1989) *Teacher Quality: An Issues Paper*. Canberra: Australian Government Publishing Service.
Schools Council (National Board of Employment, Education and Training) (1990) *Australia's Teachers: an Agenda for the Next Decade*. Canberra: Australian Government Publishing Service.
Shulman, L.S. (1987) 'Knowledge of teaching: Foundations of the new reform', *Harvard Educational Review*, **57** (1), 1–22.
Walker, J.C. (1992) 'The value of competency-based education', in Hattie, J. (ed.) *The Effects of Competence-Based Education on Universities: Liberation or Enslavement? A monograph based on a conference jointly sponsored by the University of Western Australia and Murdoch University, Perth*.
Walker J.C. (1993a) 'Competency-based standards in teaching: A general rationale and conceptual approach', in *Schools Council Agenda Papers: Issues Arising from 'Australia's Teachers: An Agenda for the Next Decade'*. Canberra: Australian Government Publishing Service.
Walker, J.C. (1993b) in Anderson, D.S. (ed.) *Higher Education and the Competency Movement*. Canberra: Centre for Continuing Education, Australian National University.
Whitty, G. (1994) 'The use of competences in teacher education', in Williams, A. (ed.) *Perspectives on Partnership: Secondary Initial Teacher Training*. Lewes: The Falmer Press.
Wilson, B.G. (1992) 'Higher education', in Anderson, D.S. (ed.) *Higher Education and the Competency Movement*. Canberra: Centre for Continuing Education, Australian National University.

Part Three
Going Beyond Initial Teacher Education

9

Competence Frameworks and Profiles for Newly-Qualified Teachers

Peter Earley

The first year of teaching has long been recognised as of crucial importance both to the newly qualified or beginning teacher and to the teaching profession. It is during this formative period that expectations and standards of performance are set, whilst receptiveness and willingness to learn are at their greatest. Induction – often defined as the process bridging initial training and employment – is generally considered to be the first stage in an ongoing programme of professional support and development. It is part of the continuum of further or continuing professional development. The process of induction should ensure that guidance, support and training are available to the new entrant, as and when needed, to secure the foundations upon which a successful teaching career can be built.

It has also been recognised, however, that the arrangements for the induction of newly qualified teachers (NQTs) have left much to be desired. Her Majesty's Inspectorate, for example, noted that induction practices were less than satisfactory or poor in about one-third of the 42 Local Education Authorities and 112 schools visited between 1988 and 1990 (HMI, 1992), a situation which had not really improved by 1992 (OFSTED,1993). Indeed, the latter survey found that LEA and school induction programmes were not always targeted at individual needs and suggested that the case for developing student profiling was strengthened by the evidence of their survey. It is, therefore, the intention of this chapter to consider the development and use of profiles – particularly competence-based profiles – with beginning teachers or NQTs to ascertain their value or worth as a tool to facilitate continuing professional development. In so doing much use will be made of a recent National Foundation for Educational Research (NFER) project which looked in some detail at effective induction practices in schools and LEAs (Earley and Kinder, 1994).

The Development of Competence-Based Profiles

The move towards the greater use of profiles with NQTs is of fairly recent origin and has to be seen against a backdrop of a number of significant changes, the most important of which have been the abolition of probation, the changing role of the LEA and the greater devolution of training funds (including those for induction) to schools. The statutory probationary period, which all teachers had to complete successfully to gain qualified teacher status, was abolished from September 1992, although it has been retained in Scotland and Northern Ireland. The move from 'probationer' to 'newly-qualified teacher' was accompanied, in England and Wales, by Government support in the form of a training grant to LEAs to establish more effective induction programmes. Since April 1992 the Department for Education, through its Grants for Education Support and Training (GEST), has helped stimulate improvements in induction and in the first year of the scheme 43 LEAs were successful in their bids for funds, whereas in 1993–94 and subsequently, all LEAs submitting satisfactory bids were supported. The DFE's objectives in supporting expenditure by LEAs and grant-maintained schools were five-fold. They were to:

- improve the links between initial teacher training, induction of NQTs and INSET during the early years of teachers' careers, particularly through the development of profiling and competence-based approaches to professional development;
- improve coordination between the induction activities of LEAs and those of schools;
- encourage provision which is carefully differentiated to meet the particular needs of individual teachers and groups of teachers who will have obtained qualified teacher status through a variety of different routes;
- help to ensure that those responsible for induction training are effectively prepared for this role;
- help to improve the quality of written guidance and other materials used in the induction of NQTs.
(DES, 1992).

As part of the NFER research – which consisted of a survey of LEAs and detailed case studies of 30 'good practice' schools in six authorities – data were gathered on all of the above DfE objectives and these have been reported elsewhere (Earley, 1993). It is the first objective, particularly the development of competence frameworks, however, which forms the main focus of the remainder of this chapter.

It is probably accurate to state that prior to the GEST funding for induction few, if any, LEAs had introduced competence-based profiles for probationers. Most if not all LEAs, however, had a mechanism for assessing probationers that made use of broad skill areas, such as those listed in the various DES (as it was then) circulars and administrative memoranda. A few LEAs had gone further and had introduced professional development profiles or records of achievement for new teachers, which were seen as eventually forming part of appraisal systems. Competence-based profiles or portfolios, as they were sometimes called, were not common although most LEAs reported that they would be welcomed (Earley, 1993).

As evidenced elsewhere in this book, there is currently much debate about the competences required for teaching and whether or not there is a need for a nationally agreed profile of skills or competences. Two recent government Circulars on secondary and primary teacher training have specified the competences which trainees should have achieved on the completion of training but have stressed that they 'do not purport to provide a complete syllabus for initial teacher training' (DFE, 1992). Even more recent developments suggest that such profiles should be based on a common framework. The Secretary of State asked the Council for the Accreditation of Teacher Education (CATE) to give initial advice on the preparation of guidance on profiles of competence for teachers (DFE, 1993b), which has since been taken forward by the Teacher Training Agency. The latter issued a consultation paper in late 1994 which, amongst other things, sought views on the structure and format of a new teacher profile and whether or not there should be a single set of descriptors or competence statements for both primary and secondary teachers. An annexe to the consultation document brought together the competences defined in DFE Circulars 9/92 and 14/93 into the following five areas:

- knowledge and understanding of the curriculum
- subject knowledge and subject application
- teaching strategies and techniques, and classroom management
- assessment and recording of pupils' progress, and
- foundation for further professional development
  (Teacher Training Agency, 1994).

The NFER Research

At the time of the NFER research – 1992 to 1993 – there was considerable variation between the different types of profile being used with NQTs, with some detailing competences and their associated performance criteria, whilst others were more open ended and less prescriptive allowing the participants a greater say on the appropriate criteria for profiling.

In the six LEAs involved in the case study phase of the research, profiles and portfolios were being used to varying degrees:

- two shire counties had developed and were using competence-based profiles;
- a metropolitan borough had devised and piloted separate portfolios for its primary and secondary NQTs;
- a London borough had used a pre-appointment personal profile to identify the main components of NQTs' training along with their strengths and areas for further development;
- a metropolitan borough had made no moves towards profiling (it was making use of a pro forma for use with classroom observation);
- a London borough had made a decision not to develop a competence-based profile but had produced an induction portfolio for NQTs.

Since the completion of the research the last-mentioned LEA decided to pilot a competence-based profile. It decided, however, not to 'reinvent the wheel' and produce its own but rather to fine tune and contextualise a profile that had already been developed. In fact the profile it successfully piloted was one which had been marketed by another of the case study LEAs – one which had been in receipt of the first round of GEST induction funding.

So what do these profiles and portfolios look like, how were they used with NQTs and what was the reaction of schools to their use? It is the intention to answer these questions by reference to the NFER case studies.

The initial survey of LEAs had identified a number who were using GEST funds to develop profiles building on and refining the so-called 'CATE competences' (i.e. those outlined in Circular 9/92 on secondary initial teacher training). Several LEAs in the north-west, for example, had been working with a university faculty of education to produce competence-based profiles and these were now publicly available for other schools and LEAs to purchase should they so wish (Smith and West-Burnham, 1993).

The two case study LEAs with competence-based profiles had devised their own sets of competences. Working parties had been established by LEA personnel with representation from both primary and secondary schools and local institutes of higher education. The CATE competences were published during this time and both working parties were able to use them to ensure that there were no obvious areas of omission. In one LEA the professional development profile (and associated competence criteria) was part of a wider support pack, whereas the other LEA had produced a self-contained document entitled 'The New Teacher Competency Profile' (for further details of how this was developed see Gifford, 1992). A brief summary of the two documents follows which shows the different approaches taken. The third example – again produced by a group of LEA, higher education and school personnel (including NQTs), largely as a result of a two-day residential workshop – was not competence-based and used the term portfolio rather than profile. There are differences between profiles and portfolios – the latter usually expects evidence of performance to be collected – but essentially both are attempts to devise instruments that can be used by NQTs, usually in conjunction with their mentors, to reflect and to act on that reflection to improve practice. They are used to document progress and achievement, and structure the process of self-review whilst helping identify individual training and development needs. (For an analysis of their use with teacher trainees see Murphy *et al.*, 1993; and with school managers see Earley, 1992.)

Example 1: Professional development profile:
- Introduction:
- what is a profile for?
- what are competences?
- Personal information
- Competency criteria:
- level 1: more than satisfied with performance/understanding
- level 2: satisfied with performance/understanding
- level 3: less than satisfied with performance/understanding
- Use of above criteria to reflect on:
- the school (10 elements)
- subject expertise (4 elements)
- management of learning (10 elements)
- assessing, recording and reporting progress (12 elements)
- further professional development (6 elements)

Example 2: New teacher competency profile:
- The aim of the competency profile
- Principles of the profile
- The profile in school and the mentor's role
- The profile: initial discussion, review targets and action plans
- Guidance notes: how to use the profile
- Unpicking competency statements:
- curriculum knowledge and planning (7 elements)
- classroom management (11 elements)
- assessing, recording and reporting (8 elements)
- Loose leaf appendices:
- tracker/year planner
- competency menu cards
- competency stickers
- answers to some of your questions

Example 3: NQTs in secondary schools: portfolio:
- Introduction
- An outline timetable of provision for NQTs
- Personal data sheets:
- personal details
- initial training details
- Job data sheets:
- job description and teaching duties
- school calendar and INSET needs
- Review sheets (each contains a list of issues to stimulate thinking and writing):
- establishing and developing relationships (7 issues)
- planning and preparation (8 issues)
- classroom management (7 issues)
- teaching and learning (10 issues)
- professional activities outside classroom (6 issues)
- Targets and actions plans (for each term)
- Classroom support visit – guidance notes. (Each NQT is entitled to at least one visit per term from mentor)
- Classroom support visit sheets (pro formas)
- Record of in-service activities

Interviews with school personnel in the above three LEAs explored the use and value of the profiles and portfolios which had been developed. In the first LEA, the professional development profile – part of a wider support pack for schools with new teachers – had not yet been extensively used or made available to all schools. Where it had been used it was regarded as a most useful self-assessment tool that would link in very well with staff appraisal. It was used initially by the NQTs themselves and then together with the NQTs' mentors to identify areas for discussion, development and action. The following interview extract is taken from an NQT who had used the profile termly:

> I've used the profile twice so far – the first time I used it I went through it with my mentor, but the second time I went through it on my own. After having done this last term, I said to my mentor that I was sure that I was a lot more negative now than in the first time. Perhaps it's because ignorance is bliss and you don't realise how little you know! My concern by the middle of the Spring term was whether I was making some kind of progression – I'd become more critical of my own practice – at the outset I think I was more concerned with such things as classroom organisation but I'm starting to think now about whether I'm really catering for individual children's needs. I looked at the profile over the Easter holidays. I went through all the sections of the profile but was unable to compare my responses with my initial responses. I think it was better to do it this way and then to compare your responses after you'd completed the profile for the second time. The plan is that I will have another

look at the profile at the end of the summer term. Yes, the profile is something that I would recommend other NQTs to use – it's useful because it covers issues which you may not even have thought of in the first place, it makes you more aware of what you should be doing as a teacher.
(NQT: middle school)

In the second case study LEA the competence-based profile was being used by all five schools in the research, in fact three of these were the schools of working party members. It should be said, however, that the positive reactions expressed by NQTs and mentors were found in all five case study schools. The LEA had undertaken an evaluation of the profile's use in all of its schools. This suggested that the profile had generally been well received and was seen as useful in promoting reflective development. It further stated that there was evidence that new teachers had become more effective as a result of its use and 'the competences had provided a sharper focus and the action-planning a more efficient structure'.

The following comment was taken from a mentor in a middle school who was not involved in the production of the profile or the associated 2-day programme of training on its use:

I think (the profile) will be very useful once we start actually getting things written down. We've had one meeting for the initial discussion ... it's a good idea to separate the competences into three categories. It's negotiated and targets are set. We decided to focus on a couple of competences from the menu card in classroom organisation and management but in our discussion (the NQT) also wanted to look at assessment (a different menu card). So we need to get going on targets related to classroom management and then, next term, look at assessment. I think we share the ownership of the profile but ultimately it will become his. I feel it will be a most useful document and also helpful for staff appraisal. Having the list of competences could help people decide on which areas they would like observed – they provide a good starting point.
(Mentor: middle school)

It had proved difficult, however, for the mentor and the NQT to find as much time as they would have liked to use the profile. A series of events within this school, including an unusually large number of staff absences had not helped. There were plans for the profile to be used with future NQTs. Similar comments about the value of the profile were expressed by the headteacher of the other school not involved in the profile's development:

The profile is new. All the suggested points of discussion have been covered. She looked at these before we sat down and discussed them. Setting the targets was quite useful because we hadn't done this before – we had a lot of informal discussion after school. The areas she's highlighted as developmental areas are areas we were already working on (assessment and record-keeping were identified as targets). I'm not sure who owns the profile, so I'd be interested to know how the NQT sees this. She's been used to identifying her strengths and

weaknesses through a programme (profile) which she used at college. She's given it to me to look at, so clearly she doesn't feel threatened by it. She's very open about expressing any concerns. She's seen my summary and we're due to discuss it. I hope she feels it's something we share. The new teacher package is excellent and it's made us formalise the targets.
(Head/mentor: infant school)

The new teacher in the same school remarked:

The profile makes you focus on things – weak areas that you want to spend some time on – so that's good. The idea behind it is that it's there to help me. We went through it together at first and chose some areas for development. We've agreed on some termly targets. I was concerned about record keeping, maths practical activities and progression in maths. So maths is the area that concerns me most; next term I'll focus on something else. I'm not sure who 'owns' the profile. At my college they had a personal profile which was quite similar to the LEA's scheme. I've given mine to the head for her to look at.
(NQT: infant school)

At the second interview (during her second term at the school) she explained that finding the time to use the profile had presented some difficulties:

We had a meeting last week but it's the first time we've looked at it this term. There are just so many things to be done and with record keeping and the children, it's just time; time to think about it. Long term it's good to do because at the end of the year it's a catalogue of how you have been developing. It's super to have it. It should continue all the time, not just the first year. It makes you think about things!
(NQT: infant school)

In the other three schools in this LEA involved in the research, as might be expected, there was a very high degree of commitment to the profile. Comments from the mentors and NQTs in these schools gave an indication of how valuable its use had proved to be. Most saw the profile as providing a framework or a focus to help structure one's thoughts about teaching and its component parts. The profile made NQTs – and significantly mentors too – ask questions about what they were doing. A mentor (not a working party member) when asked in her second interview if she was still finding the profile useful remarked:

I think the profile is excellent and I would certainly use it again if I had another NQT. It builds in reflection. The profile gives you common ground and it is laid out there in front of you. Also it's open for you to use as you wish, there are the competences spelt out and you can use those which are most relevant to you. We will choose these together, although sometimes I've made certain suggestions to her. Some of the targets we've outlined have been fairly easy to achieve, in the short term, others it's proved to be more difficult. You have to constantly work on these and develop strategies over a longer period.
(Deputy/mentor: primary school)

The NQT in the same school said:

> We mostly fill in the profile together. At the end of last term we summarised and decided what we were going to focus on. We are still using the stickers in the pack. We have got together on occasions after school to discuss the profile and the areas or competences that we need to focus on. I have found it of benefit and I would recommend the profile to be used by future NQTs, but I find a lot of the areas naturally overlap with each other and it's sometimes difficult to look at a specific area or competence. The competences are all interrelated but it's useful to get you to focus on these and to make you aware of the role of the teacher. As far as the target setting is concerned, on occasions this has been easy, other times more difficult.
> (NQT: primary school)

A head of department in another school welcomed the structure and guidance that the profile offered:

> I think anything that helps to channel what we're supposed to do and gives it a bit more structure and guidance is to be applauded. I have felt a bit at sea in the past – we go in, we observe and it's been a bit unstructured. The profile provides us with that structure – I've observed the NQT twice. I made a concrete decision not to formally observe her until after half term. The Deputy and the NQT decided upon which competences they were going to look at. The NQT and I then met and discussed it. We decided to look at classroom management and she targeted three areas on the menu cards. So we sat down and discussed No. 5 – I felt her beginnings and endings of lessons were already excellent! We discussed looking at those areas. I saw a Year 8 class last Friday specifically to look at those areas of competence. I produced and typed up a list of general comments. We unpacked what the competences actually meant. ... At the end of the exercise I felt it was very productive to brainstorm that together but I do think the process of brainstorming or discussing is beneficial for bringing things out. I'm sure it's helpful for the mentor as much as for the NQT. The problem, however, is one of time to do this. I've got one NQT, if I had more I don't know how I'd cope. It's a question of fitting it in. I'd like more time to do this properly.
> (Head of Department/mentor: secondary school)

This middle manager and the NQT went on to use the profile flexibly – they did not restrict themselves to the competences specified on the menu cards. The fact that the profile could be adapted to meet identified needs was seen as a further advantage. The NQT, when asked at the time of the third and final interview (during the third term in post), said she intended to continue using the profile in her second year. It was suggested that if teachers were used to using a profile 'then a lot of the fear associated with appraisal is removed'. The induction manager in this school saw the use of the profile as being of particular benefit to middle managers: their experiences of identifying areas of competence with NQTs was helping with the appraisal process and for managing other teachers in their departments.

In the third and final case study LEA which had developed a profile or portfolio, the reactions of teachers to their use were more mixed. Some insights were offered by an NQT at the beginning of his second term in post:

> The idea is good but sometimes it sounds too vague, I don't always see the point of filling in bits of paper when I can talk about it to someone, yet it might be a jog to your memory. If you were isolated, didn't see or talk with other teachers, then it could be good, an on-going record of how we felt, what we're doing. Filling it in can be unnecessary because the issues you're talking about in the portfolio are the ones you're constantly talking about with teachers. It's of more use to someone not in the school, who came in to see how we felt we've developed over the year. It's important not to deify the actual document – it's just a means to an end. Many aspects of the portfolio and induction from the LEA were at their most important when you're in a bad situation, when nothing is working, there's no system of support and appraisal, no forum for bouncing ideas around.
> (NQT: secondary school)

The deputy head in the same school, who had been involved in the LEA working party developing the portfolio, remarked that its completion should not be seen as an imposition or 'as just something else to fill in', a view which it was felt was held by some NQTs, whilst others were not entirely clear for what purpose it was being completed. It should be seen as 'a means to an end: to help with reflection' but to quote the same NQT at the time of his second interview:

> A lot of people were rather irritated by the process of having to fill in more documents, after a day at school the last thing you want to do is write it all out again. The aim of it was acceptable; people were concentrating too much on what's on paper, rather than listening to you. The day to day discussions with the department cover the issues of NQTs' development [well enough], so there was a lot of criticism of this rather abstract document which a lot felt they were only filling it in because it had to be filled in...not that they were against thinking, criticising or analysing – they were just irritated by the medium. I agree it's a bit laborious.
> (NQT: secondary school)

The new teacher went on to remark that, in his view, those who made most use of the portfolio tended to be those NQTs who were receiving least support. The portfolio was a document to refer to, part of a process and not the end product. It provided an opportunity to set and agree targets. This could be achieved without a profile or portfolio but its existence 'ensures targets are set and things are monitored in some schools where they might not be done otherwise'.

An induction manager in another school, also involved in the development of the portfolio, spoke negatively about it and how it was on 'the very bottom of the list of (the NQTs') priorities'. The exercise was seen very much as being paper-driven and not reflecting NQTs' concerns. This deputy remarked that the consensus view of other mentors he had spoken to at their most recent meeting was 'that it wasn't useful'. However, the portfolio had been adapted in the light of criticisms received and the deputy remarked that the following year's NQTs would be making use of it.

Within the same LEA, primary NQTs were the responsibility of a different officer and a separate profile had been developed in conjunction with a different higher education institute. Comments regarding the use of this document in schools centred around its 'long-windedness' and degree of detail, the time that was needed for its completion and the fact that it was too similar to a student profile, not treating the NQT as an adult professional. A head remarked that 'the requirements of the profile made everyone feel guilty that they were not filling them in'.

Primary NQTs on the other hand spoke more positively of the value of the document and how 'it broke everything down into sections ... which made you stop and think' or 'gave you ideas for (the mentor and I) to think how I'm progressing in the classroom'. The most valuable parts of the document were 'the tick-lists, the suggestions and the information packs'. It helped to prioritise what was needed and gave an indication of what was required in terms of development. It was felt, however, to have become 'decreasingly useful' over the year. The action planning part of the profile was also seen to be beneficial but there was a similar concern about 'just writing things down for their own sake' and the need to write out lesson plans. Again, as a result of feedback received from primary school mentors and NQTs, the profile had been revised for the following year and the process streamlined.

Concluding Comments

It is clear from the above comments that not all profiles – competence-based or not – were received equally favourably by NQTs and their mentors, although all recognised their potential as a tool to encourage the personal reflection so necessary for continuing professional development. Personal reflection or the ability to become a 'reflective practitioner' has long been regarded as an important attribute of educational professionals, yet it could be seen as more appropriate to the induction stage rather than that of initial teacher training or education, since the new teacher is now able to draw upon a wider base of experience (Turner, 1993). Indeed, it is apparent from the NFER research that the use of profiles and the ensuing discussions of the competences underpinning them can be beneficial to both NQTs and their mentors or 'critical friends'. Other research into mentoring – be it with students, new teachers or new headteachers – has, similarly, pointed to the benefits gained by both parties (e.g. Kerry and Shelton Mayes, 1995). What is less certain, however, is whether or not it is the bringing together of two professionals – one experienced, the other less so – to discuss matters to do with work, which is the key ingredient which promotes reflection and development rather than the profile or the statements of competence *per se* (see also Gifford, 1994; Hutchinson, 1994).

Nevertheless, it has been said that competence-based profiles do provide the all-important agenda or backcloth to enable such discussions to take place, whilst also offering a common language and understandings. In addition, the processes underpinning them encourage targets to be set and action-plans to be carried out and monitored. It is not that these activities cannot take place without a profile, it is just that they are more likely to occur where they are in existence.

Perhaps the most important issue of all is one of time and how it is used in schools. Time has to be found for such professional activities to take place but it is well known that time is in short supply in schools and other more pressing concerns may be given priority. As training budgets are increasingly devolved to schools will some decide to use their time and resources in other ways wherever possible? For profiles to be a valuable developmental tool for NQTs and for the schools in which they work, they will need the support of senior management along with appropriate resourcing. Already some schools (and LEAs) are attaching specific sums to NQTs for induction purposes – an entitlement or voucher to be spent in meeting their training and development needs. Profiles may therefore act as a mechanism for quality control of the induction provision; in effect ensuring a framework exists to support the ongoing development of the NQT. As schools become self-managing institutions and the LEA's role changes then profiles may be a mechanism for guaranteeing that at least some induction support is forthcoming. But in the final analysis their success will largely hinge on the degree to which schools are prepared to invest in their most importance resource. As Gifford found in her evaluation, the main factor affecting the success of profiling was the school's commitment to professional development and to 'investing in people'. This in turn determined how well mentors were able to perform their role (Gifford, 1994).

An issue that did not emerge as a major factor in the NFER research but needs addressing is the degree to which competence-based profiles are able to serve both formative and summative purposes. The profiles in the case study schools were clearly being used in a formative sense, indeed they were seen as 'owned' by the NQTs themselves, although virtually all mentors and induction coordinators expressed the view that they hoped they would be shared documents. If profiles are to be used for other purposes, such as recruitment, deployment or promotion, then the chances of their being used meaningfully are likely to be reduced. There is already some research evidence that target-setting, be it associated with profiling or appraisal, is being regarded with a degree of suspicion by some teachers who fear it might be used in deciding which staff members are the first to go, if or when redundancies are to be made (Earley, 1995). There are interesting parallels here with teacher appraisal and some of the difficulties currently being experienced with a professional development model increasingly being used for accountability purposes.

It is also interesting to note that few of the competence-based profiles make specific reference to the development of 'personal qualities', which are generally regarded as essential for successful teaching. As other contributors to this volume have argued, the nature of professional competence is problematic and cannot simply be represented by behavioural models, as exemplified, for example, in Circulars 9/92, 14/93 or the TTA's amalgam of the two. The term 'capability' is sometimes seen as more appropriate for professionals, stressing as it does judgements about values and the purpose of action. Professional competence is complex and holistic and requires the ability, for example, to make judgements, act creatively and innovate as well as acquiring basic skills. Competence-based profiles may well emphasise the latter, although it could be argued that until the basic or threshold competences have been demonstrated there is little chance of moving beyond competence and proficiency and becoming an expert practitioner. The omission of 'personal qualities' may be more serious, especially as recent work on management and other professional groups suggests that personal competences are fundamental to effective practice, and that an absence of the requisite qualities cannot be substituted by technical or functional competence. The work undertaken in Northern Ireland, and reported earlier by Geoff Whitty, delineated the personal and professional characteristics, knowledge and skills needed of an effective teacher. Personal qualities must at some stage be addressed and profiling should therefore include a consideration of this key aspect of the successful professional.

Competence-based profiles are being increasingly used in schools and this in part has been a result of GEST funding. In the light of recent developments (e.g. the establishment of the Teacher Training Agency) it seems reasonable to assume that profiling will become more widespread and used to inform both initial teacher training, induction and continuing professional development. The evidence regarding the use of profiles as a developmental tool has been outlined by drawing on the findings of a recent NFER research project. The process of professional support for teachers in the early stages of their career that profiling promotes could go some way in overcoming many of the criticisms of induction levelled by HMI and others. They should not, however, be seen as providing the means of meeting all of an NQT's needs. As Menter (1995) has recently argued, profiling may be a partial answer to the transition or continuity problem from initial training into the profession but in itself it is not enough. Profiling does not deal adequately with the affective domain and yet as numerous studies of NQTs and probationers have shown, if there is one thing that new teachers value highly it is the opportunity to meet with others in similar situations to themselves. Any induction programme should therefore ensure such needs are catered for; indeed such needs may well be identified through the use of a profile. Competence-based profiles can be responsive to identified individual needs and provide 'a structure for focused discussion and reflective action' (Gifford, 1994). Above all, they can be a useful tool for providing that all-important professional foundation and in helping to promote the notion that professional development is continuous.

References

Department for Education (1992) *Initial Teacher Training (Secondary Phase)* (Circular No. 9/92). London: DFE.

Department for Education (1993a) *Initial Teacher Training (Primary Phase)* (Circular No. 14/93). London: DFE.

Department for Education (1993b) *The Government's Proposals for the Reform of Initial Teacher Training*. London: DFE.

DES (Department of Education and Science) (1992) *Induction of Newly-Qualified Teachers* (Administrative Memorandum 2/92). London: DES.

Earley, P. (1992) 'Using competences for school management development', *British Journal of In-Service Education*, **18** (3), 176–85.

Earley, P. (1993) 'Initiation rights? Beginning teachers' professional development and the objectives of induction training', *British Journal of In-Service Education*, **19** (1), 5–11.

Earley, P. (1995) *'Managing our greatest resource': The evaluation of the Continuous Professional Development in Schools project*. Oxford: CBI Education Foundation/NFER.

Earley, P. and Kinder, K. (1994) *Initiation Rights: Effective Induction Practices for New Teachers*. Slough: NFER.

Gifford, S. (1992) 'Surrey New Teacher Competency Project', *British Journal of In-Service Education*, **18** (3), 159–65.

Gifford, S. (1994) 'Evaluating the Surrey New Teacher Competency Profile', *British Journal of In-Service Education*, **20** (3), 313–326.

HMI (Her Majesty's Inspectorate) (1992) *The Induction and Probation of New Teachers, 1988–1991* (HMI Report 62/92). London: DES.

Hutchinson, D. (1994) 'Competence-based profiles for ITT and Induction: the place of reflection', *British Journal of In-Service Education*, **20**, (3), 303–312.

Kerry, T. and Shelton Mayes, A. (eds) (1995) *Issues in Mentoring*. London: Routledge/OU Press.

Menter, I. (1995) 'Running in, please pass', *Times Educational Supplement*, **13 January**.

Murphy, R., Mahony, P., Jones, J. and Calderhead, J. (1993) 'Profiling in initial teacher education', *British Journal of In-Service Education*, **2** (3), 141–46.

OFSTED (Office for Standards in Education) (1993) *The New Teacher in School: A Survey by HMI in England and Wales 1992*. London: HMSO.

Smith, P. and West-Burnham, J. (1993) *Mentoring in the Effective School*, Harlow: Longman.

Teacher Training Agency (1994) *Profiles of Teacher Competences – Consultation on Draft Guidance*. London: TTA.

Turner, M. (1993) 'The role of mentors and teacher tutors in school-based teacher education and induction', *British Journal of In-Service Education*, **19** (1), 36–45.

10

Competency in the Mathematics Classroom – The Example of Equal Opportunities

Leone Burton and Hilary Povey

Introduction

No clear agreement yet exists about the notion of the 'competent' teacher. Among the most important factors which make such agreement difficult in relation to the teaching of mathematics are epistemological questions about the nature of mathematics as a discipline and related educational questions about why we are teaching the mathematics we teach. For example, when considering the kind of discipline portrayed as mathematics, two contrasting paradigms underlie the public documentation which supports the UK National Curriculum and, indeed, many similar attempts in other countries (see Burton, 1994). One of these, the transmission model of 'objective' knowledge, underpins public syllabus documents. The other, the construction model of learning, directs much guidance given to teachers. These two approaches make very differing demands on teachers' knowledge of mathematics, and of how pupils learn mathematics and have very different implications for conceptions of 'competent' teaching. Indeed, Alan Schoenfeld (1988: 146) has drawn attention to the fact that students can be taught well in the sense that they achieve on public measures of performance but learn:

> some inappropriate and counterproductive conceptualizations of the nature of mathematics as a direct result of their mathematics instruction.

So, even the apparently uncontroversial requirement to have knowledge of subject matter is not so straightforward. Problems of construing 'competence' are especially severe wherever change in existing school practices is seen to be desirable. We decided to look at equal opportunities as an area where change is sought since we take is as a premise that much of the time, in many schools and mathematics classrooms, equal opportunities do not exist for many learners, or teachers. Focusing on equal opportunities was a means, for us, to ask questions about the exercise of judgements, knowledge and skills by beginning mathematics teachers. We believe that this helps to identify the strengths and weaknesses of the use of competences to draw lessons for other areas where change to existing practices might be sought.

If we assume that, at the least, all pupils are entitled to equal access to mathematics, a competent teacher must be one within whose classroom such entitlement is built into those areas over which the teacher has sole responsibility and monitored in those areas which are interactive, or pupil centred. None the less, research evidence continues to show just how difficult it is to implement such requirements, even for experienced teachers (for example, see Forgasz, 1994).

For student teachers, a place to begin might be by placing equality of opportunity as necessarily on the agenda through competency statements. The mere existence of such statements of competency certainly alerts students to a requirement that a response should form part of lesson planning and implementation. However, as with any other aspect of lesson planning, the statements do not, of themselves, constitute situated direction or advice nor can they possibly take into account the student teacher's positioning with respect to equal opportunities. As a consequence, evidence can be found to support the warnings in the literature of a retreat into a simplistic, behaviourist, tick-list type response despite the existence of substantial supporting documentation prepared by University staff and practising teachers.

None the less, it has been our experience when working with prospective teachers of mathematics that the issue of equal opportunities is one that is taken seriously, information about it is welcomed, and student teachers tend to rate it highly on their learning agendas. However, empirically, the equal opportunity map in mathematics classrooms is not being substantially re-drawn. Can the competency debate help us through this maze?

Beginning Teacher Needs

Our concern here is with the needs of beginning teachers. We are assuming that, in the student phase, information and case study material is used to establish a need for the consideration of equal opportunities in the mathematics classroom, to deal with different personal positions and to begin to unpick the complexities of the issue. During the practice teaching, students' responses to the learning demands of different pupils and their awareness of the ways in which gender, 'race', class and disability construct and are constructed by them and their pupils should naturally feed the dialogue between them, their mentor teachers and their university tutors. The difficulty, as we see it, lies in the conflict between:

- the 'precise specification of behaviours to be learned' (Tuxworth, 1989) with evidence for competency being gained from the assessment of these behaviours; and
- the inability of specifying the particularities, similarities and differences likely to be encountered by the beginning teacher as she moves from one pupil to another, one class to another or one school to another.

The general conception of competence which informs our work is similar to John Elliott's (1991:18) when he suggests that:

> we could develop a broad competency-based teacher education curriculum to support intelligent practice in unstructured, complex, and fluid educational situations. It would radically differ in its conception of teaching competence to the behaviourist conception embedded in the 'social market' perspective and the model currently promoted by the National Council for Vocational Qualifications (NCVQ). In as much as this curriculum would aim to develop those abilities which are related to a capacity for situational understanding, the conception of competence which underpins it is highly consistent with the 'practical science' perspective.

Our model of the competent teacher has three components which are inter-dependent. One requires the teacher to engage with an epistemological position which recognises that mathematics learning is situated, socially and culturally, and consequently cannot be differentiated from pedagogy. The second demands a reflective practitioner whose reflection is integral to decisions taken in the classroom. The third involves embracing responsibility for achieving and asserting a 'voice' with respect to teaching and learning informed by theory *and* practice, and the authority that that assumes.

We believe that the only appropriate means through which such a curriculum can be explored is a profile and the process is one of recording and reflecting upon growing awareness and responsiveness to the demands of that awareness. Early information which alerts student teachers to the imbalances of power in the mathematics classroom is used in developing classroom profiles of similar data. Later, student teachers are expected to show knowledge and skills about the content and methods of teaching and their equal opportunities' implications. Later still, planned responses to classroom situations and intuitive responses to unplanned events provide further developmental information. Competences therefore set an agenda for the course which the student can use to make decisions about the evidence to be offered to support a competency claim. Such evidence could be, for example, written reflections, an assignment or based on a discussion of a classroom event.

The learning needs of the beginning teacher are thus derived from analysis of the many factors possibly affecting their pupils' encounters with mathematics. Far from obscuring the complexity, or practising a sleight-of-hand with tick-lists, the process emphasises it and alerts beginning teachers to its situatedness. Competency, in this scenario, is not a one-off judgement but a threshold crossed by the beginning teacher to signify the start of a journey.

Such a general outline was the structure for an action research project which focussed on raising gender issues in the initial teacher education curriculum for a cohort of mathematics PGCE students at Sheffield Hallam University. The results of the initiative were overwhelmingly positive in the short term, with student teachers avowing attitude change and able to detail ways in which bias could be mitigated within the context of the mathematics classroom (Povey and Johnson, 1991). None the less, we were left with a concern that 'competency' judged at the moment of qualification might hide, for these students, difficulties and pressures which would lead them away from their avowed intentions. Below, we detail the results of conducting follow-up studies of two beginning teachers.

Joanna and John

Both Joanna and John were members of a cohort of mathematics PGCE students who participated in the action research project. At the end of the course, Joanna and John had a very similar competency profile with respect to equal opportunities. On the form which was used to record teaching practice assessment by both schools and the students' tutors, there was a section asking for appraisal of equal opportunities aspects of their work (Table 10.1).

PROFILE CATEGORY	CRITERIA FOR HIGH RATINGS	Very High	High	Average	Low	Very Low	CRITERIA FOR LOW RATINGS
EQUAL OPPOR- TUNITIES	Student effectively promotes equality of opportunities in the classroom						Student shows little or no aware- ness of EO issues and these are not addressed in classroom practice

Table 10.1 Extract from teaching practice report form

Joanna was awarded one *average*, two *high* and one *very high* and John one *average*, two *high* and one borderline *high/very high*. Before their final practice, the students had been asked to give some specific examples of classroom practice or other aspect of behaviour in school that would

merit a *very high* mark in this category. Joanna included in her list:
- use of names/occupations etc. from different cultures, classes and both sexes that don't subscribe to the stereotypical image;
- display posters etc. that show other cultures (e.g. Islamic art patterns) or women in maths etc;
- catering to all needs, being especially aware of bilingual problems and acting accordingly, or having support material for low attainers;
- encouraging of mixed groups for working with regard to gender, ability, race;
- positive encouragement equally for same criteria e.g. not girls for neatness, etc;

John's examples were:
- lessons which use resources and ideas which show men and women in non-stereotypical roles, discussion of this;
- introduction and use of materials from other cultures, discussion of this;
- teaching time shared equally between boys and girls;
- tackling sexist, racist comments as they arise in the classroom;
- careful use of language.

Both Joanna and John provided a reasonable list indicating a level of awareness which would presumably contribute to the awarding of an appropriate competency statement. How the levels of awareness affected classroom behaviours and were incorporated into their reflections by the students of course is not indicated. None the less, at this point both students seemed equally alert to the connection between equal opportunities and at least some aspects of classroom practice.

The picture 2 years later, however, was very different, not yet particularly in how effective their classrooms were in providing equal opportunities but in what seemed to be the potential for change they still possessed. Joanna and John were both observed for 2 days in school, at work in the classroom, associating with colleagues and generally partaking in the life of the school. They were each interviewed as were their heads of department and members of the senior management of the schools. Portraits were drawn of the new teachers at work and of the settings in which they found themselves. There is space here only to draw out one or two indicative details.

When asked directly about equal opportunities, Joanna's response was: 'I don't often think of whether they're girls or boys.' Commenting on aspects of classroom organisation and ethos often associated with mathematical achievement in girls – for example providing opportunities for discussion, for working in relatively open-ended situations, or for tackling tasks involving posing the problem for oneself (DES 1989:20 f) – she voiced the conviction that: 'the old didactic methods have to be brought back in ... the [PGCE course] would do students a favour [to equip them with these] because it comes as a bit of a culture shock.'

Joanna seemed highly competent and already very 'professional', was regarded by management when she began as 'not a typical probationer' because of her maturity and competence, and yet nevertheless could only derive personal confidence from an exemplary performance which, most significantly, would be judged *by others* to be so. She had positioned herself within the department in such a way as to present the 'acceptable face' of innovation ('good ideas' for teaching fractions and so on) but she did this from a location within a conservative tradition which would be more likely to offer protection from the critical judgement of others. She had 'internally adjusted' (Lacey, 1977) to the norms at the more traditional end of the spectrum of those prevailing in the school and seemed extremely unlikely to become in the future a motive force for change. Joanna would undoubtedly be deemed a competent teacher and we certainly would not want to disagree with that. But her agenda for teaching was now heavily influenced by a transmission model of mathematical learning; involved 'treating everyone the same'; and generally appeared to endorse the taken-for-granted assumptions of contemporary schooling.

By comparison, John's agenda still involved, for example, a commitment to working on gender issues in his classroom (in the lesson observed, consciously trying to eradicate the dominance of the boys, albeit not yet with a great deal of success); an awareness of the relevance to teaching of 'personal development, to be open-minded about things'; and a conviction that it was important for the staff group 'to inspect our own attitudes and beliefs and approaches' with respect to racism in order to begin to work for change within the school. John claimed that his fundamental outlook had remained unchanged. When the opportunity arose to become involved in the school's equal opportunities working party he had done so; when it became defunct he claimed to be 'doing nothing' but as he recreated the story of his time at the school it became clear that he had been much more active in the whole school context than he remembered himself as being: 'I'd forgotten all this, I'm interested now ... I did display a certain amount of interest in certain areas ... oh it's all coming back to me now.'

He had been discouraged but now said: 'it's something that I think perhaps I ought to develop more and perhaps might in the future ... what I ought to look for is a school that was sympathetic, where I could feel comfortable working'. He was not yet at this stage in any sense a 'gender leader' (Rudduck 1994) but he had retained as strongly as ever his commitment to equal opportunities: there was no suggestion of the 'that's-alright-in-college-but-the-real-world-is-different' kind. The socialisation process had not countered or undone the attitudes and convictions with which he had started teaching. Although the issue of equal opportunities might currently be largely in abeyance, the potential for and will towards future work was apparent. (He has subsequently seen through his intention to seek out a school which will allow him to develop these ideas further and is working positively for change in his new environment.)

The school settings in which Joanna and John found themselves gave no obvious clue as to why their differences were emerging. Again there is space here only to offer indicative details of the two schools. For example, although John's school was mixed and had a balanced intake of boys and girls, *all* the senior management team were men and, in terms of the organisational ethos of the school, there was a very 'male' atmosphere. It was difficult to gain access to the senior management despite prior warning and agreement and the general picture was that decision making was not genuinely consultative nor democratic but was essentially authoritarian. The school produced a prospectus for parents, a reasonably substantial document of more than 25 sides which contained much useful information as well as attempting to give an overall impression of the ethos of the school. Throughout the brochure there was no mention of equal opportunities and as far as we could discover the school had no equal opportunities policies. The mathematics department provided an environment more congenial to equal opportunities. There was a stated departmental commitment to equal opportunities, a concern for the achievement of all pupils and an atmosphere of openness to new ideas.

Joanna's mathematics department was not dissimilar to John's in that there was a commitment to shared decision-making, value attached to being 'forward thinking, not standing still, having initiative' and a willingness to work at equal opportunities issues. Her experience was unlike John's, however, in the whole school context. The school prospectus, early on and prominently, included a paragraph on equal opportunities; the management style of the school was open and consultative. It was easy to gain access to the senior management team who were generous with their time and attention. Of the senior management team, four were men and three were women and there were a number of strong, respected and effective women in relatively senior positions. It is true that, despite acknowledgement of the relevance of equal opportunities to the promotion of achievement and the generally thoroughly civilised atmosphere prevailing throughout the school, there were aspects of the underlying culture which were hostile to anti-sexism and which might make it quite difficult for attitudes and ethos to change. Nevertheless, the context was one in which there was room for manoeuvre and where suggestions for development and change would be listened to by most and welcomed by some. If anything, therefore, Joanna was under less pressure than John to compromise on the view she espoused as a student; the school setting did not seem to account for the divergence between their responses to beginning teaching.

What seemed to emerge as a significant difference, however, was between their 'ways of knowing' (Belenky *et al.*, 1986). John was influenced by ideas, understood himself and his practice in relation to those ideas, used theoretical descriptions to see, articulate and try to understand himself and his experiences. Dissonance between those descriptions and his practice and experience troubled him and potentially demoralised him; it also, however, enabled him to resist simply accommodating himself to the status quo and to the 'common sense' of his particular environment. He saw himself as having both the authority and the right to evaluate the different perspectives of senior, experienced teachers and to synthesise his own, original perspective as a result.

For Joanna, it almost seemed as though theoretical descriptions were a bit of a nuisance. Her guiding principles and the tools she used to grasp and understand herself and her experience seemed to be located elsewhere, perhaps in a 'metaphoric way of thinking' (Calderhead, 1992: 20). She wanted to bring her theoretical descriptions and her practice into line but gave the impression that she would never do this by work at a theoretical level, where the relationship between ideas and their implications were analysed. Rather the ideas must give way to a new formula which 'represented' what she currently did. She used external authority both within her teaching itself and in her decisions about how to teach. About her teaching she said she had come to a realisation that:

> what I had to teach was all the nitty gritty, the fundamental ways that it is difficult to get across other than by saying 'this is what you do, this is how you do it'.

This fitted in with her response to a question about what she had discovered was important about teaching since leaving the university. She replied:

> don't think you know it all, sometimes you can go into a school and they think 'She thinks she knows it all' ... as well as bringing new ideas you have a lot to learn and a softly, softly approach and not 'This is what [the University] told me, this is how you do it.'

The authority might be, at different times, the school or the university but rarely, if at all, Joanna.

If these indications are correct, there are two consequences with respect to competences. That part of our formal university assessment which might seem to fit within a competency framework did not allow us to distinguish between Joanna and John at the level of ways of knowing and consequently did not contribute to an understanding of how their views and practice would develop in an area where change to existing practices is sought: one was equipped to maintain a critical distance from existing practice and the other was not. Much more important than this predictive aspect, however, is how the framework of assessment affected what students and tutors thought the course was essentially about. It would suggest that unless a competency framework can support the development of an epistemological perspective that moves beyond received knowledge, that values 'the joy attendant upon intimacy with an idea' (Belenky *et al.*, 1986:102) and that fosters the capacity in students to 'jump outside the frames and systems authorities provide and create their own frames' (Belenky *et al.*, 1986:134), it will fail us in promoting equal opportunities.

Competency as a Response to Reflection

In an area like equal opportunities where change is a necessary condition of 'entitlement', teachers need to be able to stand back from their existing practice, to work on it, to keep it under critical review while they develop those practices in line with their changing understanding as well as the conditions and pressures in schools. This requires of the teacher an ability to re-define what, for her or him, being competent means. Such a continuing re-definition is provoked by day-to-day experiences and what is learnt from them, together with the theoretical context into which they can be placed. To be effective, therefore, is dependent upon:

- an explicit understanding of one's own theories in order to understand how they affect attitudes and behaviour as well as to work on them to bring about change;
- grappling with the theories of others to assist the reflective process through which observations and experiences are interpreted and critiqued;
- accepting one's own responsibility for justifying and substantiating one's theoretical position and acknowledging that this authority lies with oneself.

This reflective cycle is 'central to the process of developing flexible teachers who will continue to learn after qualification and who will be able to respond to new challenges and opportunities in the future.' (Eraut, 1989:175) However, it is also a central element in the capacity to resist internal adjustment and incorporation, both of which, in supporting the status quo, are hostile to promoting equal opportunities. The differences between Joanna and John, especially in the ways in which they use theoretical descriptions and do or do not search for relationships between these descriptions and their practices, exemplify the degree to which competency at qualification cannot ensure the process of development of which Michael Eraut wrote. Neither, we would suggest, can the brief encounter with a PGCE course of teacher education, especially one which is sited in the pressurised environment of a school where the articulation and interrogation of theories cannot have a high priority.

Inevitably, this leaves us wondering how much it is possible to develop a reflective practitioner through a short course of teacher education and how much, at qualification, is characteristic of individual students themselves? For example, in the case of Joanna and John, their characteristics of thinking seem reasonably deeply embedded. Furthermore, how significant to the process of reflection are the material conditions in the schools in which they work? In developing profiles of competences which reflect the complexities of learning in school are we committing the fatal error of looking for predispositions which existed prior to training and assuming that they have been acquired as part of the training process? If we believe, as we do, that responsiveness to the demands of an equality perspective is always necessary, highly unpredictable in its demands, and constantly changing, and also that demands are always situated with a teacher and her particular pupils, in a particular class, in a particular school, perhaps this very ideosyncracy indicates that far from looking for competency statements about beginning teachers, it is at least as important to work on the situatedness in schools. How far is it possible or reasonable to place a responsibility on a teacher education student to be responsive to material conditions which are antagonistic to the issue? We none the less continue to be committed to the notion of education as an agency for change.

These questions, and others, are part of a research agenda springing from a particular epistemological perspective. The view of knowing on which it depends is responsive to enquiry, personal as well as cultural, problem-situated and negotiated. This view of knowing is equally applicable in the mathematics classroom where it is related to pupil activity, negotiation of meaning, collaboration and the use of representation to support reflection on the learning of mathematics. This is a fundamentally different paradigm which provokes classroom behaviours and organisation distinctive from that which believes mathematics to be fixed, objective and self-evident. A teacher who adopts the former paradigmatic stance will look very different in the classroom to a teacher who approaches mathematics as a non-negotiable knowledge-based body of content and skills. As long as the two traditions are regarded as equally valid, or, at the least coexist, it would be unfair to judge competency in one by criteria appropriate to the other. Cobb, *et al.* (1992:575) describe the distinction in terms of the mathematics classroom tradition which they characterise by 'four aspects of mathematical activity – problems, solutions, explanations, and justifications'. They refer to the two traditions as 'school mathematics' and 'inquiry mathematics'.

> The differences between the two traditions concern the quality of the taken-as-shared or normative meanings and practices constituted in the two classrooms ... meaningfulness was relative to the classroom mathematics traditions. This

contention reflects the view that students generally experienced an activity as meaningful if they could cope in the interactively constituted instructional situation ... students who participate in a school mathematics tradition typically experience mathematical understanding when they can follow procedural instructions successfully. In contrast, students who participate in an inquiry mathematics tradition typically experience understanding when they can create and manipulate mathematical objects in ways that they can explain and, when necessary, justify. (Cobb *et al.*, 1992:597–8)

Both teachers described in this case study material:

> were authorities in the sense that they initiated their students into particular interpretive stances. In the course of these interactions, their students learned which mathematical activities were acceptable, which needed to be explained or justified, and what counted as a legitimate explanation or justification.' (Cobb *et al.*, 1992:597)

From a reading of the case study material, neither teacher would be considered to be other than competent; but competent in very diverse ways, some of which conflict with specified value positions on, for example, the nature of mathematics.

If the judgement of competency is based upon pupil competency yet another layer of complexity is added. First, the pupils were developing different competences in the two classrooms. In the 'school mathematics' tradition pupils were developing competency in following instructions whereas those in the 'inquiry mathematics' classroom were learning to explain and justify mathematical activities often in ways that appeared to be not necessarily consistent. That is, compared to the 'school mathematics' one-correct way, alternative formulations and/or explanations were positively encouraged by the other teacher. As Alan Schoenfeld (1988: 165) made clear:

> What the students in the target class learned about geometry extended far beyond their mastery of proof and construction procedures. They developed perspectives on the role of each, which in turn determined which knowledge they used – or failed to use. Similarly, their views about mathematical form, 'problems', and their role as passive consumers of others' mathematics, all shaped their mathematical behavior.

However, pupil competency is not only a product of what a pupil knows or can do. As David Clarke (1994) demonstrated, a judgement of pupil competency at mathematics is a product of the interplay between ability, self-concept and, most importantly, classroom conceptions of competence which are derived from the social context. The hierarchy derived from the classroom conception of competence can be powerful enough to over-ride both ability and self-concept. 'Such is the degree of consensus about what behaviors constitute competence that pupils are located in rank order within the resulting hierarchy with a high degree of consistency across all participants.' (Clarke, 1994: 62). The result can be, as in the case reported, that two children achieve equivalently but one is labelled 'good at maths' and the other academically unsuccessful. The outcome in the case of the unsuccessful student was that he

> acquiesced to a role, determined for him by the high school community, characterised by a passive approach to learning, a non-academic class profile, and by disruptive classroom behavior. (Clarke, 1994:73–4)

Thus, we have come around full circle to the equal opportunities' implications of such type-casting by what is an, apparently, uncontested and 'objective' judgement.

Conclusion

A 'school mathematics' tradition has failed generations of potential learners. In part, it is that failure which the equal opportunities approach to mathematics learning aims to correct. Behaviouristic competency lists which reflect an atomistic, fragmented view of knowledge and an epistemology based on reproduction are no more likely to succeed than have previously attempted strategies since it is the epistemological basis which is faulty. Consequently, advice to beginning teachers to be firm disciplinarians first and relax afterwards or to get the skills first and worry about the contexts later is highly unlikely to generate competency in the way in which we have been discussing it. Such advice depends upon a notion of skills being independent of values and epistemology.

In this chapter, we have adopted the position that increasing competency is a function of three things. One is the recognition of the interdependence of epistemology and pedagogy. The second is reflective practice and the third the assumption of authority with respect to one's own positioning. These must be established from the first encounter with the complexities and problematics of the classroom. With respect to equal opportunities, this demands an understanding of the impact upon individual learning of placing enquiry at the centre of classroom practice. However, given the prevalence of 'school mathematics' in our classrooms, a beginning teacher who rejects that approach to teaching may be isolated, unsupported and pressurised at precisely the time when she is most in need of the colleaguial community. On the other hand, we would claim that the reflective practitioner is more likely to implement an 'inquiry' view of mathematics in her classroom having herself uncovered the power of reflection to assist in analysing and critiquing her classroom experiences and that such a view is necessary to a classroom with an equality perspective. Equally, effective reflection and an enquiry based epistemology build authority in the learner whether he or she is a learner of mathematics or a developing teacher. Such authority we see as being necessary to underwrite educational growth and embrace change.

We are therefore asking of our beginning teachers that they adopt a much more challenging tradition than the one which is currently widespread and that they do so, in part, to address aspects of school-based behaviour and attitudes with which society, as a whole, has failed to cope. However, it is impossible to untangle these threads. Given that we wish to ensure that *all* learners have equal access to mathematics, teacher competency can only, in our view, be built upon our current understanding of what it means to learn mathematics. Since complexity is now a well-accepted feature of the mathematics classroom, it must be embraced rather than attempts made to avoid it. Embracing the complexity means abjuring 'solutions' and, rather, looking for 'best-fit' and being ever vigilant to the possibilities of improving that fit. In this case, the best use to which competency statements can be put is in helping to open an agenda for a continuing discourse which analyses practice in all its dimensions.

References

Belenky, M.F., Clinchy, B.M., Goldberger, N.R. and Tarule, J.M. (1986) *Women's Ways of Knowing: the Development of Self, Voice and Mind*. London: Basic Books.

Burton, L. (1994) (ed.) *Who Counts? Assessing Mathematics in Europe*. Stoke-on-Trent: Trentham Books.

Calderhead, J. (1992) 'The professional development of teachers in changing Europe', in Leino, A., Hellgren, P. and Hamalainen, K. (eds) *Integration of Technology and Reflection in Teaching: a Challenge for European Teacher Education*. Proceedings of the seventeenth annual conference of the Association for Teacher Education in Europe, Lahti: University of Helsinki.

Clarke, D. (1994) 'The transition to secondary school mathematics', in Robitaille, D.F., Wheeler, D.H. and Kieran, C. (eds) *Selected Lectures from the 7th International Congress on Mathematical Education*. Sainte-Foy, Quebec: Les Presses de l'Universite Laval.

Cobb, P., Wood, T., Yackel, E. and McNeal, B. (1992) 'Characteristics of classroom mathematics traditions: an interactional analysis', in *American Educational Research Journal*, **29** (3), 573–604.

Department of Education and Science (1989) Education Observed: *Girls Learning Mathematics*. Stanmore: Department of Education and Science.

Elliott, J. (1991) *'Three Perspectives on Coherence and Continuity in Teacher Education'*, paper prepared for the UCET Annual Conference, November.

Eraut, M. (1989) 'Initial teacher training and the NGVQ model', in Burke, J. (ed.) *Competency Based Education and Training*. Lewes: Falmer.

Forgasz, H. (1994) *Society and Gender Equity in Mathematics Education*. Geelong, Vic.: Deakin University Press.

Lacey, C. (1977) *The Socialisation of Teachers*. London: Methuen.

Povey, H. and Johnson, S. (1991) 'Integrating gender in teacher education: mathematics', in Boulton, P and Coldron, J. (eds) *Gender Work in Progress*. Sheffield: Pavic.

Rudduck, J. (1994) *Developing a Gender Policy in Secondary Schools: Individuals and Institutions*. Buckingham: Open University Press.

Schoenfeld, A.H. (1988) 'When good teaching leads to bad results: the disasters of "well taught" Mathematics Courses', *Educational Psychologist*, **23** (2), 145–166.

Tuxworth, E. (1989) 'Competence based education and training: background and origins', in Burke, J. (ed.) *Competency Based Education and Training*. Lewes: Falmer.

11

Competences and the First Year of Teaching

Pat Mahony

Background to the Project

In 1992 a Local Education Authority (LEA) in London initiated a project to develop a profile of teacher competences for use with Newly Qualified Teachers (NQTs) and their teacher-mentors. The project team consisted of one LEA Inspector and three members of staff from different Higher Education Institutions (HEIs). Our work was informed by our experiences of developing competence frameworks in initial teacher education (ITE) and by the literature identifying the complex issues raised by competence based approaches to teacher education. Each of us was responsible for different elements of the project and within our small team there existed a range of commitments to competence based approaches to teacher education – from the severely sceptical to the positively enthusiastic. We did however, share a view about the importance of appropriate support for teachers in their first year of teaching.

The 'Need for Something'

It has become almost a cliché to claim that induction forms the weakest link in the professional development of teachers. Even before the government rescinded the formal mandatory requirements which covered the probationary period for beginning teachers (DfE, 1992a), LEAs differed markedly in relation to the quantity, quality, content and principles underpinning provision (Sidgwick, Mahony and Hextall 1993). In addition to the abolition of the probationary year, the delegation of funding to schools further weakened the role of the LEAs as providers of support for NQTs (Earley 1992). This is not to say that there was no recognition of the fact that NQTs needed further professional development. It is identified in Circular 9/92 (DfE, 1992b) and guidance given in Administrative Memorandum 2/92:

Assistance for NQTs
After taking up appointment the NQT should be able so far as is practicable:
i) to seek help and guidance from a nominated member of staff who has been adequately prepared for the role, and from the Head of Department where appropriate;
(DfE, 1992a; para 9)

Government grants were available to support the shift from LEA provided induction to more school based provision and teaching competences were mentioned as part of this process:

> The Department's objectives in supporting expenditure by LEAs and GM schools on induction training are to:
> improve links between initial teacher training, induction of NQTs and INSET during the early years of teachers' careers, particularly through the development of profiling and competency based approaches to professional development.
> (DfE, 1992a)

Predictably there was much concern about whether the shift to school-based induction was a sensible move. The findings of HMI did little to reassure critics that schools would be able to provide the necessary support:

> Schools varied greatly in the quality of support offered to probationers. Informal support was almost invariably good, but well-structured provision was much less common. Only a minority of schools had an established induction programme or a policy statement on induction. Schools under LMS are likely to be expected to assume an increasing responsibility for the induction of new teachers. It is important that LEAs provide guidance which will assist schools in formulating effective induction policies and practices.
> (HMI, 1992)

Of course it could be argued that the point of the government grant was precisely to enable LEAs to provide this guidance, however not all LEAs were successful in their bids for the grant and thus were placed in a position where they had neither the resources nor the power to translate policy into practice.

Many other concerns have been raised about the changed arrangements for induction. For example, the basis on which a school chooses mentors for NQTs, how the mentor's role is defined and how it is monitored were already questions raised by Menter and Whitehead (1992) in the light of their experiences with the Articled Teacher scheme and it seemed likely that these would re-emerge in the context of induction. There is no acknowledgement within the official documentation that these are important issues. Even if one were to ignore these difficult questions, it is still not easy to resolve the most straightforward, logistical anxieties. Who is responsible for ensuring that the evaluation of the induction phase is undertaken in a fair way? What is the appropriate timing for such evaluations and in a world of tight budgets upon whom can their resource implications fall? Most urgently, for the sake of the new teachers themselves and for the teaching profession in general, what kinds of protective safeguards can be built into the procedures and how does the shift away from statutory probation impinge on conditions of employment?

More important from the point of view of the discussion on competences, the official documentation does little to clarify the conceptual confusions which abound in this area nor quieten the critics of competence-based approaches to teacher education. Underpinning the shifts in language and meaning contained in various paragraphs of Administrative Memorandum 2/92 is a fundamental and unacknowledged tension between the use of 'profiling and competence-based assessment' for the purposes of enhancing professional development and its utilisation for the quite other purpose of providing a 'licence to teach'. In its ambiguity it also raises, but does not resolve, questions about exactly what constitute the procedures for the 'adequate' completion of the induction phase. It assumes that the debate concerning the whole question of teacher competences is resolved, that competence and profiling procedures for initial teacher education are firmly in place and that these can be unproblematically translated into procedures for induction with notions of progression built into them. In addition there is slippage between the ideas of competences and the notion of teacher appraisal. Until now these have come from quite different directions and have been seen as having different purposes.

Given all this and despite our various concerns about competence-based approaches to teacher development, we believed that – provided the nature of the profile framework, its purposes and the processes developed for its use were sound – there were a number of potential advantages in developing a profiling scheme for NQTs, their mentors and others interested in the quality of further professional development. Many of these advantages paralleled those already identified in relation to student teachers (Murphy *et al.*, 1993).

Uses of profiling teaching competence for the NQT
- Help to make explicit the skills, knowledge and understanding necessary to the development of their practice.
- Help them articulate their own decisions about appropriate teaching strategies.
- Help them see learning to teach as a developmental process and learning to teach better as a long-term concern.
- Help them focus their reflections and evaluations about their own practice – what they have achieved and what they have yet to grasp.

- Help them to set realistic future goals and to be involved in the process of assessing to what degree they achieve them.
- Provide them with a positive (and transferable) experience of what it means to support learners by involving them in monitoring their own progress.

Uses of profiling teacher competences for the Mentor

- Provide a framework or set of parameters which will support a focused approach to further professional development.
- Help generate productive professional debate with the NQT about what models of good practice are being assumed. It is important that differences in emphasis between mentors in school and tutors involved in ITE do not become, in the eyes of beginning teachers, contradictory demands leading to feelings of powerlessness and frustration.
- Provide a shared language in which these professional debates can be conducted.
- Focus attention on the degree to which opportunities really are available for the NQT's development.
- Help clarify what realistically can be achieved in the first year of teaching and what should be a matter for continuing professional development.
- Help clarify the issues in the debates about what aspects of further professional development ought to be sited where.
- Focus attention on the fact that the relationship between professional development and assessment is not straightforward (see Chapter 3).
- Help raise issues about the role of the mentor and the purposes of the mentoring, the educational needs of mentors and the time required to adequately fulfil this role.

Uses of profiling teacher competences for a wider audience

- Focus attention on the need for proper professional development for teachers from the cradle to the grave, by making explicit what is involved in maintaining practice of a high quality.
- Enable comparisons to be made with our colleagues in other countries, particularly those in Europe.
- Enable comparisons to be made with graduate programmes in industry and commerce and provide evidence where teaching is treated as a poor relation in terms of funding for training.

It was within the context of the sense of policy chaos, described earlier, and our beliefs in the potential (realisable or otherwise) of a profiling scheme that the project took place (see Chapter 3).

The Project

One of our concerns within the project was to begin to develop an account of NQT competence generated by the NQTs and mentors themselves. Previously the LEA had tried using a framework based on Circular 9/92 and was dissatisfied with the way it seemed to provoke a dry and bureaucratic response from mentors. Therefore we believed it was important, in order to maximise ownership of the profiling scheme by those who would be using it, not to impose the competence descriptors from 'on high' but rather to invest some time in eliciting from both groups, their views on desirable developments in the first year of teaching.

Eleven mentors and 16 NQTs attended meetings on different occasions at the LEA's Professional Development Centre. They were asked to identify what ought to be the characteristics of NQTs by the end of their first year of teaching. As Johnson (in Carter *et. al.*, 1994:56) describes the process:

> Personal constructs were elicited using Repertory Grids (Kelly, 1955) .... From the Repertory Grids elicited for each individual, all elements and constructs were transferred to cards. A structure of meaning analysis was undertaken to exhibit the pattern of relationships in the responses for each group.

The results were sent back to both groups for comment and amendment and the final data used to form the framework for the LEA's new profile of NQT competence.

The project neared completion at the point when Circular 14/93 (DfE 1993) was published. Our impressions were that the elements identified by mentors and NQTs and the language in which they expressed them were very different from those set out in 14/93. This might be thought to be unremarkable; there is after all no definitive 'truth' about the nature of teaching contained in the official documentation and nor is one claimed. It was, however, somewhat surprising given that the mentors were already working with the 9/92 framework which is not dissimilar to 14/93 and they were well used to commenting on the progress of NQTs according to its categories and in its language, albeit in a way which was perceived as 'dry and distant' (Carter *et al.*, 1994). To explore the matter further and using all the data which had been generated by the project, the teachers' statements were compared with the competences as laid out in 14/93. This it was felt would provide another voice on the subject of teacher competence.

First the mentors' and then the NQTs' statements were mapped where possible on to the relevant DfE competences. This exercise did not of course yield any firm conclusions about what experienced or new teachers 'really' believe is important in teaching but it did provide insight into the priorities of busy teachers as expressed after a day in the classroom. Notwithstanding the potential for misinterpretation of the mentors' or NQTs' comments and given the possibility of variously interpreting 14/93, some interesting results emerged.

DfE Competences not Mentioned by the Mentors

A significant number of the 14/93 competences were not mentioned. There was relatively little comment which fitted within 'Curriculum Content, Planning and Assessment', although we shall see later that *planning* figured highly when seen as having wider application. 'Further Professional Development' was also not mentioned and in relation to 'Teaching Strategies', mentors simply did not express themselves in a way which indicated even a remote match with the DfE's way of describing practice.

As an explanation of these results, it cannot be that mentors were unaware of the statutory obligations of teachers, many of which are implied or directly stated by the DfE competences. These formed a routine, everyday part of their professional lives and were for some time high on the political agenda. We know too, from the evidence of their assessments of NQTs' progress, articulated against the earlier 9/92 draft of the LEA profile, that they were well able to work within a DfE model of what constitutes competent teaching and to understand and interpret its discourse. It could be that the mentors interpreted the question which we asked them as an opportunity to set their own priorities and in this respect what they produced could be seen as deliberately oppositional to the official version of the competent teacher. Alternatively, it could be that what was omitted was regarded as so self-evident that they viewed it as not requiring mention or that in the short time available they focused on what they considered to be other priorities: perhaps they needed longer to complete the task, given that, in common with many experienced teachers, their knowledge about what teachers need to know and understand to develop competence has over time become an implicit part of their professional practice. The comments from this mentor when she returned the first draft of the results provide some evidence for this view:

> I found several of the sections disappointing and even embarrassing! I do hope this is only a first draft. So much of it needs more careful thought and rephrasing and I haven't time or confidence to do it alone. I think the nature and timing of the meeting was not conducive to the serious consideration which I think such a document needs.

DfE Competences not Mentioned by the NQTs

In comparing the data from the NQTs with the competences as listed in 14/93 a rather different picture emerges. Difficulties as to where to place their comments in relation to the DfE competences were much reduced by virtue of the fact that the language in which they expressed themselves was much more akin to the official descriptors. They may not have *meant* what officials at the DfE mean but what they said was in many cases virtually identical. This could suggest that the government's vision of a competent teacher is currently being successfully achieved within existing, HEI provided courses of primary initial teacher education. Alternatively, it could be that as new teachers they had not yet reached the point where their knowledge had become tacit but were rather still self-consciously trying to come to terms with their responsibilities. Very few of the 14/93 competences were left unmatched by the NQTs. These were in the areas of:

Assessment and Recording of Pupils' Progress

2.4 Newly qualified teachers should be able to:
2.4.4 provide oral and written feedback to pupils on the processes and outcomes of their learning
2.4.5 prepare and present reports on pupils' progress to parents

Further Professional Development

2.7 Newly qualified teachers should have acquired in initial training the necessary foundation to develop:
2.7.3 the ability to recognise diversity of talent including that of gifted pupils
2.7.8 vision, imagination ... in educating their pupils.
(DfE, 1993)

As with the mentors we could speculate about the reasons for these omissions. It could be that these competences, in the NQTs' minds, are incorporated in more generalised comments about practice. Or it could be that in some cases they form part of the routine of professional life and that in others they are perceived as marginal to the main task of teaching 30 children day after day. The fact that no NQT ever mentioned 'vision or imagination' (aspects which often figure in professional conversations with student teachers) does perhaps signal that successful induction into the relentless and exhausting 'hard graft' of the first year of teaching occurs very fast. Whether these NQTs will rise to re-discover their vision and imagination may depend in part on the ethos and culture of their school: whether it is a school in which there are opportunities to work in genuinely collaborative ways, or whether it is 'an egg-crate' school (Fullan and Hargreaves, 1992) in which teachers are isolated physically and professionally.

So far, discussion has centred on areas omitted by either mentors or NQTs. Let us now turn to another scenario and consider the areas mentioned by mentors and NQTs but omitted by the DfE.

Mentors and NQTs Agree to Differ with the DfE

A large number of the statements from both mentors and NQTs could not easily be mapped on to the DfE competences. These fell into a number of categories the largest of which by far for both groups was what might be called 'professional and personal qualities'. Mentors expressed professional qualities as the 'ability to be adaptable and flexible', 'the ability to accept constructive criticism' and 'willingness to learn'. 'Stamina' 'hard work', 'effort' and 'energy' and the responsibility to maintain these while 'maintaining a sense of perspective and realism' were deemed to be significant. Personal qualities such as 'tact', 'humour', 'self-esteem' 'open-mindedness', 'compassion', 'lack of self-importance' or 'humility' all give clues about what for these mentors, was an ideal NQT. While it could be dangerous and open to much abuse to debar new entrants to the teaching profession on the grounds of personal qualities, it does seem that for these mentors this was by far their greatest priority and concern.

Similarly, NQTs put a high priority on being flexible and adaptable with a number of their statements apparently coming from the heart: 'good at thinking on your feet, e.g. when the video blows up'; 'coping with sudden changes of routine' and 'flexibility – to exchange ideas and negotiate resources'. 'The ability to seek and use advice', 'discussing problems rather than bottling it up', the 'need to be receptive and adaptable to feedback' and the 'ability to evaluate advice' were all phrases which mirrored the mentors' comments. The 'ability to work alone' was significant for a number of NQTs and presumably marked a shift from their experience as students, where they would have had more opportunity to work alongside other adults in the classroom. 'Being open to ideas', 'being methodical', 'being resourceful, sensitive and receptive' were all personal or professional characteristics deemed to be important, as was 'the ability to cope with the workload'.

The other large group of cards from both groups which could not be readily mapped on to the DfE competences concerned teachers' 'attitudes to and relationships with children'. Mentors rated 'empathy with children', 'ability to set up a dialogue with pupils', 'ability to reassure individuals', 'refusing to dislike individual pupils' and 'open-mindedness towards pupils' potentials' very highly and these may all have been expressions for what one mentor called 'child centredness'. An interesting issue emerges at this point as to whether it would be possible for a teacher to develop the DfE competences to an acceptable level and yet thoroughly dislike children. It may also be that the current official preoccupation with teachers' subject knowledge has had little profound impact on those actually doing the job. It could even be on this evidence that the increased time in school for student teachers is likely to operate against the former Secretary of State's objective of eliminating child-centred ideology from the initial education of teachers.

Similarly, NQTs produced a large number of statements in this category though not as many proportionately as the mentors. NQTs spoke in terms of 'being prepared to spend time building relationships with children', 'encouraging independence in children', 'building children's self-worth' and 'valuing children's opinions', though they framed their expressions in more formal language than the mentors whose warmth towards and identification with children was much more strongly expressed.

In the areas of 'planning, organising and managing', mentors seemed to be working with a more complex model than the DfE. According to the Circular 14/93, NQTs should be able to use knowledge of the curriculum to plan lessons. It was evident that according to the mentors, knowledge of children, of classroom management and of teaching strategies were all needed to inform planning for children's learning. Thus terms such as 'planning for special needs', 'planning for differentiation', 'planning for flexibility', 'reflection in planning' and 'planning for individual match' were used frequently. Mentors also understood what has to be managed by teachers in much broader terms than is expressed by 14/93. According to mentors everything about teaching and teachers (including stress and 'the self') has to be 'managed', while DfE talks in more limited terms of managing 'time'.

For the NQTs, as with the mentors, 'planning', 'organising' and 'managing' covered a much wider range of activities than suggested by DfE. Everything had to be planned; short term and long term, work for individuals, groups and whole classes, as a team member and as an independent individual teacher, for the everyday routines and for crises. Everything had to be managed too whether this be time, classrooms, children's learning, resources for learning or the movement of children round the school. Similarly everything and everybody had to be organised, demonstrating a sharp awareness that teaching for effective learning requires minute attention to detail.

One other area of discrepancy between the mentors' and the DfE's accounts emerged. First, mentors did overtly mention 'awareness of equal opportunities' whereas it could be argued that the DfE competences have to be interpreted by those who already possess such awareness to be made explicit. This omission is somewhat surprising since for a number of years, the British government has remained a signatory to a European declaration which commits member states to including Equal Opportunities in teacher education.

On the other hand, NQTs mentioned 'equal opportunities' surprisingly little given the alleged obsessions of their ITE college tutors. 'Teaching children with English as a second language' and 'knowing the expectations of the Muslim community' may well reflect the fact that the NQTs had not yet absorbed into that body of knowledge which for experienced teachers becomes implicit, ways of meeting the specific demands of teaching in an ethnically mixed environment.

Other smaller though significant groups of NQT statements which could not entirely be mapped on to the DfE competences, as these are expressed, were 'having aims and objectives', 'to know, implement and *critique* the National Curriculum'.

Mentors, NQTs and DfE Agree

Some of the mentors' comments did easily map on to the DfE competences. By far the largest categories where this occurred were:

2.6.2 create and maintain a purposeful, orderly and supportive environment for their pupils' learning
2.6.1 establish clear expectations of pupil behaviour and secure appropriate standards of discipline.

This was also the case for the NQTs and many clues were given in their responses, as to *how* 'discipline' might be achieved and maintained. 'Ability to organise and manage the learning environment to maintain control', 'ability to gain and keep attention', 'ability to formulate and maintain classroom routines over the year for an atmosphere conducive to work' and 'ability to establish a safe, secure framework to show the boundaries of acceptable behaviour' were all comments which showed the NQTs as having grasped that 'discipline' is not something isolated from other aspects of teaching. Sometimes, more specific strategies were revealed: 'highlighting positive behaviour where possible' and 'ability to use school discipline codes to establish class rules'. Within all of it perhaps their anxieties occasionally peeped through: 'gaining a variety of strategies for managing disruptive behaviour', 'ability to keep disruptive children calm', 'ability to deal with arguments so the children are not aggrieved', 'what to do with a child who is constantly wanting attention and exhibiting challenging behaviour?' and 'interrogation skills for dealing with fights, to be just and for children to know it will be so.' Finally, NQTs apparently felt it was legitimate to expect them to be able to provide 'evidence of criteria for discipline' and a 'rationale for discipline strategies'.

A notable feature of both mentors' and NQTs' comments which mapped on to the competence referring to the development of 'effective working relationships with professional colleagues (including support staff) and parents' (2.7.2), was the breadth of understanding about what this involved. Beyond general comments such as 'can form good relationships with colleagues' and 'puts effort into relationships with colleagues', there were pointers from both groups as to the kinds of qualities needed, such as 'demonstrates friendliness and flexibility with colleagues'. NQTs made many more comments than did the mentors about classroom support and the way this had to be planned for, organised and managed.

NQTs seemed particularly preoccupied with relationships with parents and again, beyond the general comments referring to building positive relationships with parents, particular references seemed to be made to their own experiences. Comments such as 'ability to sort out problems between parent/child', 'ability to negotiate with parents honestly but tactfully', 'ability to act rationally with parents' and 'ability to calm down parents' hinted at a host of stories waiting to be told.

Finally NQTs did seem to be concerned with 'critical awareness in educating their pupils' (2.7.8), much more so than the mentors. The 'need to be able to step back from situations', the 'ability to justify classroom practice', 'having a rationale for classroom practice' and the 'ability to evaluate own practice' all seemed to mark the fact that the NQTs attached importance to reflecting on, reviewing and being able to articulate and justify their practice. This may be because these NQTs had been introduced to teaching within an ideology of teacher education in which 'reflective practice' was emphasised or it may be that their relative lack of experience and confidence generated the need for explicit review and self-monitoring (or both).

Conclusions

Three different discourses were found to exist within the material described above; how the mentors describe competence is very different from the account given by the DfE. How the NQTs describe it is superficially closer to the DfE's account but on closer analysis it seems that for them the whole business of teaching is more challenging and requires more thought, self-examination and review than anybody seems to appreciate. Both mentors' and NQTs' statements implied a view of teaching as complex, as fundamentally involving children and relationships with others. They would undoubtedly argue that the DfE account could be improved by the additional recognition that teaching centrally involves building positive, professional relationships with children and that the opportunity to acquire the relevant knowledge about children is made available to teachers early on in their education.

There was no evidence that either group was inclined to reduce their accounts of teaching to simple, discrete check-lists of behaviour, quite the contrary. When asked to group the statements under more general headings they found it difficult because 'everything links up with everything else'.

The project did reveal how easy it is for NQTs to become swamped in their first year of teaching by the nuance and particularity of the sheer volume of what they have to deal with. It would seem that a competence framework could support them to move beyond the immediate priorities set by life in the classroom by reminding them of the broader dimensions of the teacher's role and of the importance of further professional development, negotiated against the profile framework.

Given the number of substantial differences between the mentors' and the NQTs' priorities and the language in which these were expressed, it cannot be assumed that a profile framework could merely be picked off the shelf and interpreted uniformly. It would seem then, that school-based induction programmes should begin with a number of professional conversations between mentor and NQT about what a profile of competence means to the parties involved – how they understand the particular document being used, to what extent they agree with it as an account of teaching and what they want to amend or emphasise. The profile can support and focus these conversations but cannot replace them and thus it would seem that competences cannot, on their own, fulfil the early promise of functioning as 'a bridge' between ITE and the first year of teaching.

As with any learning, the profile will depend for much of its success on the rapport which develops between NQT and mentor (a point emphasised by the mentors). This rests as much on the competence of the mentor to mentor (rather than teach) as it does on the receptiveness of the NQT. In addition, a process for using it has to be developed and proper time allocated. These in turn are not without their problems (see Chapter 3). To clarify the real professional demands on mentors, as well as NQTs, perhaps it is time to begin to develop a profile of mentor competence?

References

Carter, J., Devlin, P., Mahony, P. and Johnson, G. (1994) *Competence-based Approaches to Professional Development: Newly Qualified Teacher and Mentor Perspectives.* Wandsworth: LEA.

DfE (1992a) *'The Induction of Newly Qualified Teachers'*. Administrative Memorandum 2/92. London: HMSO.

DfE (1992b) *'Initial Teacher Training (Secondary Phase)'*, Circular 9/92. London: HMSO.

DfE (1993) *'The Initial Training of Primary School Teachers: New Criteria for Courses'*. Circular 14/93. London: HMSO.

Earley, P. (1992) *Beyond Initial Teacher Training: Induction and the Role of the LEA.* London: NFER.

Fullan, M. and Hargreaves, A. (1992) What's Worth Fighting For In Your School. Buckingham: Open University Press.

HMI (1992) *The Induction and Probation of New Teachers, 1988–1991.* London: HMI.

Kelly, G. (1955) *The Psychology of Personal Constructs.* New York: Norton.

Menter, I. and Whitehead, J. (1992) 'Response to request for information on mentoring', seminar paper, Bristol. (Unpublished observations.)

Murphy, R., Mahony, P. and Calderhead, J. (1993) 'Profiling teacher competences in initial teacher training', *Journal of Teacher Development*, **3** (2), 141–146.

Sidgwick, S., Mahony, P. and Hextall, I. (1993) 'Policy and practice in the professional development of teachers', *International Studies in the Sociology of Education*, **3** (1), 91–108.

Part Four:
Other Professions Approach Competences

12

The 'ASSET' Programme: The Development of a Competence-Based Honours Degree in Social Work

Richard Winter and Maire Maisch

Introduction

The idea of the ASSET (Accreditation of Social Services Expertise and Training) Programme was born in 1989, as part of a widespread concern to ensure that vocational education and training should derive directly from the needs of the workplace. The work of the NCVQ had begun to address these concerns at the lower levels of vocational activity, but little had then been done to explore the applicability of the emerging concepts of competence and work-place assessment at higher vocational and professional levels. At the same time, the professional validating body for Social Work, (the Central Council for Education and Training in Social Work, CCETSW), was seeking to develop a national post-qualifying framework of education and training which would be flexibly responsive to the needs both of employers and of the profession itself.

Anglia Polytechnic University was one of the first higher educational institutions to develop a modular credit based system across the whole of its course provision. It also had close collaborative links with Essex Social Services Department, which had a high commitment to training and was committed to reviewing and improving the operational benefit from this investment. As a result of this collaboration, and of the concerns which existed nationally and within Anglia, it became clear that a radical re-appraisal of existing modes of post-qualifying training was both necessary and feasible. It was agreed that a new and more appropriate model, which derived from the needs of the workplace and could be assessed within the operational context, could be generated. A proposal was therefore developed and submitted to the Higher Education Branch of the Employment Department, who agreed to fund the work.

The primary aim of the Project was to explore the viability of the work of the National Council for Vocational Qualifications in the context of 'Professional' Higher Education, to develop 'an advanced competency based, workplace assessed, modular and credit accumulation model of postqualifying education and training in social work in Essex'. In doing so, the project would meet the 'skills needs' of employers and entitle participants to the award of an academically validated degree. The project would, therefore, formulate a degree level vocational qualification in terms of workplace competences, and thus build a bridge between the procedures required for awarding academic credit and those required for accrediting vocational practice. At the same time, to ensure the transferability of the vocational credit which was awarded, the project would ensure that its sytems, procedures and outcomes articulated with the emerging national requirements for the award of professional credit.

Throughout the project, the Project Team worked very closely with the members of Essex SSD Training Section to ensure that the implications of the Project for the organisation's training development and delivery were recognised. The Project Team liaised with Social Services managers and assembled groups of practitioners to carry out a functional analysis of the professional social work task, and the tasks of specialist child care practitioners in particular. The results of this analysis were disseminated to a wider professional social work audience, and the products modified in the light of feedback. 'Core' assessment criteria (i.e. applicable throughout the programme) were generated from research undertaken, and these were related to an analysis of the concept of 'professional' development and to criteria used to indicate academic 'honours degree worthiness' in a variety of established honours degrees.

The Project Team had to explore the interface between this new model of training and development, the concerns of other sub-systems within the employer organisation (most notably the Planning, Inspectorate, and Research Sections) and the concerns of the Trade Union representing the staff. They also explored the relationship between the academic and professional aspects of these developments and the quality assurance, credit accumulation, and validation processes within the university.

Once these complex issues had been resolved in principle, and a comprehensive Student Handbook had been written as a support to work-based and self-directed study, a pilot study was established to test and refine the model of training and credit acquisition which had emerged.

The programme was formally validated in March 1992, and the first cohort of 30 participants from the Social Services Department began work on the Programme in September. In March 1995 the first 13 candidates were awarded their degree through these procedures. There are currently (in 1995) more than 80 social work staff enrolled on the programme, from Essex, Cambridge and Suffolk.

The ASSET Model of Professional Development and Training

The ASSET model (Figure 12.1) is a competence-referenced, work-place assesssed, modular method of training which incorporates the following characteristic components:

- *Modules*. Each module comprises a 'unit of competence' consisting of a set of competence statements ('elements of competence'). These were derived through a research process based on the functional analysis of employment competences described by groups of practitioners and validated by means of a questionnaire and by comparison with a study of practitioners' narratives of critical incidents.
- *Core Assessment Criteria* applicable to each unit of competence.
  These were derived through a research process consisting of:
  – a general theory of the nature of professional occupations, i.e. what they require in terms of ethical responsibilities, knowledge, interpersonal understanding, and continuous learning;
  – a study of examiners' reports upon Honours Degree examinations and course work, in a variety of vocational and academic fields;
  – a study of practitioners' rankings of their own lists of personal constructs concerning qualities required by the professional role;
- *Relevant Evidence* which may be submitted to demonstrate possession of the competences through fulfilment of the core assessment criteria.
- *A Module Action Plan* negotiated between the candidate, the work-place supervisor, and the tutor, which specifies the elements of competence in terms of the candidate's particular work context and responsibilities, and indicates how the assessment criteria will be fulfilled and what documentation will be developed as evidence. It will include plans for the candidate's practice to be observed, and may include plans for specific learning experiences.
- *Training Support*. The module action plan may prescribe various training experiences which will support candidates in acquiring or demonstrating the specified competences. These may include in-house training events, attendance at higher education courses, and 'structured professional experience' such as visits, consultations with specialist colleagues, and brief placements in relevant work contexts.
- *A Portfolio of Evidence*, containing evidence demonstrating each element of competence at the standard specified by the core assessment criteria.

- *Accreditation of Prior Learning*. Candidates are encouraged to submit authenticated evidence of prior certificated learning. Candidates may present this evidence initially, to claim exemption from a module or modules (up to half of the total programme). Evidence of prior *uncertificated* learning may be incorporated in the module portfolio, along with current practice-derived learning, to demonstrate the specified elements of competence.
- *Work-place Support*. The candidate's line manager may act as the official supervisor with responsibility for providing support for the work, and will be one party to the negotiation of the module action plan. All supervisors undertake training modules to prepare them for this support role, and this also earns credit within the award. The final assessment of the candidate's work is *not* carried out by their line manager but by *another* supervisor.
- *Peer Support Group*. All candidates are attached to a peer support group. Its purpose is to provide intellectual, emotional, and professional support. This may be on an informal basis, or (more frequently, as it has turned out) the peer group may be the main form of support for candidates undertaking modules, through a sequence of carefully structured meetings. In this case the role of the work-place supervisor is of reduced importance.
- *Academic Guidance*, concerning the general operation of the Programme procedures and up-do-date specialist information, provided by the tutor, i.e. professional training staff or higher education staff.
- *Assessment*. Elements of competence involving mainly evidence derived from workplace observation are assessed in the workplace by a supervisor (*not* the candidate's line manager) or by a member of the candidate's peer group, with guidance from the tutor. Elements of competence not including evidence from workplace observation are assessed by the tutor. When all elements are passed, the module is passed. When the requisite number of modules have been passed, the academic award is made and professional credits registered with the professional body.
- *Quality Assurance*. All assessment processes are subject to normal academic and professional quality assurance procedures.

Problems Encountered and How They Have Been Resolved

How Could the Appropriate Level of Work be Specified?

This was a major challenge: 'competence statements' describe requirements, but were we concerned with matters such as 'arrives punctually' or (alternatively) 'initiates organisational change'? The question of 'level' would be crucial for academic validation. We attempted to converge upon this issue through three different approaches:

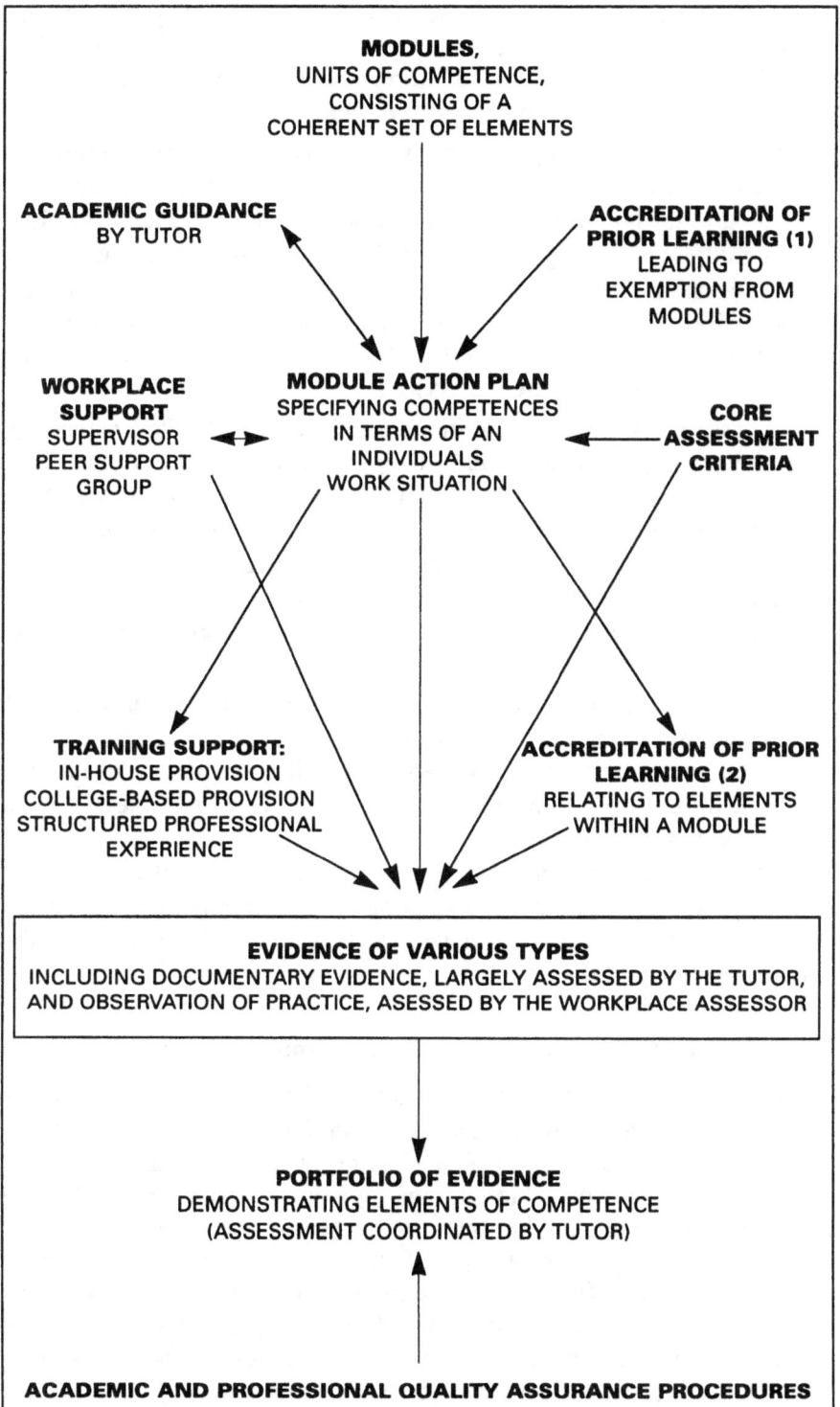

Figure 12.1 Relationships between the components of the model

1. We constructed an elaborate theoretical model of the specific nature of professional work, including: continuous learning through practice, awareness of the limitations of current expertise, affective awareness, and responsibility within a framework of values.

2. We carried out an empirical study of the categories used to identify 'Honours Degree' work by examiners in a variety of disciplines: Education, Nursing, Environmental Planning, Law, English Literature, and Biology. From a total of 150 examiners' reports about 80 phrases were collected (some positive, some negative), provisionally divided into qualities of communication, knowledge, argument, evaluation, activity, 'general qualities' (e,g., 'well-balanced') and intellectual processes.

3. We asked a group of practitioners to generate the key categories ('constructs') they used in thinking about their work and their colleagues (using the Kelly 'repertory grid' method). They were then asked to rank order these constructs in terms of their importance as required qualities for social work practice. A total of 29 qualities were ranked first or second (out of ten): some were practical, some were emotional, some were intellectual, but most were 'general' (e.g. 'positive', 'sensitive').

The results of these three studies were then integrated to produce a set of 'core assessment criteria' (see Appendix 1). This document is used throughout the assessment process and its detailed specifications provide a general indication of the sort of competences which are relevant for a degree-level professional award.

Used in this way, the core assessment criteria document also enabled us to tackle another problem: the adaptation of current university and social services department training provision so that it could be included in the assessment framework.

How Should we Decide the Content of the Training Modules?

An important principle for our work, taken from NCVQ and the Employment Department Standards Methodology Unit, was that the content of vocational curricula should be derived 'from employment'.

There is a danger that this may merely come to mean 'prescribed by industrial lead bodies', rather than 'prescribed by academics', but in our case it meant that the work was based on empirical studies with groups of practitioners, drawn from Essex and the London Borough of Greenwich SSDs. We asked them to describe the detailed requirements of their role in terms of its overarching purpose, i.e. (in the case of social work) 'to identify and provide for the needs of vulnerable groups and/or individuals'. This process ('functional analysis') was carried out twice, once with mixed groups of practitioners (to create 'general social work' modules) and once with child care practitioners (to create 'child care' modules). Altogether, 52 practitioners took part in these initial discussions, and the first draft of the descriptive analysis was amended in the light of comments from a further 175 staff.

This does not mean that the module content is a verbatim reproduction of practitioners' descriptions; a considerable amount of rephrasing and reorganisation was necessary to obtain a consistent style and structure. Nor does it mean that the modules simply describe what social workers actually do; the process of functional analysis (moving continually from general purposes to specific requirements) encouraged staff to articulate a sort of 'practical ideal' – a version of their work which is both demanding and realistic, and can thus provide a set of feasible objectives for developmental work.

The results of the functional analysis were checked by means of comparison with another empirical study. Practitioners were asked to write about a 'critical incident' from their recent practice, and these accounts were then analysed in terms of professional decision-making issues, using the method of 'dilemma analysis' (see Winter, 1982). Comparison showed a satisfactory degree of overlap between the results of the two approaches. The final stage of the work was to organise the practitioners' statements into units which (as the Standards Methodology Unit Guidelines suggested) would be large enough to have 'independent value' in employment and small enough to constitute a manageable commitment for a full-time staff member. For this, the modular units of the Anglia Polytechnic University credit accumulation system (based on a notional 75 hours of student learning) provided a helpful structure. (A sample module, showing the texture of the competence statements, is given in Appendix 2.)

What is the Appropriate Format for the Presentation of Competences?

ASSET competences (see Appendix 2) are not presented in the NCVQ orthodox format of elements, performance criteria, and range statements. There are good reasons for this:

- Practitioners' statements did not become progressively more concrete as they described what their role required; after a certain point they invoked the continual need to exercise discretionary judgement, in the light of underlying professional aims and values.
- The assessment criteria are therefore embodied in a set of 'core' criteria which elaborates the general level of the work. These criteria must be fully met in the work for each module: each element must implicitly conform to all of them and must also explicitly demonstrate fulfilment of at least one of them. In this way the 'atomisation' of 'performance criteria' is avoided.

- The texture of professional work involves a continuous combination of intellectual, ethical, and affective awareness. Realistic and workable competence statements need to preserve the unity of this texture, rather than segregating value judgements as 'performance criteria' and treating 'personal skills' as separate from the requirements of practice.
- 'Range statements' are too simplistic a treatment of the relationship between individual instances and general capabilities; insistence on a comprehensive 'range' may be quite unrealistic, given the special focus of an individual's practice. Instead, therefore, the ASSET Programme requires individual candidates to draw up a detailed 'module action plan' (MAP), which 'maps' the general requirements of the module competence statements onto the details of their recent and/or forthcoming practice. What sort of evidence is required (and how much of it) thus becomes a matter for negotiation, planning, and fine judgement.

How can Workplace Competences be Academically Assessed?

There were two aspects to this problem: (i) the question of evidence and (ii) the question of 'grading'.

The Nature of Appropriate Evidence

An assessor's report of a practice observation in the candidate's workplace is the form of evidence which receives overwhelming emphasis in the NCVQ literature. But professional work always involves making important decisions, and these always need careful documentation, in case of future queries (or even litigation), so that other forms of evidence, which are just as much part of the candidate's 'practice', are readily available. We therefore began by drawing up a long list of all the different types of evidence (more or less directly arising from practice) which candidates could present to demonstrate the required competences. This created for candidates a helpful sense that they had control over the assessment process.

However, in order to ensure that candidates could have access to the files relating to their previous work, we found it necessary to ask the Department to make an official statement to the effect that work for the Programme constituted a legitimate professional interest and was compatible with normal rules of confidentiality. We also found that we did not need to introduce a separate category of evidence concerning 'knowledge-and-understanding': since this is always implicit in professional practice, it is frequently inherent in the competence statements; alternatively it can be made explicit by the writing of a brief 'commentary', explaining how the documentary evidence (a) demonstrates the competence statement and (b) fulfils one or other of the core asssessment criteria.

The Question of Grading

In many ways this was the single most difficult problem of the whole project. On the one hand the classifications of an honours degree enforce normative grading: a few 'outstanding', rather more 'above average', most 'average', and a smallish number of 'relatively weak'. On the other hand the NCVQ/Employment Department model of competence requires criterion-referenced (pass/not-yet-pass) assessment, and social work professionals gave powerful reasons for the inappropriateness of giving a grade or a percentage mark for practice in the workplace. Our proposed solution to these dilemmas has four aspects:

1. We offer candidates a choice between two alternative awards: an honours degree and a 'graduate diploma of professional studies'. The degree will involve them in having their work graded, whereas the graduate diploma (equivalent to the degree in all but name) is awarded on a pass/fail basis only, which allows them to avoid grading at the cost of gaining a qualification whose academic status is slightly ambiguous.
2. We instituted two stages of assessment:
    (a) The assessment of individual elements of competence (which may involve the observation of practice by a colleague) where the question is simply: has the candidate presented sufficient evidence?
    (b) The assessment of the module as a whole, which is carried out by the tutor and which may or may not be graded, depending on the award sought by the candidate.
3. Consequently, we needed rules concerning the ratio of workplace observation to 'other' evidence, as follows. On the one hand, to ensure overall 'practice relevance', all modules (for both awards) must include at least one element where the evidence mainly derives from workplace observation, and at least one recording (audio or video) of practice. On the other hand, to ensure that, where candidates seek the honours degree, the final grading is based on a sufficient proportion of the work to be acceptable to the university senate, no more than two elements in any one module may be based on workplace observation.
4. Assessors may continue to give formative feedback to candidates, on a 'pass'/'insufficient-evidence-as-yet' basis until either the work is passed on to a second assessor for the final assessment (who may still return it for further work) or the maximum period of registration for

the module elapses. (The candiate is only allowed to register twice for the same module; when the maximum period elapses for the second time, the module is deemed to have been failed. However, this maximum period is set at several times the anticipated average period of time required for the work.)

How Can Candidates Manage the Operational Pressures of the Workplace in order to Prioritise their own Professional Development?

Everyone who participated in the pilot programme found it unexpectedly difficult to set aside the necessary time to work on the Programme because of the intense and continuous pressures of the workplace, i.e. the permanent inadequacy of available resources in relation to clients' needs. A starting point here is the managerial issue: managers, one might say, need to give a lead in supporting practitioners' attempts to prioritise their own training. But how can this be achieved? To say that we need to 'change attitudes' or 'change organizational culture' expresses the problem, not the solution. Where would we look for the 'levers' for such changes?

In any case, the participants did not blame managers; they blamed themselves for their own 'lack of self-discipline', but this only points to a further dimension of the problem. In a work situation which is so highly determined by external deadlines, it actually may be very stressful to be given, suddenly, so much responsibility for organising one's own time and to decide upon one's own purposes. Perhaps, therefore, one side-effect of the Programme was to reveal to participants the extent to which they had been socialised into dependency upon the very external pressures which they resented. In this way, a Programme one of whose key purposes was to enhance morale through providing an opportunity for staff to take control of their own professional development could result, ironically, in undermining participants' self-confidence. This has alerted us to the fact that 'flexibility' and 'freedom' are not simply unmixed blessings but one side of a general motivational ambiguity with which the Programme procedures will have to come to terms, if it is to succeed.

Advantages of The ASSET Model

The ASSET model attempts to combine the clear expression of standards with the flexibility and complexity of professional levels of employment. It is based upon a recognition that the workplace ought to be the main resource for professional learning and attempts to specify the arrangements which will be needed if this recognition is to become a reality. As a result, the model has a number of positive and distinctive features:

- Its competence statements have been derived from practitioners' statements and extensively checked and revised through a widely

distributed questionnaire to staff.
- The module action plan preserves a substantial degree of individualisation within the guidelines and objectives laid down by the competence statements.
- The list of core assessment criteria provides a full indication of the level of work required, and draws its authority from an elaborate research process. It is used systematically to provide a unique but fundamentally straightforward 'two-dimensional' assessment process.

The procedures of the model provide a coherent framework for:

- demonstrating that practice already meets required standards of competence;
- planning further learning which will enable required standards of competence to be met;
- demonstrating the relevance of prior learning.

By focusing the learning process on employment practice, the model avoids the necessity for lengthy secondments, and thus widens the opportunity for accredited and supported professional development. It thus has a potential for contributing to equal opportunities policies, to access policies, and to the improvement of staff morale.

'Conclusion' – Issues Arising From The Project

An innovatory general model of the relationship between training and professional practice has been developed, which combines some procedures derived from NCVQ with others derived from higher education practices. The model is now established and has been successfully established in the area of social work, and is currently being piloted in the area of engineering, through a partnership between the university and the Ford Motor Company (The Ford ASSET Programme – 'Accreditation and Support for Specified Expertise and Training').

However, there were and remain a number of issues which the project to date has highlighted but has not been able to resolve:

- The priority which operational (as opposed to training) branches of organisations give to staff learning and assessment activities remains problematic. So long as managers regard 'training' as an encapsulated activity which is removed from or remote from operational realities and needs, this will continue to be the case even where, as in the case of the ASSET Programme, the learning and training takes place within the work place and is assessed in relation to its practice implications.
- Most Programme participants are accustomed to the insulated and structured world of traditional training events or courses – many of which, historically, have had no formal assessment requirement. When faced with the need to generate, within the workplace, evidence of the

learning which they have achieved, they are brought face to face with the dilemma that, to do so, they must divert time and emotional energy away from a direct response to pressing operational needs.

Hence, two general questions can be posed, which relate to the ASSET model and indeed to the work-based NCVQ model of training:

1. Under what conditions does it actually (as opposed to theoretically) become 'easier' to undertake vocational/professional development in the workplace, rather than in a location which is insulated against the pressures of the workplace, i.e. a 'classroom'?
2. What is the relationship between models of professional training and development and the structure of operational and managerial roles within an organisation?

However, what continues to inspire the programme team is the unremitting enthusiasm of the participating practitioners, whose commitment is manifested in the high quality of their work for the Programme, and this in turn inspires confidence that the ideal of 'relevant' and 'effective' professional training can – in the end – be embodied in a genuinely 'educative workplace'.

Acknowledgements

The ASSET Programme was funded by the Employment Department; their help and support throughout the work was invaluable.

This chapter is based on the official Programme Report published in 1992, written by Richard Winter and Maire Maisch in conjunction with Paul Stanton and Anne Hilton.

Further information about the ASSET Programme, including a set of project research papers, can be obtained from the Chelmsford campus of Anglia Polytechnic University. A book describing and discussing the Programme in detail, *Professional Competence and Higher Education: The ASSET Programme* by Richard Winter and Maire Maisch, is to be published by Falmer Press in 1996.

References

Winter, J. (1982) 'Dilemma analysis – a contribution to methodology for action research', *Cambridge Journal of Education*, **12** (3).

Appendix 1: List of Core Assessment Criteria

NOTE: All criteria must be implicitly demonstrated in the evidence for each element in each module; the evidence for each element must be explicitly related to one of the criteria; particular attention should be paid to criterion number 1 throughout the work.

CRITERION 1: 'Commitment to Professional Values'

Demonstrates understanding of and commitment to professional values in practice, through the implementation of anti-discriminatory/anti-oppressive/anti-racist principles.

This involves demonstrating:

- awareness of the need to counteract one's own tendency (both as a person and as a professional worker endowed with specific powers) to behave oppressively;
- respect for dignity/diversity/privacy/autonomy;

CRITERION 2: 'Continuous Professional Learning'

Demonstrates commitment to and capacity for reflection on practice, leading to progressive deepening of professional understanding.

This involves demonstrating:

- willingness and capacity to learn from others, including clients/supervisees/colleagues;
- recognition that professional judgements are always open to question;
- ability to engage in self-evaluation, recognising and analysing one's strengths and limitations.

CRITERION 3: 'Affective Awareness'

Demonstrates sensitivity to and understanding of the emotional complexity of particular situations.

This involves combining sensitivity with effective management of emotional responses in the course of professional relationships.

CRITERION 4: 'Effective Communication'

Demonstrates ability to communicate effectively in complex professional contexts.

This involves communicating in a form and manner which is clear, sensitive, and appropriately varied in style and medium according to particular audiences and purposes.

CRITERION 5: *'Executive Effectiveness'*

Demonstrates ability to pursue the stages of a chosen approach in relation to a clearly established purpose.

This involves demonstrating decisiveness combined with sensitivity in making difficult judgements in response to complex situations.

CRITERION 6: *'Effective Grasp of a Wide Range of Professional Knowledge'*

Demonstrates an understanding of the relationship between various types of professional knowledge, and an ability to apply this understanding effectively through practice.

This involves demonstrating:

- comprehensive knowledge and critical evaluation of professional methods/policy/procedures/general theory/research findings/ legislation;
- ability to relate specific details to other contexts and to general principles.

CRITERION 7: *'Intellectual Flexibility'*

Demonstrates an open-minded awareness of alternatives.

This comprises demonstrating the ability to analyse issues in terms of dilemmas and/or to analyse situations in terms of continuous change.

Appendix 2: General Module 7 (Unit of Competence 7) Planning, Delivering, and Evaluating Intervention

Elements of Competence

To demonstrate this unit of competence, candidates need to:

1. Assess the client's situation in relation to their needs and to available resources, legal and statutory provisions, and departmental systems and policies; and decide whether intervention is appropriate.
2. Involve the client and others in making a comprehensive plan, analysing short-term and long-term implications (financial, social, and personal).

3. Argue persuasively to colleagues and managers for the validity of the planned intervention, while remaining open to others' interpretations, and add any agreed amendments.
4. Interpret statutory provisions in relation to a particular practice situation, and exercise appropriate statutory and discretionary powers.
5. Analyse the limitations of current views and policies concerning resources.
6. Evaluate the outcomes of the planned intervention and re-negotiate client's agreement with goals, methods, and evaluation criteria.
7. Manage the dilemmas arising from tensions between personal, professional, and community values and local and national policies, to negotiate acceptable courses of action.
8. Recognise and explore strategies for handling the stress arising from the relationship between the client's emotional conflicts and the worker's responsibilities.

13

Exploring Competence in Nursing and Midwifery

John Schostak

The changes that have taken place in social expectations over the last quarter century have placed ever-increasing demands upon professionals. As new visions of 'professionality' have taken the stage, so debates about what it means to be competent have taken place between those who would defend older positions and those who argue for the new. In nursing and midwifery these debates were stimulated by the introduction of Project 2000 in nursing and pre-registration diploma direct entry for midwifery. These changes were not just about raising the qualifications of the nurses and midwives but about re-defining the nature of the occupations in professional terms. Putting it in crudely simplified terms: for nurses, the change could be characterised as one from being 'handmaidens to doctors' to becoming increasingly independent problem solvers and decision makers. Midwives could argue – although some would dispute it occurred in practice – that they have always enjoyed an independence of decision making. Nevertheless, there is a parallel move to be discerned in the direction of increasing professional autonomy. In each case, educational changes have focused upon the development of generic care, holistic approaches, care in the community, placing the client's needs at the centre of decision making. It would be difficult to overstate the extent and the complexities of the changes and the pressures that staff have endured during the 1980s and 1990s. Suffice to say that these have been enormous. Although the effects of the changes are far from being over, I think it would be true to say that the ways in which educational and clinical staff have responded place these professions at the forefront of any debate on strategies for educating professionals in practice. Since decisions in these professional areas may mean the difference between life and death this adds a particular edge and intensity surrounding the debates. Focusing principally upon two projects – ACE and TYDE – in nursing and midwifery I want to explore the relation between professional action and decision making and what it means to be competent.

The ACE Project was funded by the English National Board for Nursing, Midwifery and Health Visiting (ENB) during the period July 1991 to June 1993.[1] Its object was to explore issues relating to the assessment of competence on all the branches relating to Project 2000 and non-diploma courses in nursing and both diploma and non-diploma 18-month post-registration midwifery courses. Fieldwork was carried out in East Anglia, London and the North East. Although the project in no way attempted to paint a national picture the nine colleges of nursing and midwifery and their associated student placement areas provided a rich and useful data base more fully reported in Bedford *et al.* (1993).

The TYDE project[2] was much larger in scope, attempting to cover *all* 3-year undergraduate programmes in nursing and midwifery and a range of 4-year programmes (Bedford *et al.*, 1994). This project extended the debates about competence from diploma to graduate levels. It raised the simple yet oddly disturbing question: so, what's the difference between diploma levels of practice and graduate levels? This in turn raised the uncomfortable possibility that graduate care might be considered by a client to be more competent than diploma level care hence leading to potential legal issues about the quality of care in a given case. Any answer to such an array of issues has to delve deeply into the nature of professional action, an issue that the project could only hope to raise and sketch exploratory approaches and outline issues for debate not answer.

What is Competence?

To say a professional is competent has a comforting ring, particularly if the client is facing major surgery. Comforting or not, competence is an elusive quality to define for purposes of assessment. Ask what people mean by competence and answers will often be vague and conflicting. At a minimum we were frequently told that a competent professional must at least be safe to practice. However, what exactly did that mean? It could refer to having the up-to-date knowledge, skills, attitudes and confidence necessary to engage in particular procedures. However, when asking for concrete examples it was clear that an action considered safe in one situation and its particular context might not be safe in another. An action defined safe by one side of a debate or professional sub-group could be branded unsafe or inadequate by another. Thus there was no recipe list which could be applied to all situations in all contexts that was true for all parties in a given area of professional debate. In short, the meaning of 'safe' is open to interpretation. So open, in fact, that it may have no essential meaning and should not beg the question that 'competence' is some real entity or phenomenon; rather it may be more like a unicorn, a mythical construct. As with all mythical constructs, the effects of belief may well be real in their consequences but that is quite different from saying the construct itself has a real referent. We began our quest in that spirit:

> The study of the assessment of competence would seem straightforward if it were not that considerable controversy and confusion over what is to count as 'competence' takes place at every level in the system. One way of beginning the analysis of the 'assessment of competence' is to ask such questions as:
>
> - what function it serves within a symbolic system or social process
> - how it is related to other elements or features
> - how it is accomplished as a practical activity
>
> What characterises human activity is its symbolic dimension. That is to say, it is not enough just to observe a behaviour or an action, one has to ask what it means within a complex system of thought and action. Key concepts are regulative agents in a system. In other words, they generate order, they give a pattern to behaviour such that each element is related to each other element. Every element can be analysed for its function in the system. Meaning, however, is not open to inspection like a physical object. What is said is not always what is meant. What one intends to mean is not always what is interpreted by others to mean the same thing. The intended outcome of an action may have unforeseen consequences because it has been variously interpreted, or because the system is so complex it defies accurate prediction. (Bedford *et al.*, 1993:11)

Nevertheless the notion of competence remains a useful focus for organising discussion about definitions from different perspectives: clinical and educational staff, managers, students and various professional and official bodies. In our interviews and analyses of course and assessment documentation we found versions and combinations of all of the following:

- a set of behaviours that can be analysed in functional terms;
- a set of legal or quasi-legal demands/criteria;
- a set of course, assessment and other institutional texts setting out agreed criteria;
- a particular discourse that is employed inside or outside of particular occupational cultures to legitimate or justify professional decision making and action;
- a dialogic or critically reflective process through which theories/ hypotheses/values are contested in order to develop and maintain professional practice;
- a convenient myth covering a hotch-potch of views and practices, or referring only to a contemporary subject of debate amongst professionals serving only to displace critical attention from the real issues of social, cultural and political life to which professionals should be attending.

Myth or not, frameworks for thinking about and assessing competence abound whether these are academic, official, unofficial. At that level, competence is a social reality or construct, if not real in itself, then real in its effects in terms of people organising activities with reference to something they label 'competence'. There is, in a sense, something of an inversion in this approach to understanding competence. It may be that competence is a 'null concept', a 'hole', a 'void' the purpose of which is to have no essential meaning so that it can be used as a justifying principle for social action. This is perhaps rather like the 'x' in an equation such as $2 + x = 4$, or $1 + x = 4$. The number to be filled at 'x' varies in the interests of ensuring that both sides of the equation equal out. It is a tautologous system, self-referring, self-defining:

> We're competent as a qualified nurse because we've satisfied the system that requires us to demonstrate it. We've passed the assessments etc so therefore we are competent. That's one definition.
> (ACE^3: education manager: p.33)

Debunking the term may mean that in no longer being dazzled by its ideological and political importance, we see that action 'x' is called competent when it does not disturb the tranquility of the norm, the expected, the vested interest in ensuring that all the paper-work at the end of the day adds up. The norm, of course, can be constructed in a multiplicity of different ways. It can be done through a professional body such as the UKCC or the ENB, or a governmental body such as the DoH. Or it can be constructed through a process of research which would perhaps involve asking various 'experts', or those that peers identify as models of good practitioners, to give their accounts of good practice, to tell their stories of good decision making, to provide descriptions of what makes a good practitioner and so on. From this can be produced various impressively detailed categories and sub-categories that in turn can be reduced to theoretical frameworks involving say cognitive, emotional, behavioural, social dimensions in producing a model of professional competence. Whatever such strategy is employed, if it is essentially self-referential (that is, professionals define who is professional and what counts as professional) no matter how sophisticated and complex the twists and turns may be, it does not escape the circularity of its tautological structure.

If competence is only about ensuring that every action is accounted for within the accepted formulae for defining competence, then the fact of the client dying because a life-saving action outside the formula was required may be a matter of regret but it is not a matter of incompetence. This may be a cynical view of 'competence' but it is one which is implicit in much talk about 'public accountability': it is about 'covering your back' and at worst about finding an appropriate scapegoat.

In short, then, to call some action competent has as a key function the role of legitimising it, or at least seeking to legitimise it. At this point it acts within an institution, a professional association, and a system as a unifying device for organising beliefs, actions, and general professional discourses. It becomes a grand 'X', a symbol in the sense of a national flag which the mere act of waving in times of war is enough to rally people to one side or the other, enough to lead people to offer their lives in the service of the flag. If asked, who would stand up and publicly say that 'competence' is not something that professionals should strive to attain? Competence as understood in this way has less to do with safety, good decision making or life saving action and more to do with the legitimation, and politics of professionalisation, of showing 'whose side you're on'. If this is so, then to seek to define the competence of an individual is to miss the point, a very complex point. In this view, competence is not an *individual* attribute of some kind, it is an *intersubjective* framework for organising experience, knowledge, interpretation, understanding, judgement, decision making and action. This shift from individual performance to intersubjective frameworks-for-analysis is important because it effects the choice of an appropriate paradigm within which to develop educational strategies and post-qualification professional development and to define and implement the task of assessment.

Identifying Paradigms

Check-lists of competences are increasingly being seen as not the answer:

> I mean generally people I think in nurse education aren't happy with competency based training. We think it concentrates on performance, skills, the technician... and doesn't take sufficient account of the development of the individual. The cognitive, the intellectual, the reflective practitioner. And certainly this is a worry since one of the major things about Project 2000 ... at Diploma level, is that it strives to develop cognitive and intellectual skills which enable the person to be reflective, a critical change agent at the point of practice, but also someone who can resource their own learning, their own continuing education and direct that and influence all of those things as an equal partner with all sorts of other professions. And I'm not sure that the competences necessarily reflect that side of the professional role...either of them (pause) is certainly better but I think the very fact that they are still cold competences, which has a very clear manual task related definition.
> (ACE: p.36)

In this one extract we see the effects on thinking of two distinct paradigms. The 'cold competences' paradigm being largely rejected in this particular extract we called behavioural or technicist[4] and were essentially quantitative in approach:

> Technicist and behaviourist approaches to the assessment of competence are

predicated on the notion that predictability of outcome is possible in human activity. They assume situations sufficiently controllable to enable learning to be measured in terms of pre-specified outcomes.
(ACE)

These approaches focused upon the individual and the activities of the individual in terms of observable, measurable, controllable factors. Its earliest exponents included the 'scientific management' of Taylor (1947); the behaviourism of Watson (1931) and then Skinner (1953); the mental measurement of people such as Burt (1947), Thorndike (1910) and Yerkes (1929); and the kinds of programmed learning advocated by Gagné (1975), the influence of which can still be seen even in the more visually sophisticated computer aided learning of today (see Fox *et al.*, 1992); Schostak 1988). In a medical context this is clearly illustrated by Dunn *et al.* (1985:17):

> ... competence must be placed in a context, precise and exact, in order for it to be clear what is meant. To say a person is competent is not enough. He is competent to do a, or a and b, or a and b and c: a and b and c being aspects of a doctors work.

Such lists of procedures, skills and knowledge which an individual must be competent to do or know about can be almost indefinitely expanded (Bloom 1954, 1956 are early examples; see also Evans, 1987; Medley, 1984).

The problems inherent in these approaches were summarised in the ACE report as:

> Firstly it splits the 'expert' theorist from the practitioner who becomes the person who *applies* theory that can be assessed. Secondly, it places greater emphasis on the assessment of performance criteria than it does on the assessment of knowledge. Thirdly, it fails to take any account of the complexity and dynamism of human interaction and organisational processes.
> (p.25)

In contrast the alternative paradigm took its focus to be not measurement but meaning, interpretation, reflection, dialogue and emphasised:

> actors as agents in their own definitions of and approaches to competence and its assessment. Appropriate structures with their mechanisms and procedures to produce desired outcomes are developed by reflection upon workplace practice. Such structures are continually negotiated and redefined because work is both dynamic and situationally specific.
> (p.25)

Both kinds of paradigm could be found underlying nursing and midwifery assessment practices. The story of nursing and midwifery over the last decade is one of transitions and of oscillations between transition points at a multiplicity of levels. It is not a story of smooth, clear transitions and transformations as may be told in fairy stories of frogs becoming princes and cinderellas becoming princesses. These are stories told by politicians at press conferences. The full complexity of these changes is a story that cannot be told here. The central transition which places into full focus the debate on competence is the move from apprenticeship to reflective practitioner.

Quantitative approaches are more easily applied to occupations which can identify clear procedures, behavioural skills and routines. They become increasingly difficult to apply to occupations which demand such *qualities* as flexibility, judgement, and risk taking in unpredictable arenas and contexts for action. When nursing, for example, was conceived of as a handmaiden role for doctors, then the premium was on nurses having serviceable skills that a doctor could rely on. As nursing has become increasingly complex in its scope with the focus on decision making and the construction of care plans so the notion of competence has shifted from observable categories of behaviour or performance to broad themes. The example from a midwifery assessment schedule shown in Figure 13.1 is typical in that it takes a broad theme which is not fully specified. The judgement is left to what may be called an 'accredited witness', that is, a qualified assessor. The burden of judgement is thus shifted from exact specification in the document to professional judgement by an accredited judge.

> In this example, an agreement between assessor and student defines whether the 'competency' has or has not been met. There is the potential for greater triangulation of views, but once signed, there is no further evidence available for an independent examiner. The validity of the assessment is thus still dependent upon the credibility of accredited witnesses.
> (ACE: p. 69)

The 'accredited witness' became an issue within the ACE report. What it meant was that the only evidence that a competency had or had not been achieved was the accredited witness whose signature appeared on the documentation. The training and trustworthiness of the accredited witness thus became crucial since no other independent evidence existed that could be reassessed by an external moderator. Indeed, the research showed that the quality of 'accredited witnesses' varied considerably raising the disquieting issue that unsuitable, even dangerous[5], students may well pass. To increase the evidence base the following alternative approach dispenses with the listing of categories that can be ticked and instead provides general statements as follows:

> The nurse assists the client, as an individual or in partnership with the family, with daily living skills and activities.

(Performance criteria)
Performs a post natal examination, explains the significance of the findings to the midwife, gives correct advice to the mother in relation to:

	Intermediate interview (formative) achieved/not achieved				Final interview (summative) achieved/not achieved			
S = student								
M = midwife								
achieved								
	S	M	M	S	M	S	M	S
signed								

breasts	– prevention of nipple damage suppression of lactation
abdomen	– involution of the uterus abdominal tone
perineum	– healing, hygiene
lochia	– changes
legs	– oedema, tenderness

competency achieved:

signature:..

date:..

Figure 13.1 Midwifery assessment schedule

This then is supplemented with a list of sub-statements:

- maintaining high standards of nursing care;
- Assisting with the activities of living to promote self-care and reduce dependence;
- others are listed.

Instructions are given in the student profile document as to how to proceed. A series of interviews is required where 'the learning needs and expected learning outcomes will be discussed and mutually agreed'. Completion of the document requires all experience gained and teaching given during the placement to be recorded in the appropriate section.
(ACE: p.69)

Increasingly, the burden of proof is shifting from ticks on an assessment document, to the provision of evidence that can be independently re-examined. The learning contract is perhaps the most developed version of this approach to date. For example, page one of a contract asked three basic open-ended questions:

- What have I achieved to date that is relevant to this module?
- What do I need to achieve during this module?
- What did I achieve during this module?

Page two and subsequent pages of the document were structured in terms of three broad parallel columns with the headings:

- Objectives to include competences.
- Resources and strategies achievement.
- Evidence and standards for reflection.

> The contract was set out on large A4 pages, the blank areas to be filled in by the student and validated by an assigned member of staff. The space available for the student was sufficient to allow the development of an essay. Objectives and competences were identified and discussed in relation to resources and strategies. Completed examples showed the inclusion of descriptions of practices and experiences, supported by referencing of relevant literature. As a result, the final product was very close to being a research based assignment. There was a very considerable body of evidence provided as to what exactly a student accomplished, together with integrated understanding of the knowledge informing that practice.
> (ACE: p. 73)

Where the demand by the behavioural/technicist paradigm for clarity and exactness implies intolerance for ambiguity, 'greyness', uncertainty – all aspects of actual everyday situations, the alternative paradigm explicitly recognises the 'messiness' of social life and everyday practice. In doing so, the simple lists of performance criteria prove to be inadequate to the complexity of the process of professional action and reflection. Thus the discourse of competence is increasingly replaced by a broader more complex discourse of dialogue, debate, critique, evidence.

Apprenticeship and the Reflective Practitioner

It could be argued that training prior to Project 2000 was essentially that of an apprenticeship. Hence a substantial change is implicit in removing the centre of training from the clinical setting to that of the college or university. It subverts workplace apprenticeship. Nevertheless, it raises the question, how can one be assured that the new forms of training will still lead to qualified people who are competent to perform safely when as previously argued check-lists of competences are not enough?

The issue is quite difficult to conceptualise in any clear and distinct way. The move to a discourse of reflective practice has, on the one hand, what may be called a hermeneutic rather than an analytic structure; and on the other, an existential rather than an abstract form. This double structure has the effect of locating a given *person* within a *concrete context* rather than a role (analysable into functions, procedures and duties) which is in a formal abstract structure (specifying role relations, mechanisms and laws or rules). What is drawn into the debate is a notion of self reflexivity which is loosened from the narrower confines of what counts as professional competence:

> I feel a lot of the time nurses lose sight of the prime reason that they are there, and that is the patient. Because it's so easy to do because there's so much else going on. And a professional person is able to constantly pull themselves and say, 'Now hang on, what am I doing? Where am I going? It's not good enough just to measure myself against the competences and say, "Oh well I come up to that standard".'
> (ACE: p. 38)

The argument implicit here is that professionality is a continuous process of critical interrogation of action in light of the 'prime reason'. What ever the prime reason is, it must operate as a rationale, a *raison d'être* which:

- unifies experience, that is, draws it all under one significant umbrella of apparent coherence, defining the professional quest as 'Now hang on, what am I doing?' in relation to the 'prime reason';
- gives meaning to professional and personal life;
- situates the professional within a binary relationship: that is, professional and patient/client.

The intellectual framework within which this thinking takes its meaning has been informed recently at a general level by Schön (1987) and at a more specific level by Benner (1982, 1983, 1984). However, does it reduce or increase the role of apprenticeship? The neophyte who begs entrance needs above all recognition that they too 'look like' a professional. What better way than to model one's self upon the other who has achieved such a status in the eyes of other professionals and of clients/patients? Apprenticeship, whether formal or informal in nature, satisfies such an existential need to locate oneself in an occupational discourse and is hence resurrected in the reflective practitioner model:

> She's the sort of midwife I would like to be. She doesn't rupture membranes and apply scalp electrodes unless there's a need for it. But the women are always given an option, everything is discussed with them, she always finds out what they want first and will always comply with their wishes as far as she can... Things like pain relief you can have a big influence on that by the rapport you establish. I've seen Kay talk to women with first babies who haven't needed any pain relief at all, which to me is pretty impressive. Whereas with other midwives it's, 'I think you need an epidural', just because it's easier for them, they don't have to give all the support. ... Some (midwives) will get in an epidural and wheel in a television so they don't have to talk to them. You just sit there and think, 'Oh God, I don't want to be here.'
> (ACE: p.103)

This is a very typical kind of account, which through its conversational structure situationally and existentially locates self and other into a workplace matrix of subject positions, actions, procedures, typical events and so on as competence is again seen to be an intersubjective matrix which positions individuals into such subjective slots as neophyte, beginner, advanced beginner, proficient, competent, expert and even model practitioner as key professional positions together with creating further slots such as layperson, client (including bad client, troublesome client, ideal client and so on) and patient. These 'slots' organise the form of reflection that will take place in terms of: e.g., 'am I like or not like person "x" who is considered 'competent/incompetent' by person "y" who is an authority on the situation or "my examiner/employer"? Placing the matrices of subject positions for work, competence and assessment together there is then a multiple axis for the situating of individuals into organisational and professional space which can generate a kind of fusion or merging of performance, work, occupational discourses and competence which are summed up as 'experience':

> ... some of the skills come with experiences of life and I think intuitiveness. I could work with a student and I could say, 'What do you see in this patient?' and the student could say, 'Well she looks fine.' Now intuitively I might say, 'Well I don't think she is' and I can't explain why I think that. It's come with experience...so that I don't think can be taught. That is something that has to be acquired throughout as they go on.
> (ACE; staff nurse: p.39)

The clarity and distinction yearned for by positivists and outcomes measurers of all denominations becomes untenable in the face of this kind of ineffability involving intuition, 'experience', a 'something' to be acquired. If we were describing the action of steam engines all would be relatively simple. At least there would seem some commonsense basis for talking about cause and effect. However, in the world of social action even if knowing all the variables and how each effected the other were possible it would not necessarily help to predict appropriate courses of action. This is because social action occurs in a 'strange place'. The place in question is made strange in the sense that it does not exist in a physical location as such. Its space is that of the virtual reality, the symbolic universe of meanings, values, understandings, beliefs. It is a space where there are no laws equivalent to the laws of gravity or of mechanical cause-effect. The apple that hit Newton was not acting ironically, nor arbitrarily, nor whimsically. People do. Social space is textured through levels of meaning, plays of meaning, repressions and denials of meaning. Intentions are masked, erased, transformed. Nothing is stable, univocal, identical throughout time. In this universe competence is:

> transient. I think it (pause) you glide in and out of competence and I don't think you have it for ever and a day erm and yet our notion of it really is that when

you're competent that's it and you always are forever more, so it needs nurturing.
(ACE)

It may be the case that a tree will still materially exist if there is no one left to think of it, but what about competence? Its very nature (or 'materiality') is that of an intersubjective thought construct. It needs continual nurturing through conversation, the construction of repertoires of discourse about competence else it will not exist.

Being a reflective practitioner does nothing to alter the fact that one is situated by prevailing discourses of competence, professionality and those of particular occupational and organisational cultures. It is the attitude of the reflective practitioner that matters. It is here that educational action makes the difference. Students may be socialised through identification with a master/expert to fit better the prevailing norms and frameworks. Or they may be educated to generate the critical attitude necessary to reveal the inherent contradictions, confusions, obfuscations and conflicts underlying everyday situations and hence reduce the power of the master–apprentice relationship. The difference can be analysed in the process of case comparison and contrast that was developed in the TYDE project (Bedford *et al.*, 1994) as a way of modelling the reflective process in practice as follows:

> Having decided that particular features of the current situation are sufficiently like a previous set of comparable cases then options for possible courses of action can be identified and assessed in the light of their suitability for the current case given its particular features. The course of action chosen is then monitored to see the extent to which it leads to predicted outcomes or solutions. If there are differences from the expected then a further search of comparisons and contrasts with previous cases is set in train and modifications made. This process of case comparison provides an account of what may be called dynamic case generalisation and can be schematised (as shown in Figure 13.2).
>
> In the diagram (Figure 13.1) case 1 (c1) is identified as sharing similarities with both c2 and c3 and the current case. These similarities offer solutions s1 as associated with case 1, s2 as associated with case 2, and possibly s3 as associated with case 3 for courses of action. If the current case is more like c1 than c2 then the options most closely associated with c1 (say s1) may be chosen (than say s2 which is more closely associated with case 2). However, through monitoring, differences may be observed that lead the professional to see similarities with say, c3 which may lead say to option s3.
> (Bedford *et al.*, 1994:142)

This account provides a limited approach to reflective practice which never really goes beyond the presentation of a given problem situation to look at a wider context. As case is compared to case, professional knowledge accumulates over time. The sheer weight of case lore evidence

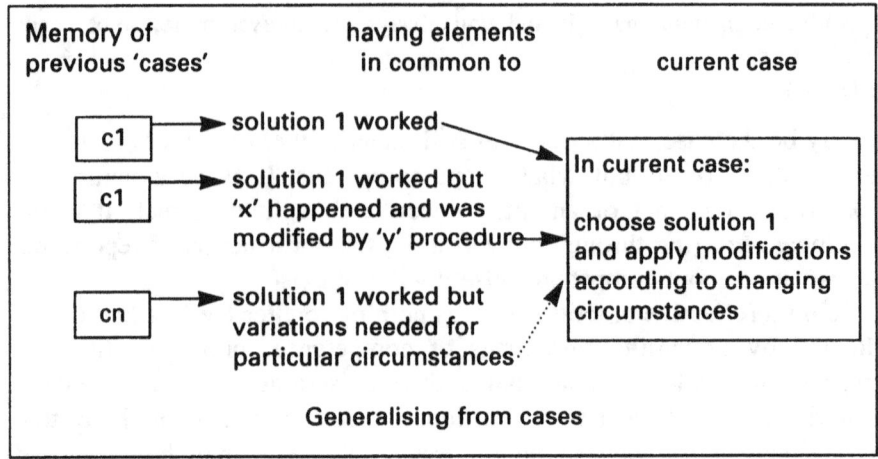

Figure 13.2

may well close down any further analysis. Yet it is often all that is meant by being a professional. Nevertheless:

> Professional critique comes into being when reflection goes beyond the single instance as the focus in order to understand the single instance in its wider embedding contexts. Only through such a process of contextual analysis can alternative, more far reaching decisions be made. Schematically (Figure 13.3).

Solution 6 (s6) requires a shift of attention from the immediate circumstance facing say, a road accident victim, to a society wide investigation of why such accidents occur in the first place. A professional who treats the immediate needs of the victim yet does not pursue the wider political agenda is, of course, not incompetent. However, the professional who reflects critically at all levels is acting in a way that is ultimately qualitatively different and may pursue longer term goals that will have far-reaching social benefits. It is this latter point that turns the debate from being one about competences to the nature of professional action itself.

Conclusion

The competency debate has diverted the agenda. Rather than lists of competences that must be achieved, the move towards the reflective practitioner has brought into focus the complex nature of professional processes and action within a society wide context. The professions generally seem currently bogged down under the weight of the competence rhetoric which is not really appropriate to handle such complexity. Some of the effects of this are seen in the field of nursing and midwifery which is struggling to develop realistic professional education that can make a difference in practice. Some considerable advances are being made within nursing and midwifery as many institutions move to establish procedures

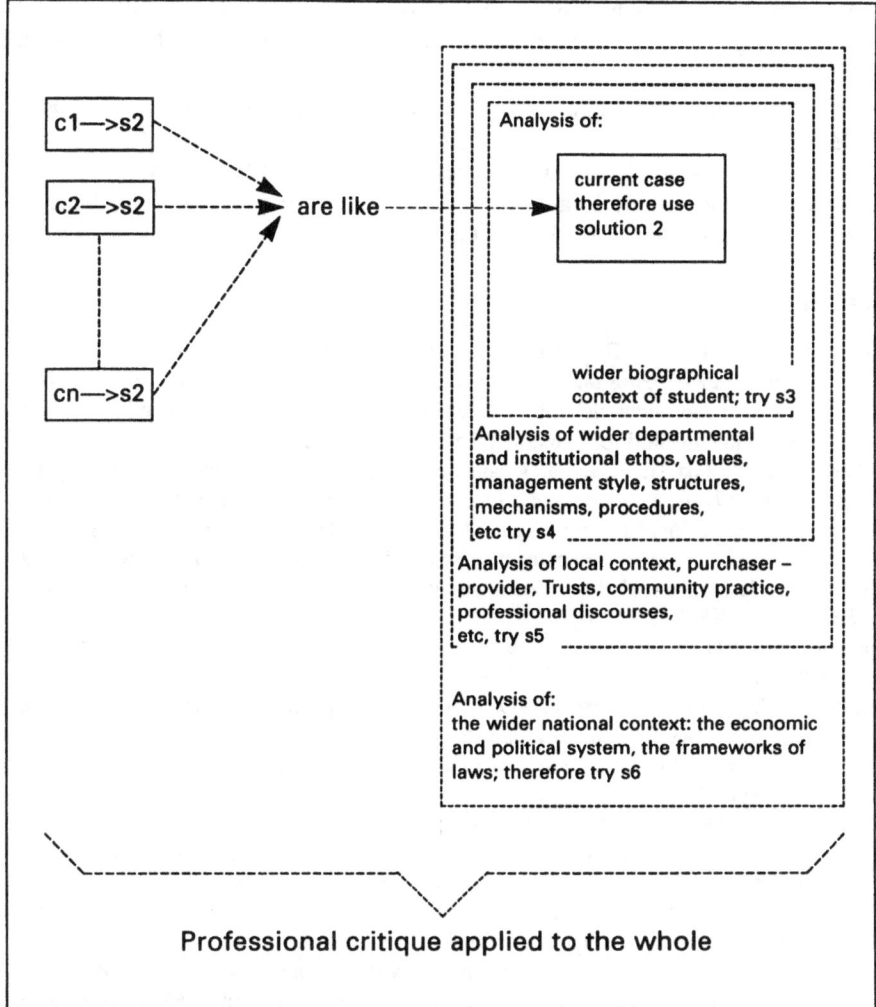

Figure 13.3 (From Bedford et al., 1994:147)

for the development of more appropriate evidence bases for reflection and assessment. It is my view that only if the whole rhetoric of competency is thrown off can a real advance in the quality of professional practice be made through the development of a community of reflective practitioners who make public their evidence bases for decision making.

Notes

[1] This was a joint venture between the University of East Anglia, the Suffolk and Great Yarmouth College of Nursing and Midwifery and the Suffolk College of Higher and Further Education (now known simply as the The Suffolk College). The Co-Directors were John Schostak and Terry Phillips; project co-ordinator was Jill Robinson and the full-time field researcher was Helen Bedford.

[2] This is a 3-year project also funded by the English National Board for Nursing,

Midwifery and Health Visiting. The Co-Directors were John Schostak and Terry Phillips and it was carried out at the Centre for Applied Research in Education, UEA.
[3] ACE will be used to signify where extracts are taken from the ACE report, Bedford et al., 1993.
[4] A fuller discussion of these approaches can be found in the report.
[5] We were made acutely aware of this issue when recent student nurse Beverly Allett was convicted of murdering babies.

References

Bedford, H., Phillips, T., Robinson, J. and Schostak, J. F. (1993) *The Assessment of Competences in Nursing and Midwifery Education and Training. The ACE Project Final Report*. Norwich: School of Education, University of East Anglia; London: English National Board for Nursing, Midwifery and Health Visiting.

Bedford, H., Phillips, T., Leamon, J. and Schostak, J. F. (1994) *Interim Report of the Evaluation of Three Year Undergraduate programmes in Nursing and Midwifery (TYDE) Project*. London: English National Board for Nursing, Midwifery and Health Visiting.

Benner, P. (1982) 'Issues in competency-based testing', *Nursing Outlook*, **May**, 303–309.

Benner, P. (1983) Knowledge in clinical practice', *Image: The Journal of Nursing Scholarship*, **XV (2)**, 36–41

Benner, P. (1984) From *Novice to Expert: Excellence and Power in Clinical Nursing Practice*. California: Addison-Welsley.

Bloom, B. S. (ed.) (1954) *Taxonomy of Educational Objectives. Handbook I: Cognitive Domain*. New York: D. McKay & Co.

Bloom, B. S. (ed.) (1956) *Taxonomy of Educational Objectives. Handbook II: Affective Domain*. New York: D. McKay & Co.

Burt, C. (1947) *Mental and Scholastic Tests*. London: Staples Press.

Dunn, W. R., Hamilton, D. D. and Harden, R. M. (1985) 'Techniques of identifying competences needed of doctors', *Medical Teacher*, **7 (1)**, 15–25.

Evans, N. (1987) *Assessing Experiential Learning. A Review of Progress and Practice*. Harlow: Longman for Further Education Unit Productions.

Fox, J., Labbett, B., Mathews, C., Romano-Hvid, C. and Schostak, J. (1992) *New Perspectives in Modern Language Learning*. Sheffield: Learning Methods Branch, Employment Department, Sheffield.

Gagné, R. M. (1968) *The Technology of Teaching*. New York: Appleton-Century-Crofts.

Gagné, R. M. (1975) *Essentials of Learning for Instruction*. Hinsdale, Ill.: Dryden Press.

Gagné, R. and Briggs, L. (1974) *Principles of Instructional Design*. New York: Holt, Rinehart & Winston.

Medley, D. (1984) 'Teacher competency testing and the teacher educator', in Katz, L.G. and Raths, J. D. (eds) *Advances in Teacher Education*, Vol. 1, New Jersey: Ablex.

Schön, D. (1987) *Educating the Reflective Practitioner*. London: Jossey-Bass.

Schostak, J. F. (ed.) (1988) *Breaking into the Curriculum: The Impact of Information Technology on Schooling*. London: Methuen.

Skinner, B. F. (1953) *Science and Human Behaviour*. New York: Macmillan.

Taylor, F. (1947) *Scientific Management: Comprising Shop Management, the Principles of Scientific Management [and] Testimony Before the Special House Committee*. London: Harper Row.

Thorndike, E. L. (1910) 'The contribution of psychology to education', *Journal of Education Psychology*, **1 (5)**, 5–12.

Watson, J. B. (1931) *Behaviourism*. London: Kegan Paul, Trench, Trubner.

Yerkes, R. (1929) *Army Mental Tests*. New York: Henry Holdt.

14

The Role of a Small-Scale Research Project in Developing a Competency Based Police Training Curriculum

John Elliott

Introduction

In 1984 the Home Office commissioned a 2-year fundamental review of police recruit training from the Centre for Applied Research in Education (CARE) at the University of East Anglia. In response to the Scarman Report on the Inner City riots the recruit training system had already been changed, the main substantive changes being the development of a Social Skills of Policing curriculum which operated in parallel with instruction in the law and police procedures, and in workplace training attachment to a trained mentor, called a Tutor Constable, on a one-to-one basis.

These initial post-Scarman changes acknowledged that initial training must include more than the acquisition of technical knowledge and skills if recruits are to be deemed competent to patrol alone on the streets. What the Scarman Report stimulated was not so much a shift towards competency based training but a gradual reconstruction of competent policing. The context of this reconstruction was the design and development of a new police training curriculum. The identification and clarification, through research, of what constituted competence did not occur prior to, and in isolation from the curriculum design and development process, as so-called rational output/input models of planning suggest. Research into competences was initiated at a relatively late phase of the process, well after the specification of rationale, aims, and principles governing the organisation and selection of content.

The UEA review of the police training system explicated and critiqued the assumptions about policing which underpinned its learning objectives, in the light of information it gathered about the problems of contemporary policing in a multi-cultural society. On the basis of this critique the review team came up with detailed proposals for radical change, and then collaborated with the Home Office's Central Planning and Training Unit (CPTU) to develop and implement these proposals. It was only then, having evolved a general model of good policing, and of the kind of curriculum organisation and content required to foster it, that it was appropriate to embark on the task of describing those capacities exercised in good practice more precisely, to provide criteria for structuring and assessing learning activities criteria. The process by which the new national curriculum for the police training system in England and Wales evolved was one of 'curriculum-led assessment' in marked contrast to the 'assessment-led' process of developing the national curriculum for schools. As I hope to demonstrate during the course of this chapter the former is a more appropriate way of clarifying competences in the context of professional education and training than the latter.

In all its phases, from 1984 to 1989, the work of the UEA(CARE) review was an interactive process in which research informed development and development informed research. And this was undoubtedly due to the willingness of the Home Office and the Police Training Council to allow a group of university researchers to participate in the decision-making process and influence the pace and timing of decisions.

What follows is an account of how the competences manifested in good patrol practice were gradually clarified during the course of the review's work in evaluating, designing, and developing the police training curriculum.

Evaluating Stage 1 of the post-Scarman curriculum

The UEA(CARE) evaluation, known as the Stage 2 Review (since it followed on from initial reforms conceived as Stage 1 of a more far-reaching process of change), heavily criticised the prevailing form of assessment on the grounds that it:

- discriminated in favour of the technical knowledge and skills; and
- encouraged instructional methods which dissociated their acquisition from a realistic appreciation of actual policing situations and the dilemmas and issues they pose.

Recruits were taught to apply knowledge and skills to situations which were largely defined in terms of their legal/procedural significance, and therefore as relatively non-problematic with repect to how the law should be interpreted and applied in them. The SSOP component functioned in virtual isolation from the legal procedural component and although its content consisted largely of 'potted' social psychology it was felt that assessment by objective testing was inappropriate. The outcome was that trainees refused to take it seriously. It was left to the mentors to cope with the trauma recruits experienced when they 'hit the streets' and found themselves having to exercise discretion in the ways they interpreted and enforced the law. The curriculum had rarely faced them with the complexities of decision making on the streets.

The review team began to fundamentally rethink the National Curriculum for police recruits in a form which supported intelligent judgement and decision-making in the kinds of situations officers handled on patrol, and to consider what changes in the organisation of the training and operational systems were necessary for its successful implementation. In 1987 the Home Office published the final report of the Stage 2 Review (MacDonald *et al.*, 1987), which included 143 recommendations for curriculum and organisational change.

Designing a new police training curriculum

The report proposed a new 32-week foundation course to replace the previous pattern of introductory, initial, and local procedures courses followed by workplace training (amounting to 27 weeks in total). It was modular in form and interspersed periods of work-place training with periods of classroom based training in the Home Office Centres.

Module 1 consisted of 4 weeks observational as opposed to direct experience of police work in the divisions to which the recruits would be attached.

Module 2 consisted of 10 weeks in the Home Office Centres following a curriculum which integrated the development of technical knowledge and skill with the development of broader capacities for intelligent judgement and action. This 'integration' was to be achieved through a core curriculum of ethnographically constructed case studies depicting the range and variety of incidents/situations officers have to handle on patrol, and the dilemmas and issues they pose.

Module 3 consisted of a 5-week attachment to a trained Tutor Constable in which the recruit would observe and discuss the officers' handling of situations and be given guided opportunities to undertake practical tasks for themselves.

Module 4 consisted of 4 further weeks of training in the protected environment of the Training Centres with a focus on the more complex and 'messy' cases officers have to handle, where the interpretation and application of the law is most problematic and dilemma ridden, e.g. domestic disputes and suspected child abuse. The recruits then returned to their divisions for 5 more weeks of workplace training, attached this time to a different Tutor Constable to provide them with an opportunity to compare policing styles. In this second workplace training attachment the recruit was given more opportunities to exercise initiative, discretion and independence on patrol while the Tutor 'stands off' but monitors performance, provides feedback and opportunities for discussion, and assists with establishing personal development targets.

The Foundation Course concluded with a 1-week assessment module in the recruits' local force training centre. Here the emphasis is on forming a judgement about the extent to which s(he) is competent to embark on independent patrol. The process involves the recruit in a review of his or her development through the Foundation Course. During that period s(he) will have kept a self-assessment log and engaged in assessment dialogues with trainers, tutor constables and divisional training officers, all of whom will have contributed to a continuous assessment process in the light of a common set of competence criteria. It was envisaged that the same competences would be continuously developed throughout the modular structure of the Foundation Course, regardless of whether the learning activities occur in the classroom or the workplace. To understand how such continuity was possible it is necessary to understand the rationale, aims and principles which underpinned the foundation course proposals.

The rationale stresses a professional approach to patrol policing and argues for the adoption of a reflective practitioner model (Schon, 1983) as the central aim of recruit training. Such a model marks a radical departure from the established view of professionals as infallible experts by virtue of their mastery of a body of certain and authoritative knowledge. It reconstructs the relationship between practitioners, their professional knowledge and their clients in terms of capacities for involving clients in a discursive process of reflective deliberation about complex, dynamic, and unpredictable situations. The adoption of such a model was justified on the grounds of its consistency with new conceptions of the police role that had emerged within the police culture in the wake of the Scarman Report. For example, the working party established by the Home Office Police Training Council post-Scarman had drawn attention to the following 'professional dimensions' of the Constable's role:

> it calls for the exercise of a high degree of intelligence;
>
> it is concerned with maintaining the peace as well as enforcing the law, and involves the exercise of a wide range of social and interpersonal skills;
>
> it should be client-centred, orientated to the service of the community and answerable to it;
>
> it requires a commitment to high ethical standards governing relations with members of the public;
>
> it requires officers to develop their understanding of the social and cultural contexts of law enforcement.

Later the Metropolitan Police (1984) proposals for Continuing Constable Development both reflected these dimensions of the professional role –

drawing a similar distinction between technical and social skills and placing the latter at the centre of its professional model – and developed it at a more fundamental level. The proposals viewed the capacity of officers to self-monitor operational situations and their own conduct in them as fundamental to the exercise of relevant professional skills in policing situations which were characterised as complex, fluid, and unique:

> a self-monitoring of interpersonal interactions can be undertaken, and conscious strategies embarked upon, ensuring a flexible response to varied situations, resulting as appropriate in more sensitive or assertive communications.

Having clarified a model of professionalism the review team then formulated a general aim and set of goals for a new curriculum which it believed to be consistent with the model. The curriculum would aim:

> to develop those qualities of judgement and skill which are necessary for the reflective performance of the police role within a pluralistic and multi-cultural society.

Six broad categories of competence were then listed as curricular goals implied by this aim:

> the ability to interpret and apply the law in a manner which is sensitive to the social and cultural contexts of policing situations;

> the ability to investigate, including (a) observational skills in discriminating those aspects of situations which are relevant to making informed and valid judgements, and (b) interviewing skills of eliciting authentic acccounts from suspects, witnesses, and colleagues;

> the ability to participate in open and free communication with suspects, witnesses and colleagues;

> the ability to represent/report incidents and situations according to criteria of accuracy, fairness, and relevance;

> the ability to evaluate the social effects of general policing policies and strategies;

> the ability to self-monitor one's own performance and conduct in the police role.

These general competences appeared to have a certain 'face validity' but we would have liked at the time to have grounded them more in empirical research. Time and resources did not permit during the review and reporting phase, but as I shall explain later we had an opportunity during the 'development phase' to redefine the competency specifications in the light of a small-scale research study.

The rationale, general aim and goals of the new training curriculum had evolved through discussion between members of the review team and a specially convened working group of the Police Training Council Steering Committee on Probationer Training. Once a degree of consensus had emerged on such matters the working group turned its attention to scrutinising proposals for a new course structure. In the light of its evaluation data the review team defined a set of structural principles to inform the construction of a new Foundation Course. It argued that the professional model, aim and goals could only be realised through a course which:

- fostered continuous interaction between training in the centres and workplace training;
- ensured that periods of Centre-based training are short enough to allow for the effective transfer of acquired knowledge and skill to the workplace;
- allowed actual policing practices and procedures to be experienced in sufficient depth and breadth to ensure adequate application, reinforcement,and contextualisation of the knowledge and skills acquired in the training centres;
- controlled recruits' experience of the occupational or 'canteen culture' and avoided 'sudden immersion' as a terminal experience;
- enabled the 'canteen culture' to be experienced gradually and progressively and provided regular opportunities in non-operational settings for continuing reflection about such experience in the light of professional standards;
- facilitated a gradual and progressive transfer of control over training processes from Central Services (Home Office) to Local Forces;
- required major problems in course development to be resolved collaboratively between Central Services and Local Forces.

Such principles were accepted by the PTC working group and shaped the modular structure of the course the review team negotiated with them, and subsequently, with their help, through the committees of the PTC (negotiations and consultations with the interested parties were a continuous feature of the review team's work throughout the evaluation, design and development phases).

The principles embodied a curriculum theory which included a theory of experiential learning. The latter explains the differentiation of the modular course in terms of three types of experiential learning. Three ways of experiencing the realities of the workplace were delineated: observational experience (module 1), vicarious experience through case studies (modules 2 and 4), and direct practical experience (modules 3 and 5). This view of experiential learning enabled the review team to design a curriculum which allowed recruits to develop progressively their reflective capacities by experiencing the realities of policing in forms which provided varying levels of protection against the socialising power of the 'canteen culture'.

Senior police managers tend to be wary of the view that beginners best learn from 'early immersion into direct experience'. Recruits are 'sworn in' with full police powers from the day they arrive in their Force. Learning from their mistakes in the workplace is a risky process for the organisation. Unlike teaching the workplace is the streets and therefore much more open to public scrutiny and complaint. The status of recruits as trainees cannot exonerate since they are in possession of full police powers. There are no student constables; only constables serving a 2-year probationary period. The public and visible nature of police performance makes police managers aware of the ways in which the police culture at the operational level shapes attitudes and behaviour on the streets. They tend to be sceptical about the extent to which the negative aspects of occupational socialisation can be counteracted by supplying sufficient numbers of qualified high quality Tutor Constables (mentors) at a time when operational requirements are fully stretching available human resources.

Hence, a tendency to rely on the initial training in the Home Office Training Centres to produce the professional attitudes desired prior to the induction process in the workplace. The ethos in these Centres emphasised quasi-military virtues like 'obedience to authority', 'discipline', 'appearance', 'punctuality', and 'team-work'. The trainers in them frequently justified the quasi-military process of social conditioning documented by the review team in terms of a 'slippage theory' of resistance to contaminating elements in the 'canteen culture'. The theory was that the conditioning process would prevent too much 'slippage into the mire' when it was encountered in the workplace, and it persisted in spite of evidence to the contrary. The Stage 2 proposals for a modular foundation course, which provided for the development of reflective capacities through an experiential learning curriculum which gradually and progressively inducted recruits into operational practice, provided an alternative solution to the problem of how to help recruits resist the undesirable aspects of the workplace culture.

According to Schon (1983) the professional draws on a repertoire of cases experienced in the past to interpret a present situation and decide upon an appropriate course of action in it. Professional knowledge is stored in the long-term memory in contextualised rather than abstract propositional form. In providing opportunities for police recruits to experience real situations through observation and the study of case materials the curriculum aimed to help them construct a repertoire of reflectively processed situational understandings which they could draw on during their periods of 'on-the-job' training and subsequently during their post-foundation probationary period. Useable practical knowledge can to an extent be acquired independently of direct immersion in workplace practices, and knowledge so acquired in more reflective, protected and safer learning environments may do much to complement and support the process of 'on-the-job' learning.

Having outlined the professional model, the structural principles, and the curriculum theory which underpinned its proposals for the Foundation Course, the review team's report went on to state criteria for selecting, organising, and handling curriculum content (Metropolitan Police, 1984: 121–126), and principles governing the process of assessment. The latter were as follows:

- the purpose of assessment should be primarily diagnostic with a view to informing diagnostic decisions;
- the assessment process should involve the production of regular diagnostic profiles;
- diagnostic profiles should be constructed by both the recruit and his/her trainers along agreed dimensions (e.g. consisting of core competences), and compared in discussion between them;
- trainers should, following a diagnostic discussion, advise the recruit on what to do to improve their capacities and skills. This advice should be recorded on the profiles;
- recruits should be given the responsibility for deciding any action they ought to undertake following a diagnostic discussion. These action-steps should be recorded on the profiles;
- at each diagnostic discussion the profiles should be reviewed in the light of the records of advice given and action-steps planned after previous discussion;
- peers should be invited to contribute to diagnostic discussion and assessments of each other's learning.

Such principles were derived from, and were therefore consistent with, the professional model, aims and curriculum principles underpinning the modular foundation course. The emphasis is on self-assessment within an overall process of an assessment discourse between trainees, their trainers, and peers which is aimed at improving their capacities for reflective practice. The main assumption behind this emphasis on self-assessment is that reflective capacities can only be developed reflexively; i.e. through a form of meta-reflection which focuses not so much on the observable aspects of performance as on the the personal qualities it manifests. The principle of assessment outlined in the Stage 2 Report are based on the view that since reflective capacities are personal qualities manifested in performance and not reducible to a predefined set of behavioural responses or indicators, they can only be developed through an assessment process which has self-assessment at its core. The development of capacities for reflection always involves a meta level of reflection which is fostered and sustained through the kind of diagnostically focused assessment discourse described in the report. This is why the adoption of the reflective practioner model of professionalism entails a form of assessment which rather than externally structuring and shaping the learning experiences of trainees and the pedagogy of their trainers becomes an intrinsic feature of both. In the education of professionals as reflective practitioners, the development of competence implies the development of meta-competence, i.e.capacities for personal self-development such as 'self-reflexivity', through an assessment process which takes a dialogical and collaborative form.

Researching the Generic Characteristics of the Good Police Officer

In 1986 the Police Training Council gave the go-ahead to the review team's proposals for a new probationer training curriculum in England and Wales. A UEA(CARE) team, led by the author, were contracted for a further 2 years to assist the Home Office Central Planning Unit – responsible for course design and instructor training at the level of probationer training – with the task of developing and piloting the new modular foundation course. The Metropolitan Police had participated at the review stage but their training centre at Hendon was not part of the national system catering for the other 43 forces. For various reasons they decided they couldn't reorganise their training to conform to the new course structure and remained interested observers of the development without becoming directly involved in it. UEA(CARE)'s role in the development phase focused on three key areas of development:

- the production and piloting of ethnographic case study material;
- the development of an assessment system;
- the development of evaluation strategies for gathering information about the change process.

The rest of this chapter will address the second area only. The author and other members of the UEA(CARE) team had become familiar with some of the 'job competence' research carried out by McClelland (1976) and his associates of McBer and co-workers at Harvard. McClelland (1973) argued that competence cannot be behaviourally defined as performance indicators when it refers to a person who has performed well in complex and unstructured situations. This is because what constitutes an appropriate behavioural response cannot be determined in advance. In this context competence doesn't simply consist of techniques and skills which can be directly derived from an analysis of the jobs people perform. Such behaviourally definable responses may be necessary conditions of competent performance, e.g. procedures for interviewing suspects, taking statements, making arrests, issuing summonses and warrants etc. But they do not differentiate the person who does the job correctly from the one who does it well. What differentiates the latter, according to McClelland and his associates, are the personal qualities individuals bring to a job and which are manifested in the way they form judgements about the situational context and decide what constitutes an appropriate response to it. What is therefore crucial to assessing competence in handling unstructured situations, is a description of those personal qualities, or 'generic competences', which demarcate individuals who perform well from those that merely conform to the requirements of the job.

It should be clear from the above account why the UEA(CARE) team saw the McBer approach to 'job competence assessment' relevant to developing a profiling system for the modular foundation course. It had already identified support for intelligent and reflective practice in unstructured policing situations as the major rationale for the modular foundation course, and made an initial attempt to specify the key elements of competence the course would need to foster. The McBer approach to job assessment, in contrast to the more conventional tasks/functions analysis approaches, provided a possibility for developing a more grounded account of the 'competences of the reflective police practitioner'. The approach in broad outline can be summarised as follows (Spencer, 1979):

> Convene an expert panel of experienced practitioners and observers of the job to 'develop a list of hypothesised characteristics of people who do the job well'. Each characteristic is rated in terms of:
> (a) the extent to which it distinguishes superior from merely acceptable performers;
> (b) its significance for education and training;
> (c) the extent to which job openings could be realistically filled if it were an entry requirement.
>
> Those characteristics which are positively rated in all these respects provide a set of hypotheses about the critical characteristics of competence to be tested.
>
> Select two samples of practitioners on the basis of the intuitive judgements of those who interact with them in the workplace, i.e. immediate supervisors, peers, and subordinates. Judges are asked to select a group of superior performers and a group of performers who merely satisfy minimally acceptable standards. McBer associates claim that the more 'distanced' from face to face interaction the assessors are, the less valid and reliable are their judgements.
>
> Conduct a recorded 'behavioural event' interview with each individual in both samples. Each practitioner is asked to come with a recently encountered situation/event, which they found complex and difficult to handle, in mind. S(he) provides an account of the situation/event and how s(he) handled it, while the interviewer seeks clarifications, elaborations, justifications etc.
>
> Analyse interview recordings/transcripts in each sample; identifying patterns of practitioner response in terms of the capacities and skills ('competences')

they manifest. Identify generalisable characteristics of interviewees in each sample.

Compare and contrast the analyses, identifying differentiating characteristics.

Determine internal validity through follow-up observations of practitioners performing in the workplace, and external validity through structured interviews (coded in terms of the prior analysis) with another pair of samples.

Klemp (1977), reviewing McBer studies employing this methodology, identified a number of characteristics which superior performers across a range of public service professions appear to share in common. He groups them in three broad categories: conceptual, interpersonal, and motivational.

- *Conceptual:*
  - discerns thematic consistencies in diverse and complex information and communicates them to others;
  - understands different sides of a controversial issue, and what is at stake between the different parties;
  - learns from experience by observing and reflecting on one's own behaviour in the context of interaction with others.
- *Interpersonal:*
  - discerns the thoughts and feelings of clients and co-workers ('accurate empathy').
  - promotes feelings of efficacy in others, which includes (1) positive regard for them; (2) supporting them, and (3) controlling feelings of hostility and anger liable to render them powerless and ineffective.
- *Motivational:*
  (a) Achievement motivation:
  - willing, under certain circumstances, to take moderate risks to achieve something novel and original ('the innovator');
  - sets time-phased and realistic goals;
  - seeks feed-back on one's own performance;

  (b) Power motivation:
  - learns interpersonal networks and uses them to influence situations and events;
  - influences others by identifying a shared and superordinate goal;
  - identifies work-group coalitions with regard to both their level in the hierarchy and their orientation to organisational goals.

The UEA(CARE) team felt that all these clusters of 'generic competences' could be linked to the aim of developing reflective practitioners. The conceptual cluster perhaps links most obviously. All the characteristics described are aspects of 'situational understanding', which includes the self-reflective dimension. However, all the other clusters can be viewed as constitutive capacities of reflective practioners. The interpersonal cluster are all aspects of the 'empathetic behaviour' which promotes the trust necessary for access to reliable and authentic information about issues and problems in social situations. The achievement motivation characteristics are all aspects of that search for excellence which underpins reflective practice and those listed under power motivation are indicative of the belief that whatever the situation, there is always something one can do to improve it. This assumption – what Klemp calls 'cognitive initiative' – also underpins reflective practice.

We were therefore interested in the extent to which police constables identified in the workplace as superior performers shared the characteristics listed above more than those who were simply regarded as average performers conforming to minimally acceptable standards. More generally we were interested in the extent to which agreements in the workplace about who the superior performers of the constable role are, compared with the merely acceptable performers, did indeed discriminate qualities evidenced in practice.

In collaboration with the Central Planning and Training Unit I embarked on a small-scale investigation during the autumn of 1988, assisted by Police Inspector Shadforth of its Directing Staff. The time-scale in which to undertake it if it were to inform development was extremely short and this ruled out working with the McBer methodology on large samples. We decided to interview 24 officers – 12 designated 'superior' and 12 'acceptable' – drawing on three Police Divisions situated in different parts of the country and representing a spread of policing environments: the urban connurbation, rural, and 'new town'. Although we were criticised for planning to proceed with such a small sample, the only alternative was not to proceed at all. Moreover, the context was one in which the CPTU had launched into a consultation exercise by asking police forces across the country to submit lists of abilities for consideration as assessment criteria, and indeed senior police officers on the joint CPTU\UEA Probationer Development and Training Team were busy compiling lists on the basis of their experience. I felt that even a little evidence, however limited, could provide a significant corrective to the 'aggregated introspections' of senior officers, whose validity should not simply be presumed. I felt that the sample was sufficiently large and representative of different policing environments to begin to explore the extent to which:

- The cross-professional characteristics cited by Klemp might explain any differences between the performances of officers judged to be superior and those judged to be merely acceptable.
- Any distinguishing 'generic' characteristics might be identified, and conceptually linked to reflective practice.

Arrangements for the study were formally negotiated in the first instance with Chief Constables and followed up by visits to operational commanders to clarify procedures for selecting and interviewing officers (Elliott, 1989). The study was a sensitive one ethically because it depended on interviewees not knowing about the categorisation process. Local Police Federation representatives were consulted before proceeding and fully informed of the proposed procedures. The initial formulation of hypotheses using a specially convened expert panel was dispensed with on the grounds that McBers' findings about cross-professional characteristics, reported by Klemp and Spencer, and the lists compiled by forces and senior officers at CPTU, already constituted worthwhile hypotheses to test in analysing the interview data.

The collaborating Inspector and myself carried out 23 interviews (one constable proved unobtainable), working throughout them as a pair. In the end 22 interview recordings were transcribed and analysed (one proved to be untranscribable). The two interviewers analysed the transcripts independently, but the categories for analysis were developed in the following way. First I selected a small number of transcripts from the total sample and worked progressively through them listing the characteristics they evidenced. In doing so I was obviously influenced by the McBer categories but tried at the same time to remain open to evidence of other characteristics in the data. Both were familiar with the McBer findings and approach to analysis. When the transcripts no longer yielded many new characteristics upon analysis a list of categories was compiled, but before they were used as a framework for analysing the rest it was decided to test their validity from a police perspective.

The five transcripts used to generate the categories were given to 20 supervisory police officers during a course they attended at CPTU. Each was asked to mark sections of transcripts which they intuitively judged to be indicative of good policing. They were then asked to review them and identify the qualities they evidenced. Following this individual work the supervisors were placed into four groups and asked to identify the items they could agree on as characteristics of good policing. The four lists were then synthesised and compared with the McBer findings. Interestingly there was a great deal of over-lap, as well as the inclusion of more occupationally specific descriptions. A final set of analytic categories was then compiled from my lists and the supervisor's lists and used by myself and my police associates to analyse the total sample of transcripts independently of each other.

My collaborator and I then compared and discussed our analyses and agreed that the following qualities, evidenced in 25% or more of the transcripts, appeared to be more characteristic of officers designated 'superior' than those designated 'acceptable':

- sees beyond the obvious and surface features of a situation;
- tolerates and accepts ambiguity in a situation;

- self-monitors own actions in the light of the situation and their effects on it;
- enforces the law in a manner which is appropriate and sensitive to the social context;
- takes moderate risks in deciding upon a course of action;
- learns from social networks and makes use of them in achieving worthwhile results;
- gets co-operation from and between others by identifying a common goal or shared concern.

All of these characteristics can be linked with the cross-professional competences cited by Klemp.

Both my associate and I had, while analysing the data, come to feel that we could identify who the superior performers were, and that although these impressions coincided with the workplace assessments in two Divisions they didn't in the third. Time did not permit the observational follow-up studies in the workplace as originally intended. However, it was agreed that the impressions formed during the analyses of the transcripts might be grounded in the range and variety of the abilities displayed by individuals. Each interviewer decided to rank order individuals independently according to the number of characteristics (evidenced in 25% or more of the total sample of transcripts) they demonstrated. The two sets of rankings, when compared, agreed on the placement of seven individuals in the 'superior' category. Both rankings confirmed the placements of seven out of the 12 individuals originally identified as superior performers. Out of the 10 originally identified as acceptable, six were confirmed by both rankings.

Rank ordering individuals according to the range and variety of characteristics they demonstrated in interview, suggested that it is the presence or absence of broad clusters of ability rather than specific abilities which best explain differences in perceived levels of competence. From the ranking exercise the following provisional conclusions were drawn:

- that the conceptual abilities related to capacities for situational understanding and self-monitoring most clearly demarcated the difference between superior and merely acceptable or average officers;
- that interpersonal abilities related to empathy and motivational capacities linked to needs for achievement and power also tended to be more evidenced amongst those ranked as superior performers but less markedly than the conceptual abilities.

Such tentative findings suggest that the distinction between superior and merely acceptable performers is too simplistic. Perhaps one at least needs to distinguish between those who conform to the minimal technical and procedural requirements of the job, those who do it competently by virtue of their interpersonal and motivational capacities, and those who excel at it by virtue of their conceptual capacities. What the small-scale study outlined above points to, is the importance of clarifying all these dimensions of practical competence and avoiding reductionism and atomisation for the sake of easy measurement.

The influence of this study on the final list of characteristics which finally emerged from the CPTU was marked. They were grouped as a basis for profiling in seven categories, including:

- 'monitoring personal performance';
- 'investigation' covering capacities for situational understanding;
- 'communication and relationships with others' covering abilities related to empathy and interpersonal understanding;
- 'decision-making, problem-solving, and planning';
- 'practical effectiveness' covering capacities linked to power motivation.

Under each category heading specific abilities are listed and the development of each has to be continuously assessed throughout the modular foundation course. The UEA(CARE) team argued that such atomisation was undesirable and impractical as a basis for assessing the development of competence. It proposed that such competences should be viewed as conceptually related clusters of characteristics whose development could be profiled as integrated wholes, and that specific elements within clusters should serve as criteria for, rather than the focus of, assessments. Although the argument was lost and 32 characteristics are now required to be continuously assessed in isolation from each other, most of these specific characteristics were identified through the study and can be linked to the development of fundamental capacities for situational understanding, self-monitoring, empathy with others, influencing situations for the better regardless of constraints, and achieving excellence.

Regardless of the obvious limitations of this small-scale study it helped to clarify many of the criteria tacitly employed in workplace assessments of experienced officers who are considered to be doing their job well, and what might be involved in developing probationers as reflective practitioners.

References

Elliott, J. (1989) *Qualities of the Good Patrol Constable: report of an interview study for the Probationer Development and Training Team at the Central Planning and Training Unit.* Mimeo: University of East Anglia.

Hampshire Constabulary (1984) *Beat Craft: a Manual for the Police Officer.*

Klemp, G.O. (1977) *Three Factors of Success in the World of Work: Implications for Curriculum in Higher Education.* Boston: McBer & Co.

McClelland, D.C. (1973) 'Testing for competence rather than for intelligence', *American*

Psychologist, **28**, 1–14.

McClelland, D.C. (1976) *A Guide to Job Competency Assessment.* Boston: McBer & Co.

MacDonald, B., *et al.* (1987) *Police Probationer Training: The Final Report of the Stage 2 Review.* London: HMSO.

Metropolitan Police (1984) *Constable Training: Proposals for a 30 year Career Span.* 'D' Dept, D13 Branch Project Team.

Scarman, Lord (1982) *The Scarman Report: The Brixton Disorders 10–12 April 1981.* London: Penguin.

Schon, D. (1983) *The Reflective Practitioner: How Professionals Think in Action.* London: Temple Smith.

Spencer, L.M. (1979) *Identifying, Measuring, and Training Soft Skill Competencies Which Predict Performance in Professional, Managerial and Public Service Jobs.* Boston: McBer & Co.

15

Concluding Comments

Donald McIntyre and David Hustler

A Proper Cause for Concern?

In our Introduction, we commented on the tendency highlighted by Sally Brown for the early papers on competence written for the ESRC Seminars to be reactive and indeed defensive, suggesting that the group members felt their educational concerns to be in danger of being swept aside by crude concepts of competence and by simple-minded prescriptions. Any reader of this book who has been on the lookout for such defensive stances will have had little difficulty in finding them. Most of the contributors have argued that we do have cause for concern, and that we should be worried by the restricted notions of professionality that have seemed to underlie recent competence initiatives. Hogbin *et al.*, (Chapter 4) express widely shared concerns about competence prescriptions for beginning teachers in England when they write that:

> the importance of critical reflection, the analysis of practice, the perception of theory and practice interpenetrating, the recognition of context with which competences are used, the ways they are interpreted, and the need for underpinning competences in a process of professional progression and development are all issues which have been largely ignored in the Secretary of State's circulars.

Mahony and Harris (Ch. 3) add two further sources of concern when they suggest that:

> there is nothing in recent circulars ... which remotely suggest that the nature of teaching is problematic ... the models of teaching represented render the learner virtually invisible.

That the dangers are neither imaginary nor local is attested to by Walker (Ch. 8) who suggests that even in the more optimistic Australian context:

that employers of teachers, for reasons of accountability and quality control, might come to incline to the kinds of neat, clear cut and often quantifiable measures provided by the behaviourist approach is not beyond possibility.

Nor is this sense of a need to resist destructive forces limited to those concerned with teaching. Commenting on how the complexity of professional activity is being increasingly understood, Schostak (Ch. 13) concludes that:

> the professions generally seem currently bogged down under the weight of competence rhetoric which is not really appropriate to handle such complexity. Some of the effects of this are seen in the field of nursing and midwifery which is struggling to develop realistic professional education: education that can make a different in practice .... It is my view that only if the whole rhetoric of competency is thrown off can a real advance in the quality of professional practice be made.

The only chapter in which this cause of concern is actively questioned is the Scottish chapter (6), by Stronach and his colleagues. They conclude that in the Scottish context 'the debate ... has been over-polarised' because of a failure to recognise:

> the complex processes of negotiation and domestication involved in the construction of the SOED competences themselves

and because any attempts to treat the assessment of teacher competences as a merely 'technical' problem would be:

> likely to end up being technically impossible, politically unacceptable, and practically unworkable. They will lose credibility faster then they can gain control.

They reject therefore:

> the assumption that somehow such a competence-based reform is likely to have far-reaching consequences for the quality of Scottish teaching, the nature of initial teacher training, the autonomy of the profession, the cause of liberal humanism, and so on.

The persuasive arguments leading to these conclusions are of course based on Scottish evidence and concerned with the Scottish situation. We should, however, reflect on how far these arguments could also be applied to other countries and to England in particular. For example, different as the English situation is, the implementation of any innovation on a national scale is surely at least as complex and as open to multiple influences as is the case in Scotland.

It is surely important that we should articulate the grounds on which we find crude conceptions of competence to be wrong or inadequate. On the other hand, it is also important not to over-dramatise what is happening, seeing ourselves as fighting a rearguard action against powerful and effective enemies: the power of those who would impose single-minded prescriptions for competence might depend less on their positions than on our own failure to offer practical alternatives. For example, as Barton and Elliott (Ch. 2) note, 'many institutions are using the [DFE Circular 9/92] accreditation framework to plan their secondary teacher training' even though the Circular makes it quite clear that they are not required to do so. We are pleased therefore that many of the chapters of this book are primarily concerned with positive and practical thinking about how to construe and assess competence and expertise in teaching and other professions.

Creative Thinking about Professional Competence

As we warned in our introduction, much of what has been reported in this book is 'work in progress'. The authors of most chapters have written about the thinking and debates underlying the plans that they or others have made, in some cases about their experiences of attempts to implement such plans, but in only one or two cases about schemes which have been tried and tested and with which the authors are satisfied. What this book has offered more than anything else is a collection of diverse creative ideas for construing and assessing professional competence or expertise. While the authors of the different chapters frequently make reference to each other's work, the ideas presented tend to reflect different concerns or different solutions to shared problems. There are few firmly established positions and little in the way of clear schools of thought.

That being the case, it would not be an easy task to synthesise these different ideas and we shall not attempt to do so. It may be useful, however, to highlight some of the key ideas which have been offered for dealing with professional competence more satisfactorily than in terms of a list of particular things one should be able to do.

The three chapters focusing on professions other than teaching offered three nicely contrasting approaches to competence. Winter and Maisch (Ch. 12) undertook in relation to social work perhaps the bravest task of all those reported in that:

> the primary aim of the Project was to explore the viability of the work of the National Council for Vocational Qualifications in the context of 'professional' higher education.

This implied that the content of vocational curricula should be derived from the nature of people's employment and specifically through functional analysis of practitioners' work; but although that implication was accepted, the functional analysis did not lead to the definition of competences 'in the NCVQ orthodox format of elements, performance criteria and range statements' since, among other things:

> Practitioners' statements did not become progressively more concrete as they described what their role required; after a certain point they involved the

continual need to exercise discretionary judgement, in the light of underlying professional aims and values.

Because, furthermore, Winter and Maisch were themselves committed to such ideas of professionality, while deriving the *content* of the curriculum from the functional analysis and specifying it in terms of lists of competence elements derived from that analysis, the criteria in terms of which students' competence is assessed are *core criteria*, applied to all competence elements, and derived from other theoretical and empirical studies. This creative idea of core criteria of professionality and of cross-referencing such criteria with specified competence elements is clearly generalisable to other professional contexts and offers one way in which a detailed specification of areas of competence in teaching might fruitfully be combined with wider concerns. This idea, as Whitty notes in his chapter (7), was influential in leading the Northern Ireland group to their key conclusion:

> that the professional characteristics of the teacher ought to permeate the application of the specific competences identified under the headings of professional knowledge and professional skills.

Schostak's account of developments in nursing and midwifery professional education (Ch. 13) suggests a different approach; instead of competence statements being complemented by the pervasive application of professionality criteria:

> the discourse of competence is increasingly replaced by a broader and more complex discourse of dialogue, debate, critique and evidence.

This gradual replacement appears to have happened, however, not through any explicit challenging of the importance of competence statements, but rather through a movement to make assessment in terms of competence statements more valid. Schostak shows how as a first step in this movement: 'the notion of competence has shifted from observable categories of behaviour or performance to broad themes ... not fully specified.'

Thus the judgement to be made is not through a standardised specification but rather through the expert judgement of an accredited professional witness. But since research showed that the quality of such accredited witnesses varied considerably, that first step did not go far enough: it was necessary to provide the evidence on which judgements could be based, and on which they could be questioned. Schostak suggests that: 'the learning contract is perhaps the most developed version of this approach to date'.

The starting point for a learning contract is the student's identification of learning objectives in terms of new competences to be acquired. Schostak argues, however, that the extended essay-like task which follows radically changes the nature of the discourse. The student's need to discuss context, choice of strategy, theoretical perspectives and evidence to justify learning claims, together with the need for validation and critique of the account by an assigned member of staff, makes for a more seriously professional discourse.

A third contrasting approach is that described by Elliott in his account of the development of a police training curriculum (Ch. 14). This development, he claims, was one of 'curriculum-led assessment', with the identification of 'criteria for structuring and assessing learning activities' following 'clarification of the rationale, aims and principles' of the curriculum. Thus although the criteria needed to be identified through research into policing, the nature of the criteria and therefore of the research were predetermined by the curriculum thinking. In particular, the curriculum planning was in terms of a small number of broad 'generic competences', personal qualities:

> manifested in the way [able practitioners] form judgements about the situational context and decide what constitutes an appropriate response to it.

Here then we have the most radical of these three examples from other professionals of ways of dealing with competences: a rejection of any need to specify tasks which practitioners need to be able to undertake competently. Such very abstract qualities as:

- sees beyond the obvious and surface features of a situation;
- enforces the law in a manner which is appropriate and sensitive to the social context.

are seen as sufficient and as the most appropriate terms in which to understand and to assess professional capabilities (even if with the help of more specific indicators). It is significant that Elliott, and also McClelland (1976) on whose work he builds, are primarily concerned to:

> differentiate the person who does the job correctly from the one who does it well

and their evidence and arguments are impressive in relation to that concern. However, Elliott's failure as he recounts to persuade those responsible for initial police training that 'generic competences' offer a sufficient basis for assessing the competence of entrants to the profession may be relevant to questions about differences between initial and later professional education and assessment in what are appropriate ways of construing competence.

It seems to have been initially in these other professional contexts, rather than in relation to teaching, that ambitious and confident developments have occurred in relation to the construing and assessment of professional competence. Walker (Ch. 8) notes that this has also been true in Australia; but the Australian work in relation to teaching which he describes offers an ambitious, distinctively professional and very much more self-confident account of professional competence in teaching than any yet offered in the UK. While expressed in terms of lists with sub-lists, each of the systems he reports are extremely wide-ranging in the 'areas of competence' suggested, each area of competence is defined in terms of an overall rationale and a set of generic competences, and even the multiple 'indicators of effective practice' for each of these generic competences are expressed in such cognitive, open and liberal terms as 'understanding', 'appreciating', 'acknowledging', 'demonstrating knowledge' and 'continuing to acquire knowledge'. As Walker himself comments:

> The depth and breadth of competence required by these indicators, their generic nature, and the cognitive grasp explicit in most of them and implicit in the others, demonstrates the holistic, contextual and genuinely professional character of the national competency standards developed by the NPQTL for teachers.

These Australian schemes are to some extent echoed in the UEA competences framework described by Barton and Elliott in Chapter 2, especially in that the main structure of the framework is described in terms of broad areas of competence. The UEA areas are not so wide ranging as the Australian ones, but they are described in the same kind of distinctively cognitive, value-laden, professional language. Two particular features of the UEA scheme seem distinctive and worthy of note. One is the explicit basis for the areas of competence – termed 'areas of responsibility' – as being 'constructed around a normative analysis of the teacher's role in terms of their core responsibilities', rather than through a functional 'analysis of jobs teachers actually perform'. The second distinctive feature is in the elaboration of the six core areas of responsibility not in terms of criteria to be met but instead in terms of 'questions worth reflecting about and discussing in the assessment process'. The emphasis is thus on education and on student teachers' active engagement in their own education and assessment.

A priority concern with engaging student teachers in monitoring and articulating their own learning and achievements is apparent also in the *profiling* focus of the Goldsmiths and Oxford initiatives. The Oxford approach (Ch. 5) goes against the general trend in its readiness to treat separately several different kinds of qualities seen as necessary elements of professional teaching expertise. It offers perhaps two distinctive ideas for construing competence in initial teacher education. One is its differentiation of the classroom-related part of the PGCE curriculum into two phases, in which different learning goals and different professional qualities are emphasised, the first within a framework of prespecified elements of classroom competence, the second within a much more open and student-defined framework. The other is its formulation of the prespecified elements of classroom competence, in the light of research on experienced teachers' classroom expertise, in terms of short-term classroom goals.

The Goldsmiths case study (Ch. 3), more than any other, offers an example of the kind of sustained constructive effort necessary in order to face up to the diverse theoretical and practical problems involved in taking an analytical approach to competence in initial teacher education. From an initial formulation of the task as one of making criteria explicit and involving student teachers in monitoring their own learning, while doing justice to the complexity of teaching, they moved on to successive tasks of:

- taking account of differences in the expertise required in teaching different subjects and age-groups;
- considering how to relate to 'the language of the official accounts of competence';
- trying to resolve the tension between the aim of empowering students and the need to assess them;
- confronting the equal tension caused by not oversimplifying teaching but as a result producing a profile that could be experienced as 'daunting' and also 'unwieldy';
- structuring students' learning tasks so that they could benefit most fully from use of the profile;
and much else.

As Mahony and Harris make clear, the multiplicity of issues involved means that the value of profiling systems depends not only on them being very carefully theorised but also on the creative and sensitive use of them and on the time and other conditions necessary to make that possible.

We would claim then that, as illustrated by the above examples, this book is full of constructive ideas about how to articulate and assess competence in teaching in ways which validly reflect the nature of good professional teaching. Also important, however, have been two other recurring constructive themes, one concerned with the value of 'competence' as a resource for debate, the other with the articulation of unresolved questions about competence in teaching and its development. It is to these two themes that we turn in the two remaining sections of this concluding chapter.

Competence as a Resource for Debate

It would be difficult for anyone with any responsibility for teacher education, as politician, teacher educator or student, to reject a challenge to make their understanding of the nature of good teaching explicit: inability to show such explicit understanding could easily be interpreted as showing lack of fitness for the responsibility. Furthermore, if one is faced with the threat that other perhaps less adequate understandings of teaching will be used to define one's tasks, the incentive to define one's own understandings becomes strong. And when apparently incompatible versions of competent teaching are articulated by people who need to work with shared understandings, debate becomes essential; and that in turn helps people to examine and to question the assumptions underlying their own understandings.

Perhaps for these reasons, a recurrent theme of this book has been that external pressures to spell out the qualities of good teaching have frequently led to productive debate or to opportunities for such debate. This seems to have occurred at three different levels – national, institutional, and individual – and it will be useful to consider at least one example at each level.

Walker has provided in Chapter 8 a fascinating account of Australian debates at national level. Important features of these debates appear to have been:

- the initial ignorance of university politicians of the considerable body of useful work already done on describing competency standards in ways reflecting the nature of professional work;
- the economic purposes motivating government to seek national competency standards, including for example enhancing deployment of competence through labour market efficiency and equity;
- a background in which a national standards framework for vocational education had been developed which was 'hierarchical, atomistic and behavioural';
- and yet, apparently as a result of vigorous and informed intervention by professional educators, the development of constructive negotiations which included extensive opportunities for academic research and serious debate, leading eventually to consensus on competency standards for teaching clearly informed by a sophisticated understanding of professional work.

What Walker's account suggests then is the possibility, even in what could well be seen as unpromising circumstances, of informed, rational and fruitful debate with a national government about competence in teaching. At one level, this can be seen as further evidence in support of the case made by Stronach *et al.,* (Ch. 6) that politicians' initiatives on such matters have to be negotiated into workable and widely acceptable forms. Walker himself, however, implies that a debate about competence was possible, and fruitful in bringing together different perspectives, in a way that would not have been the case for most other themes:

> It can be argued that the notion of competency is the most important conceptual link between Australian (micro-) economic policy and educational theory.

In Australia, then, 'competence' has served the interests of teachers and teacher educators in that it has been a theme that has brought them together with government, and around which they have been able to reach with government common wide-ranging understandings.

The Manchester Metropolitan case study is focused on debate at the institutional level. Hogbin *et al.,* (Ch. 4) describe the contrasting traditions and cultures, and especially the different approaches to competence, associated with different routes into teaching. They also make clear the external pressures which generated a need for innovation and for co-ordination across programmes in relation to competences. It seems that, as at the national level in Australia, so here at the institutional level, 'competence' was a resource for debate in that it led to unprecedently serious and sustained debate and investigation among people from different traditions and with very different perspectives, and to the achievement of a wide-ranging consensus about principles which should form the basis for further debate and initiatives.

Hogbin *et al.,* suggest that the extensive debate was necessary because:

> the introduction of competences into teacher education ... was itself a challenge to aspects of the prevailing culture and the conflicts engendered would not be solved by someone doing some work on them and coming up with a 'solution'. The whole institution had to come to terms with a fundamental challenge. The process uncovered complex and deeply-rooted issues best described as a series of polarities ....

The words 'fundamental' and 'challenge' seem to capture precisely the way in which 'competence' was used here as a resource for debate. Discussion of competence was fundamental in that it involved 'uncovering' and opening to question the 'deeply-rooted' ideas central to each teacher educator's conception of their professional task.

At the level of individuals' use of competence frameworks, a recurrent theme in this book has been that a primary purpose of such frameworks should be to promote thinking and debate. Competence frameworks or profiles, far from shaping curricula, should be useful tools in fostering the kinds of questioning and theorising intended by curriculum plans. Ideas about how this can best be achieved are more varied.

Barton and Elliott, for example, (Ch. 2) while severely critical of Circular 9/92 in other respects, welcome the fact that its criterial statements 'are generally specified in terms that are open to ambiguous interpretations'. The virtue of this 'resides in their potential for fostering reflection and discussion':

> We would argue that the function of an ambiguous framework of competency statements is to frame a reflective discourse among assessors (teacher mentors, university supervisors, and the student teachers) about the warrant for their actual judgements and inferences.

Accordingly in developing their own UEA framework:

> We neither believed it practical nor desirable to specify competences in a form which removed all ambiguity in interpretation and application. We wanted the framework to serve an essentially educative function and to be open to continuing reconstruction on the basis of the reflective dialogue we hoped it would stimulate among assessors. In the light of these issues we decided to turn the criteria into questions worth reflecting about and discussing in the assessment process.

At every level, the competence debate in relation to teacher education began through teacher educators taking necessary defensive action when confronted by external and generally unwelcome demands. As the chapters of this book have demonstrated, however, taking the issue of competence seriously has not only allowed teacher educators to 'domesticate' it and to make it much less threatening: it has also suggested that debate around ideas of competence can, at every level, be immensely and distinctively valuable in developing quality in teacher education.

Theoretical Issues and Practical Dilemmas

While most chapters of this book have offered positive ways of dealing with competence issues, most have also identified problems in need of resolution. It may indeed be that through the discussion of cases in their particular contexts, the chapters of this book have provided distinctive perspectives on the theory and practice of construing, assessing and seeking to foster beginning teachers' competence. We shall not attempt here a comprehensive review of all the questions raised but shall instead look briefly at three of the recurring themes which appear to us to be especially important. These are

- Realism in considering competence
- The progressive development of competence
- Summative and formative purposes in assessing competence

Realism in considering competence

Most of the writing and debate around competence, in this book as elsewhere, is about the relative merits of different ways of construing the qualities which teachers *ought* to have, to develop and to demonstrate. Necessary as that debate is, its usefulness depends upon it keeping in touch with the realities of teachers' work and of the ways in which teachers learn to deal with that work. There are, furthermore, ideological pressures on all concerned which systematically discourage such realism:

- those who would make teachers and teacher educators more accountable are under pressure to claim knowledge of how to do so;

- those who would defend existing practice are under pressure to make inflated claims about the complexity, subtlety and effectiveness of what is done;
- those responsible for the education and induction of new entrants to the profession are under pressure to offer them idealised visions both of what they should be seeking to achieve and of how they might achieve it.

Thus when Stronach *et. al.* (Ch. 6) comment wickedly that:

> the supreme irony of the 'competence movement' is ... that it never quite manages to find out the reality on which it is so insistent

they could equally – as their own evidence clearly suggests – have complained about the lack of realism of most of the protagonists in the competence debate.

Several of the chapters of this book have offered evidence which can help us think more realistically about teachers' competence and its development. Those concerned with recently qualified teachers have been especially revealing. Stronach *et al.* show that beginning teachers can be – and perhaps generally are – socialised into teaching by their pupils and their more experienced colleagues in ways that involve unlearning idealised prescriptions for competence, learning to survive in classrooms, and moving 'to a plateau of certainties with which to fortify their practice and identity'. Burton and Povey (Ch. 10) demonstrate that the use in practice by teachers of competences, learned as student teachers on a basis of good understandings, cannot be taken for granted; it may well depend both on more fundamental personal qualities than those which a teacher training course can teach and also on propitious conditions in their schools. Mahony's evidence (Ch. 11) suggests that, in comparison to government circulars, newly qualified teachers and their mentors may put much more importance on the personal qualities of teachers, on relationships with and attitudes to children, and on the need to take account of many different considerations in planning one's teaching. Earley demonstrates that the usefulness in practice of profiling instruments in facilitating NQTs' analytic thinking about their teaching depends in large measure on the importance attached to such work by schools (and by those who finance them), for example in the allocation of time for it.

The implications of such diverse insights into the life of beginning teachers are not necessarily straightforward. They will certainly depend on one's ideological position, for example on whether one sees it as realistic or desirable to aim for beginning teachers to be agents of change in schools. However, our understandings of such realities should surely influence our conceptions of the kinds of learning possible for student teachers and beginning teachers in different contexts, and thence the curricula we plan, and *finally* the terms in which we construct profiling or other such frameworks and the uses to which we put them.

The progressive development of competence

A recurring theme throughout the book has been that of progression, with the dominant question being that of how to relate competence statements to progression in teachers' professional learning. Walker (Ch. 8) raises the question in terms of the point in a professional teacher's career to which any given set of standards apply:

> Are they to be interpreted as a minimal baseline expectation of professional competence, or as expressing a statement of what it is to be a fully competent professional?

He indicates that the issue has not been clearly resolved in relation to the major frameworks developed in Australia but that:

> it is likely that in practice the position adopted will be an in-between one ... The escape clause, or concept ... is 'developing': students and new graduates are seen to be in the process of developing certain areas of competence, not to have already developed them.

Two of the English case studies offer contrasting solutions to Walker's question. Mahony and Harris (Ch. 3) report that it was:

> important in our view that new teachers understand right from the start what kind of activity teaching is ... new teachers need to understand their own development needs as a lifelong commitment

and so the profiling framework at Goldsmiths was an attempt to describe the qualities of a fully competent teacher. At Oxford, in contrast, (Ch. 5) the specification of interactive teaching qualities was explicitly seen as a minimal baseline, a set of targets for student teachers to attain in Phase 1 of their PGCE course, before setting their sights on the longer-term goal of becoming a competent self-evaluating, self-developing teacher.

The Northern Ireland case study makes a distinctive contribution in this respect. Whitty (Ch. 7) explains that the notion of minimum thresholds was rejected in favour of a developmental view in relation to all the specific competences:

> we did not see any of the competences as entirely disposed of at the end of ITT. Instead, we tried to indicate priorities for development at the respective stages rather than to imply that a competence should be entirely neglected in any of them.

Thus tentative suggestions were made about the relative amounts of attention which should be devoted to different areas of competence during initial training, induction, and the early years of further professional development. The need for such extended curriculum planning over different phases of professional education is clear, and it would be useful for theoretical models to be developed for this purpose in relation to teaching in particular. For example it would be helpful if the kind of task attempted by Whitty and his colleagues could be related to the kinds of progress which Eraut (1994: 218–19) suggests as being relevant to professions generally 'during the period before and soon after qualification':

- extending competence over a wider range of situations and contexts
- becoming more independent of support and advice
- routinization of certain tasks
- coping with a heavier workload and getting more done
- becoming more competent in further roles and activities
- extending professional capability
- improving the quality of some aspects of one's work.

It is also important, however, to take account of a very important distinction which Hogbin *et al.* (Ch. 4) formulate in terms of the two concepts of *structured professional progression* and *personal professional development*. It is the former which we have been discussing above: the specification of appropriate standards and learning for different phases of professional education and careers. The latter refers to the very varied patterns of professional learning which individual beginning teachers exhibit, and which need to be treated as of crucial importance especially at such transition points as from initial training to induction. Any adequate theoretical or practical scheme for progression in teachers' development of competence needs to take account of these interrelated but distinct kinds of progression.

Formative and summative purposes in assessing competence

A final problematic theme which runs through many chapters of this book is the tension between formative and summative assessment. It is not generally suggested that the same profiling frameworks cannot be used for both purposes: it is rather that their use for both purposes complicates the task and makes it more likely that problems will arise.

One aspect of the tension, mentioned for example by Earley in relation to NQTs (Ch. 9), is that of who 'owns' the profiles which beginning teachers and their mentors develop together. If they are owned entirely by the learner-teachers, then they can have considerable scope as formative aids to learning; but if they are to be used for awarding qualifications, or for recruitment or promotion purposes, then it must be expected that the learners' discussion of their teaching will often not reveal, nor therefore probably develop, their authentic thinking.

Other tensions relate to the nature of the qualities which are emphasised in competence frameworks, and to the nature of competence statements. The evidence about the importance of deep-seated personal qualities for good teaching is persuasive, and so summative assessment of student teachers to determine their fitness to enter the profession should properly emphasise these qualities; but it may well be considered unrealistic to attach importance to such qualities in a profiling instrument intended for formative assessment, especially in the context of a 1-year course. Similarly the emphasis put by Barton and Elliott (Ch. 2) on the value of ambiguity in competence statements as a stimulus for thought and debate seems appealing in terms of the educative function it is intended to serve; but it is surely less attractive where one is concerned with the reliability and fairness of summative assessments.

Finally, as both the Goldsmiths (Ch. 3) and Oxford (Ch. 5) accounts of their experiences suggest, the structuring of curricula, including the tasks set for student teachers, the evidence and writing they are asked to produce, and the nature of the tutorial meetings in which they are asked to participate all appear to be more difficult to plan and manage satisfactorily because of the need to take account of both summative and formative purposes in assessing competence. Yet, as is clear from both these accounts, use of the same criteria for both formative and summative assessment is a necessary condition for the coherence of the curriculum.

In this, as in most other respects, we do not offer any tidy solutions. Instead we would argue that there is clearly a need for much more empirical and theoretical research into the formulation and use of competence concepts in relation to teachers' initial professional education and their continuing professional development. We hope that the case studies in this book provide useful stimuli for such research.

References

Eraut, M. (1994) *Developing Professional Knowledge and Competence.* Lewes: The Falmer Press.

McClelland, D.C. (1976) *A Guide to Job Competency Assessment.* Boston: McBer & Co.

Index

ACE Project 168–82
accreditation 1–16
Anglia Polytechnic University 153–67
assessment frameworks 16–25, 32–9, 50–1, 56–7, 70–1, 94, 161–2, 165–7, 169–76, 190
   see also formative assessment; summative assessment; workplace assessment
ASSET Programme (Accreditation of Social Services Expertise and Training) 153–67
Australia 98–113

Barton, R. 9–27
beginning teachers *see* newly qualified teachers
BERA Teacher Education Policy Research Group 1–2
Bernstein, B. 73–5
British Educational Research Association (BERA) 1–2
Broadfoot, P. 38
Brown, S. 6–7
Burton, L. 128–40

CBI Task Force on Training 3
Centre for Applied Research in Education (CARE) 9–27, 183–98
change 46–8
Circular 9/92 3, 9–16, 88, 117, 141–2, 145
Circular 14/93 145–52
Cockett, P. 41–55
Committee of Scottish Higher Education Principles 73
competences 6–7, 48–50, 61, 89–90, 105–11, 128–9, 169–76, 192–7, 205–8
   generic 6–7, 24–6, 30, 59–61, 67, 88, 191–7
   specific 6–7, 59–61, 77–9
Competences and Teacher Education Seminar Group 1–8
Cope, P. 72–85
Council for National Academic Awards 44
Council for the Accreditation of Teacher Education 87–8

Department of Education for Northern Ireland 30, 86–97

DfE Circular 9/92 (Framework of Competences) *see* Circular 9/92
Didsbury School of Education 41–55
Earley, P. 114–27, 141
ESCR Seminar Group 1–8
Elliott, J. 9–27, 32, 52, 67, 88, 130, 183–98
Enterprise in Higher Education 43
equal opportunities 131–6
Eraut, M. 1, 136
experiential learning 188–90

formative assessment 18, 32, 34–7, 63–4, 125–6, 211–12

generic competences 6–7, 12–14, 24–6, 30, 59–61, 67, 88, 191–7
Giddens, A. 73–5
Goldsmiths' College 28–40

Harris, V. 28–40
Hogbin, J. 42–55
Hustler, D. 1–8, 42–55, 199–212

in-service education (INSET) 90–93
induction *see* newly qualified teachers
Inglis, B. 72–85

journal writing 34–6

Leat, D.J.K. 35–6
Louis, S.K. 46, 50–2

McBer Associates 25, 191–3
McClelland, D. 191–2
McIntyre, D. 1–8, 56–71, 199–212
McNally, J. 72–85
Mahony, P. 28–40, 141–52
Maisch, M. 153–67
Manchester Metropolitan University 41–55
mentors 120–2, 141–52
midwifery training 168–82

National Council for Vocational Qualifications (NCVQ) 154, 158–63
newly qualified teachers 79–83, 114–27, 128–40, 141–52
Northern Ireland 86–97
Nowlen, P.W. 109
nursing training 100, 168–82

Olson, J. 29
Oxford University Department of Educational Studies 56–71

partnerships (schools and HEIs) 4, 17, 26
pedagogical knowledge 11–14
Pendry, A. 56–71
police training 183–98
Post-Graduate Initial Training Board 44
Povey, H. 128–40
practice and theory 14, 26, 32, 52, 58, 79–82, 130
professional development 10, 52–4
profiles 28–32, 38–9, 62–71, 95–6, 115–16, 118–24, 131–2, 143–4

reflective practice 12–13, 22, 26, 29, 52, 58, 76–7, 130, 136–9, 176–80, 195–7
reliability 15–16

School Management Competences Project (England) 91
Schostak, J. 168–82
Scottish Office Education Department *Guidelines* 72–85, 88
Scriven, M. 16, 19
self assessment *see* formative assessment
social work training 153–67
specific competences 6–7, 59–61, 77–9
Stronach, I. 72–85
subject knowledge 11–14, 30, 19–20, 75
summative assessment 18, 32–4, 125–6, 211–12

teacher training, history 42–4
teaching as a profession 3, 7, 29, 31–2, 48–50, 74, 109–10
Technical and Vocational Education Initiative (TVEI) 43
theory and practice 14, 26, 32, 52, 58, 79–82, 130
TYDE Project 168–82

UCET (Universities' Council for Teacher Education) 7
Under-Graduate Initial Training Board 44
University of East Anglia 19–27, 83–98

validity 14–15

Walker, J. 98–113
Whitty, G. 1, 30, 86–97
Winter, R. 88, 153–67
workplace assessment 153–67

For Product Safety Concerns and Information please contact our EU
representative GPSR@taylorandfrancis.com
Taylor & Francis Verlag GmbH, Kaufingerstraße 24, 80331 München, Germany

www.ingramcontent.com/pod-product-compliance
Lightning Source LLC
Chambersburg PA
CBHW061443300426
44114CB00014B/1812